This page is intentionally left blank.

People Are Talking

"Kasper's writing is consistently fresh and relentlessly funny."
—*DramaLogue Magazine*

"Debbie Kasper is out to break your heart with *You're Not That Pretty*. Her collection of stories is both hilariously funny and heartbreakingly relatable. I laughed out loud and had to use my sleeve to wipe away my tears. You'll want to track Debbie and her family down and take them all out to dinner—if you dare."
—*Annabelle Gurwitch, New York Times bestselling author of 'I See You Made an Effort'*

"Debbie Kasper is one of the funniest people ever, and she can weave a tale like no other. I'm so thrilled that she has put so many of her hysterical and moving stories on paper for all of us to enjoy.
—*Amy Landecker, actress/writer/director, Transparent, Curb Your Enthusiasm, A Serious Man*

"Debbie Kasper paints with words, creating a picture better than almost anybody out there. The sentences, the turns of phrase are so exquisitely written that, over and over, I found myself stopping to reread and bask in the beauty of a sentence. Ms. Kasper delivers consistently brilliant prose. *You're Not That Pretty* is often very funny but its strength is in its raw authenticity and the depth of its heart.
—*Six-time Emmy-winning writer/producer & bestselling author, Janette Barber*

"Debbie Kasper's writing is relentlessly funny, absolutely human and touching. Her voice resonates like a female David Sedaris. I am taken by how much she reveals herself with such generosity, effortlessly mixing brazen irreverence with surprising poignancy. From the very first chapter I was completely smitten."
—*Paul Lyons, comedian, author, 'Carpe Diem, Manana'*

"Sassy, Funny, Kasper flawlessly delivers."
—*LA Weekly*

Published 2020 by *Very Fine Things Press*
Los Angeles, CA 90025
Printed in the United States of America.
ISBN:

"You're Not That Pretty"

& Other Things My Parents Told Me

Stories from the chaos

A memoir ... of sorts

Debbie Kasper

For My Parents

For doing a better job than I thought

and for Reid

"Artists are children who have survived their upbringing"

- *Somebody*

Table Of Contents

Foreword

I'm a narcissist with low self-esteem. I don't think much of me, but I'm all I think about. A therapist once mentioned that to me, summing up my entire life in one lucky guess, adding, "You're just trying to fill the abyss that is your heart."

This answered Mom's eternal question, "What the hell do you find so fascinating about *you*, Debbie?"

"There's a black hole in my chest, Ma."

"That's nice, sweetie-pie," she'd say, enveloping my head with her used smoke. I should mention—it wasn't my therapist but a doctor I sat next to on the East-bound 104. (You'd be surprised at how many professional opinions you can get for the price of bus fare.) Then Dr. Crosstown Bus says, "Your parents did the best they could." Maybe.

I grew up the only girl in a house with three boys, or as Dad called them "your stinking rotten brothers." Each had their own devious way to torture me—spiders on my pillow, chasing me with dangling reptiles, letting mice loose in my sock drawer. I'd run crying to Dad who'd say, "Good—a kid—go mix me a drink."

My parents had chucked the fifties "bible" *Dr. Spock's Baby and Child Care* for their preferred manual *The Guide to the Perfect Cocktail*. We weren't really children—we were bartenders with no tip jar.

Sure, our home had plenty of laughter and joy, but usually at someone's expense. Generally there'd be one traumatized person running off sobbing, stomping their feet, slamming a bedroom door. Sometimes it would even be my dad. Usually, it was me. Mom's sarcasm could laser in on your most precious flaw—slice it, dice it, and serve it in a casserole for dinner. To her, affection was like roast beef—only for special occasions, and even then, it might be tough and disappointing—and there would *never* be enough. Her motto was, "Expect nothing, you'll usually be right." Dad's idea of funny was to sit his toddlers on his huge shoulders and lean us over the alligator pit at the Philadelphia Zoo. To this day, I am deathly afraid of zoos—and fathers. I don't like shoulders much, either.

Danger lurked everywhere. Like a balloon in a nail factory—there was nowhere to turn where I couldn't get hurt. I'd lock myself in my room and write in my diary or skulk around the house, hugging the walls, hoping to go unnoticed, eventually heading to the warm embrace of the cookie drawer.

Early on, the four Kasper kids figured out that we were being raised by wolves with a mortgage. Until one day, my father threw us a surprise half-sister—and then there were five—until that half-sister flipped out, and then there were four and a half. There was never a dull moment at the Kasper house. It was enough to make me swear I'd never have children of my own—and I didn't (that I know of). I jotted most of it down in my diary, which was kept under a tiny lock and useless key. Full disclosure: my journal is not always completely historically or even personally accurate. For one thing—on July 28th in 1969, apparently a man walked on a moon somewhere? But for me, that day was all about my teenage acne and a Jeff who didn't call. I have no clue who Jeff was, but the acne has cleared up. I think that was Neil Armstrong, on the moon?

I grew a hard shell and a humorous slant on things. But once my self-esteem took about all the kicks it could endure, my diary and I saved up for a suitcase and moved on out in search of something else. Anything, everything.

Some of these stories get dark, and plenty of it is politically incorrect. But diaries don't lie—not completely, anyway—I don't see how Paul Newman could have had a crush on me when I was fourteen.

The sub-subconscious remembers a lot—from the day we are born. It knits together the good, the bad, and plenty of ugly and that becomes the weave of who we are. My parents are long gone. The memories—they're still trying to make sense of themselves. I hope in reading these stories that you, too, will be encouraged to find humor and healing in even the craziest, darkest, and challenging-ist (yes…I'm aware that's not a word), of times. I swear on the ashes in my father's urn—I turned out okay. But then again, others might not see it that way. Thank you for joining me on this trip to the zoo.

Debbie Kasper

A Note From The Author

Here's the thing about memoirs: One doesn't necessarily "re-memboir" events exactly as they happened. Memories can be corrupt rascals striving to make something of themselves over time—to grab center stage. Not only would it be impossible to recall everything precisely as it happened, but it would also make for a boring book. I'm supposed to remember stuff I said when I was four? Not possible—especially since I was so drunk that year.

I remember certain incidents my way. Others may disagree. I have a certain chip-on-my-shoulder kind of perspective, which sometimes clashes with theirs. For example, I remember when my brother Joe flung a five-pound metal dump truck at my head. But to hear his side of the skirmish—"I was aiming for the fish tank but Debbie's fat head got in the way." *Perspective.*

I mention all of this so I don't get slammed for a fake memoir—who wants to get "James Freyed?" Thank God Oprah's off the air, I don't need that kind of pressure from a billionaire. I have pressures all my own—which you will soon see.

Don't Have Children Debbie, You'll Just End Up Hating Half Of Them

"How come you haven't had children?" I heard ad nauseam in that whiny tone of pity. Sometimes I'd give my trademark retort, "I had one, but I forgot where I put it." To date, I am childless, a mother to no one—not such a weird thing anymore, but back when I made that choice in the seventies, it brought on a slew of questions and raised many eyebrows. Women wept, someone even hit me once. People still, to this day, ask me—when I'm even too old to adopt. But now they ask in the final past tense—pluperfect, definitive, declarative, "How come you never had kids?!?" They ask with such tender despair as if it were a mistake, as if I'd forgotten, as if I'd left the house without my pants—which by the way, I have done.

I was always too self-centered to have children. I know that didn't stop others, but I'm a narcissist with a conscience. I also never wanted to perpetuate myself—the madness of me. I just didn't want to have my own children, and the possibility of giving birth to puppies seemed remote. Truth is I never even considered a child. Even as a child, I never wanted one. I never played house as a kid, and when other little girls in the neighborhood did, I'd be the social worker who swept in and took their kids away. Not only did I not want kids—I thought nobody should have any. I started out as an average little girl—by the time I was two, I began collecting dolls because TV urged me to sing their jingles over and over until my parents' ears bled. Once I got the dolls, I'd play with them for a bit, suck in that fresh rubber doll smell, and hug them close—then closer. Five minutes later, I'd done everything you could with a doll short of disemboweling it—so that's exactly what I did.

My first doll, Thumbelina, was the soft plastic infant that TV said moved like a real baby when you wound her up. Her movements were robotic, and she looked Mongolian, but nobody seemed concerned, but me. I tore the knob out from her back to see what was inside. Nothing was inside, she was hollow, except for a few wires. Thumbelina never moved again, either. Then I sang the Betsy Wetsy song until I got one for Christmas. Betsy was the doll who you filled up with water so she could pee, hence the "Wetsy," then you'd get to change a real wet diaper—a grim warning if ever there was one. I once put lemonade in mine just to see if it was more fun, and it was for a second. Saskia, my best friend for always and ever (until she got sick of me a few years later), had the Chatty Cathy doll whose pulled string spilled out a blathering of words, "I'm Chatty Cathy, and I like you!"

Being liked by a doll wasn't much fun to me, so after the tenth time she liked me, I shot back, "Well, I don't like you!" and then I punched Cathy right in her Chatty, knocking her out of Saskia's arms. Saskia laughed uncontrollably. Now that was pretty fun.

Life changing lesson that day:

Beating up dolls: boy is that fun

By age eight, I felt about dolls the same way I felt about frogs—unless they jumped right on me—I paid no attention. Then Saskia and I invented our own game which incorporated all of our finer talents. We'd dress in sparkled ruby-colored high heels, loosely strung plastic pearls and fake little mink stoles—all of which came in our twin Flapper Girl outfits we'd gotten for our birthdays. We'd walk back and forth between our houses with the dolls in little strollers, pretending they were *really* real. Not fake real, but really *really,* real. We'd slather some of her mother's bright lipstick on our little lips, then draw uneven clown circles of rouge in the middle of our cheeks, all in an attempt to disguise our eight-year-old selves to look like mothers visiting with newborns, real newborns. There we were—three-foot flapper mothers strolling the suburban sidewalks, pushing baby buggies, missing only flasks and jalopies to complete the motif. We were betting on eight passing for seventeen, which seemed possible in our smug, delusional world. We looked more like child streetwalkers, but no one paid attention anyway. Like fire hydrants, neighbors barely glanced our way—except in emergencies. Our street skit was for us.

We'd saunter up and down the sidewalk between our two houses, stopping at intervals to pick up our children and soothe them as we'd seen the neighborhood mothers do. Then I added the twist. I'd pretend to be an abusive, crazy mother. "Stop crying, baby," I'd say the first time as nicely as I imagined a mean mother would. The next time, I'd just have to get nasty. "Shut up, you little brat!" I'd bray in a sinister voice I'd heard Vincent Price use on TV. Saskia would laugh out loud, so I'd push the charade further, "STOP CRYING BEFORE

MOMMY BEATS YOU!" Then I'd whip the doll out of the stroller, and shake-shake-shake her like a cup of pudding. "Stooooooop Cryyyyyiiing!!!" S&M comedy created right there in Cherry Valley, sparked by my desperate need for attention.

The third time my baby would cry (in my skit), I'd have to snap because she wasn't obeying me, so I would just have to pull her out of the stroller by her fake fingers, yank the flimsy arm out of the socket, throw her on the ground, and kick her across Mrs. Seckler's lawn. Saskia would roll on the ground in hysterics—even wet her pants, which made it a great day. Saskia had a full laugh at a young age. She knew funny, and beating up a rubber doll was funny—not as funny as actually drop-kicking the baby or stomping on her head or ripping my cheesy mink stole off and whipping the completely disemboweled doll with it—all of which I improvised the next time we performed the "doll-walking skit." Then, I had to reach to new stars to make the baby beatings funnier and keep the laughter coming—I already needed more. Making people laugh was clearly more forte than caring for something. My inner mother went straight to hell without passing go, without collecting two hundred dollars—and I began to aspire to something beyond what the fifties had dreamt for me. It happened that young—a comedian was locked and loaded, and in search of audiences.

If I'd become a serial killer, the neighbors wouldn't have been surprised the way they always are on TV: "Tommy was a good boy from a good home."

Mrs. Selmi would've whispered: "Debbie was a sick, *sick* little monster. She used to tear her dolls apart and throw plastic body parts all over the lawn. I found a doll leg in my pansies on Easter. Easter! I couldn't even eat my ham, and the pansies, well consider them gone! We're catholic over here. I don't know what those Kaspers are!"

Mrs. Mitrocsak might've added: "If you ask me, she was a bad seed from the get-go. She bit my daughter Nancy in the leg—like a little mutt would. She drew blood! Like a mad dog."

"That's not a house—it's a rodeo. I blame those parents," Mrs. Lutz probably would've whispered in sad disgust.

At twelve, I came into my birthright—baby sitting my much younger brothers, Robbie and Joe, or as I called it "child labor camp." Joe had a huge head that didn't even aspire to be proportionate to the rest of his body—he was shaped like a Macy's Day float. The poor kid could barely rise to a stand—his bubble gum machine head would throw him off-balance and topple him over his stubby legs. The first time my parents left me alone with Robbie and Joe, Mom warned me to watch out for Joe's "soft spot," then punctuated the warning by blowing her exhaled cigarette smoke into his baby eyes. "The baby's skull is still unformed, so be careful, Debbie. Don't slip and stick your finger through your brother's head on the top here," she said, pointing right to the spot with her Kool cigarette, almost burning his scalp. "It's like a squash—so you could poke your finger right through to his brains, and he'd be a vegetable. He really would be a squash." She and my father laughed like idiots—I was terrified.

"She's not going to stick her finger through Joe's head. She's twelve—she's a big girl now. Right, Debbie?" Dad defended. I nodded in that "We're all gonna find out soon enough" way. As far as I was concerned, they were the ones leaving their pumpkin-headed toddler with a twelve year-old. I was a clumsy preteen, so the chance of my turning Joe into a turnip was there, and we all knew it. Yet, very little could keep my parents from their weekend bridge games—even bleeding children. They'd just patch things up slipshod and dash out quickly like thieves.

I had ongoing nightmares about poking a spoon through the top of Joe's head. Why I had a spoon to his head, I couldn't tell you. Every week until I was fourteen, I'd ask my mom, "Is Joe's head done yet? Can I safely poke the top of his head now?"

"Why do you want to know?"

"I just want to touch it and maybe poke a little."

My mother wasn't exactly Ma Walton. Her idea of soothing a crying three-year-old was to say, "Do you want everyone to think you're a little baby?" How she tried to cradle us in her arms when we cried, kiss our boo-boos when we fell down, sing to us, always with a cigarette clutching onto her lip for dear life, ashes spilling down onto our little foreheads. It was like our own personal Lent. When she'd sing, she only had about a two-note range and neither one was in tune. She'd croak out, "Puff the magic dragon," then, "On top of old Smoky ..."

I'd eventually beg, "Don't sing, Mommy—ever again." She'd butt her cigarette in the ashtray kept right by my pillow on the night stand and turn out the light.

"Good night, sleep tight. Don't let the bedbugs bite. All right, then. Bye." She'd say "bye" like I wasn't going to see her when I woke up. My guess now is that there was probably only about a fifty-fifty chance that she would've been there on any given morning.

By the time I was a senior in college—to nobody's surprise—I'd fallen madly in love with the theatre and got up the nerve to ask Mom if she thought I'd be making a mistake if I didn't get married and have kids. I'd decided that I had to have a career in showbiz—I even dreamt up the metaphor early on that my career would be my child. "Showbiz is my baby! That's what I shall nurture. I will feed it, burp it, and forgive it when it pees on me. And when I am old, it will desert me just like children do." Gloria Steinem had started raving that women "could have it all!" I really didn't *want* it all, and frankly, I considered her mad rants a threat. The whole family was out to dinner, celebrating my parents' 25th wedding anniversary, which was coming off more like a wake than a celebration. After we ate, I sidled up to my mother, who was perched in a leather booth, and privately asked her, "Would I be missing out on something fantastic? Would my life end up empty if I don't pop some kids out?"

"NOOOO!" she barked. Her response didn't shock me. I knew Mom was miserable. She hadn't been out of her muumuu for decades nor cracked a smile since Nixon was elected. What surprised me was how quickly she spit it out—like she'd been mulling over this forever—a wound-up Pez dispenser waiting for someone to pull her head back for her sour opinions on life to finally shoot out. It wasn't even a nice "no," but a big over-acted one fraught with resentment, sadness, and a touch of dry vermouth—as if it weren't even a good question—as if I'd asked her if she wanted to see Alice Cooper for Mother's Day.

"It's highly overrated, anybody can have kids. But only you, Debbie, can chase your dreams," she continued, sipping her Manhattan. "Only you," she repeated intensely, trying to transfer her passion to me. "Do you think it takes talent to give birth? Do you think you have to be special? All you need is a few drinks, some sort of a man and the rest just ... happens. Don't have kids, Debbie, I beg you. You'll end up hating half of them. Here are ten bucks—don't have kids." She pulled a bill out of her purse and handed it to me to seal the deal. I bought two more drinks.

I looked at my mother through the dim lighting of the restaurant, watching her eyes moisten—a monumental event for Shirley Kasper. She'd held her emotions in with a girdle and a bottle of bourbon for as long as I'd known her. There she sat, surrounded by her husband, whom she openly resented, and her four children, whom I now knew she secretly resented as well. I wondered for a second, if I were in the half of the kids she didn't despise. We were the hideous portrait of who she would never be—the abortion of her life's dreams. Shirley was one of those housewives and mothers from the fifties who'd lost her joy, living a life she hadn't designed but kind of tripped and fell into, face down. Now, having missed all her boats, my mother started imbuing me, her only daughter, with all her hope—rooting from the sidelines for me to reach out and be something. The day I drove off to college, she practically yelled through a bullhorn from the front porch, "Whatever you do, don't you find a husband! Study, Debbie, study!"

Fat Chance!

As my mother was nearing the end of her life, I became the dutiful daughter at her bedside. It was my pleasure—I adored this woman with a kind of love that nobody would ever offer up to me. I mopped her brow. I held her hand. Before she left us, I asked the question again, when now it was really too late, "Mom, are you sure I should never have had kids?"

She half-smiled at me, "I might have been wrong about that." Then she slipped away.

Stop Biting Other Kids, You Could Get Rabies!

I don't remember my first kiss or my first day of school or meeting French fries for the first time—three events that changed my entire course of destiny (particularly the French fries). But my first friend? I'll never forget her and the exact day and moment we laid our hungry little eyes on each other. Her name was Saskia. Because of her I know how to be a friend, and I know that making people laugh is my prerequisite for an everlasting friendship. Laugh with me—I will love you forever. She changed my day, my purpose for existing. No, I'll never forget that first meet—I'll also never forget the day I lost her.

We had just moved that very day to our mostly built house in the newly dreamed suburbs. We got there before the sidewalks and the grass, so there was mud everywhere because of the rain that week. There were boards laid sloppily down over the soggy dirt connecting the lives that had just moved into the homes which looked exactly like the homes next door—and next door to that. Up and down most of the streets, all I could see were cranes and tractors, plots roped off. Moving vans were unloading people's things on other streets—more families were moving in. The sterile suburbs were bursting with 1950's energy, dying to be filled and decorated—anything seemed possible on this blank slate of dreams.

The curb in front of our house was still wet and the road smelled of tar. It was all so new it reeked of hope, but I had none, or less. I sat on the wet front curb crying because I had no friends. I couldn't imagine my future, and I had already ruined my gingham dress. My parents were inside, unpacking our life into our new home, which smelled like the future.

We'd just moved from the Parkway Apartments, a low-rent spread where tons of other young families with children lived, mostly waiting for their new homes to be built in the new world, where zip codes didn't even exist, yet. I had a playmate or two there, but only because my parents' friends made their kids play with me. I wasn't well-liked on my own since I'd bitten a baby in front of the whole sandbox. When the toddler hit my brother Reid over the head with a plastic shovel, in the sandbox, I quietly put my bucket down, waddled over to the diapered misfit, bent down and took a pretty big chunk out of his leg. Apparently, I then took a little bow and plopped back down onto the sand. My nickname became "Debbie Kasper—the terror of forty B" (our apartment number).

"Don't bite strange children, Debbie. You'll get rabies!" my father warned, "and you certainly won't make friends like that. Bite kids you know." That didn't deter me since I had no clue what rabies were, and didn't really know what a friend was, either. So I continued taking chunks out of chubby legs whenever the inclination struck me, or perhaps whenever I craved more of the young blood.

Here now, in this strange and desolate place, there were no children to bite, so far, and I wasn't allowed to leave the front mud, so I plopped myself on the curb near the freshly paved road which didn't go all the way up the street, and I wept for what I didn't yet believe in or know.

Reid was five, which allowed him to wander up the block and even around corners to check things out. He headed around a slight bend in search of signs of intelligent life. I stayed behind sobbing dramatically, trapped in my very own suburban tragedy. As local legend has it, right around that corner—a mere two doors down— my soon-to-be new best friend, Saskia, was also perched on a curb, crying. It was as if Norman Rockwell had painted the scene, two little blonde girls crying two doors and a whole world away from one another other. Reid always had a way with the girls, so he said, "Why are you crying?"

"I have no friends."

"My sister Debbie doesn't have any friends!" Reid said, promptly taking her by the hand and leading her to me. I couldn't believe my eyes, there—past my tears—was my Lord and savior rounding the bend leading a blonde four-year-old, like a fireman emerging through smoke with your beloved pet. It was the luckiest thing that had ever happened to me and still—ranks up there. What were the chances? Out of the wet dirt and the treeless streets and the cranes, what were the chances another little girl would appear just in time to be my new best friend and change my whole world? Little did we know, each of those empty houses up and down all the streets for as far as we could imagine, would soon be stuffed with children, lots and lots of children.

I don't remember that first conversation we had, but I bet it went something like:

"Will you be my fwend?"

"Yes."

"I like you."

"I wike you."

So instinctual—a pair of beagles couldn't have figured it out any faster. Saskia and I both stopped crying and immediately began playing together that day and for the next ten years. She was a year older, so she knew what to do with all the mud. We made mud pies till dusk, and we giggled. Laughter became our bond. Saskia laughed like no one else. I loved her laugh, and I loved being in charge of it, it made me feel cozy—an inside your mitten kind of cozy. Pretty quickly, I became the teller of the funny, the keeper of the joy, so much so, that I completely cornered her love and approval. I could make Saskia giggle till she'd wet her pants—still my idea of a great day. That feeling of causing someone's ultimate happiness, even if only momentarily, is a rush I've continued to chase my whole life—like a dog after a squirrel. But she was my first, and we fell in little girl love.

Saskia laughed out loud all the time, infecting everyone around her with her joy. Her laughter had an opinion to it as if it weren't just that she thought it was funny but that it was funny. PERIOD.

We spent the next ten years eating at each other's homes, building tents with bedsheets in our basements, having sleep overs, playing with our dolls, coordinating our Christmas and birthday lists to make sure we got everything we needed, with no duplicates. If she got Chatty Cathy, I got Thumbelina, and then we'd switch. We shared everything. My Barbie would spend the night in her Barbie's Dream House, and then the next night, hers would sleep in mine.

Our two Barbies shared one Ken, that's how close we were. My Barbie thought Ken was a creep, and she just used him for rides, so she was happy to lend him out.

We'd make dandelion necklaces and catch fireflies in jars, we'd play with her mother's makeup, go to sleep away camp together, and of course bunk together. We'd hold hands because we loved each other, and we didn't care who knew. If anybody said anything unkind about Saskia, I'd hit or bite them. When we weren't together, we spoke on our tin-can phones attached with strings and stretched between our bedroom windows through our adjoining neighbor's yard. We'd scream out our bedroom windows, "Can you hear me now? How 'bout now?" (I'm just sayin').

Saskia picked up Pig Latin at school and quickly taught me. We spoke it fluently to each other so we could talk about others right in front of them, further bordering up our private club with only two members—Debbie and Saskia. "You are not us," we'd say to others in ig-pay-atin-lay. Then we'd laugh the way little girls do when the world was their eclair, filled with cream. We made up little street theatre skits to perform for anybody bored enough to watch. I'd always be the star—she'd be the audience laughing uninhibitedly until everyone else fell in. Saskia made me the star of the whole block—my very first agent.

Often, I'd eat dinner at her house, which was much more proper than mine. Meals at our house looked like scenes out of *The Miracle Worker*. You could grab food off of anybody's plate you wanted, and speak with your mouth full as long as you used good grammar. The only rules were: no splashing, kicking, or putting your face right down into your plate of food and slurping. At her house, you had to sit up straight and you weren't allowed to touch your food! Not even to push it onto your fork, it was really hard. I couldn't make it through a meal without acting up until Saskia and I would both shoot milk through our noses.

When it was time, we played doctor together—just the two of us. One of us would lie on a bed, while the other placed a sheet over the other's naked body. I'd snagged a plastic stethoscope from Reid's doctor kit, allowing us to listen to each other's belly buttons. We'd do examinations, naming the body parts that were previously hidden or foreign to us. We'd make up names for most things. "This is your pee-tolater." Saskia overheard her older sister, Marcia talking, and brought the word, "virginia" into our examination room, which was probably some confused, pre-teen mish-mosh of "virgin" and "vagina." Soon, Saskia and I quickly discovered that neither of us liked being the naked one (the victim), so we opened up our free clinic to others in need of a gynecological exam done by an eleven-year-old.

"Want us to look inside your whole body?" we'd ask passing neighborhood girls. Surprisingly, we had several takers. The clinic's popularity was growing, and some days there'd even be a short line in the waiting room, until one day Saskia's mother shut its doors for good, when Barbara Glenn went screaming from the exam room, down the steps and out the front door. We'd let her know that there was something weird about her virginia part—there was an errant flap of some sort. That was the end of our OBGYN office, as well as our friendship with Barbara. There *was* something wrong with her virginia, I'd only seen three, but hers was very strange, and I felt compelled to mention it. *People need to know the truth, man.*

Saskia's and my one-year age difference never mattered a lick, until one day when it did. It had something to do with boys and her starting to notice them, while I was still shooting milk thru my nose. The minute she outgrew "us" lingers as a vivid memory, even now. She was almost thirteen and had just moved into a bra—I was one year and two boobs behind her. We were playing in the swim club pool, and Saskia was wearing a two-piece bathing suit with a fully formed sewn-in foam brassiere, to which she had little to offer. Her cups were sixties style—way too big and pointy—it looked ridiculous, like a couple of upside-down snow-cones.

I was threatened by the emerald plaid swimsuit and its pointy bra and for good reason—it was about to undo me. I was still wearing my braless girl suit with the big front bow to obscure the breast area. I had nothing going on in any way—some baby fat was gathering around my chest, trying to gain momentum, but so far ... it was nothing more than a dream.

Wearing her pink rubber nose plugs, Saskia dove into the water, and moments later when she splashed back up, her cups had completely collapsed on her. They were so grossly indented that I burst out laughing, pointing, but for the first time in my short life—Saskia didn't laugh with me. She wasn't amused—at all. All of a sudden, I wasn't funny anymore. We weren't funny anymore. Just like that.

Within seconds, her rubber bra began to poke back out slowly, and as it reformed, I took my two pointer fingers and pushed them back in so they were practically inside out on her chest, again. *There—that'll make her laugh!* Instead, she gave me a hard look, with her right eyebrow slightly arched—I'd never even seen her do that, it was so grown-up. Then she swam away fast, like she was trying to freestyle into the next year. That was the day our ten-year love affair dissolved like a fizzy in water over a collapsed bra.

My ex-best friend tossed me back to the curb where she found me, moved on pretty quickly, and started hanging out with a wilder crowd (Reid for one), and even began dating. In the mornings, I could hear her laughter on the street corner waiting for the bus to take her to high school. I'd peek out my bedroom window just in time to see her toss her head back, laughing at the bad boys' jokes. Then she started smoking—to bronze the fact that we were lost forever. I mourned the loss, but it was nothing a couple of cookies couldn't fix.

I went to high school the next year and was thrilled when Saskia would throw me a smile in the hall and flip her long hair as she disappeared into a classroom. I continued with my talent for cracking people up. I knew I was funny. Saskia had made it so I flaunted it, and it made me feel loved when classmates laughed at my antics. I didn't care what I had to do to make them laugh—put the trash can over my head? If necessary! Smash a chalky eraser in your face? I've done worse! Pull a chair out from under you? Whatever! I was crowned the class clown and made many more friends effortlessly—although none of them were teachers or principals.

Saskia and I both graduated and moved away from town, although our parents remained neighbors for several more decades. When we were around forty—we saw each other for the first time in over twenty years. There was a class reunion, and Reid had come in for it, along with many of our childhood friends. I arrived at the party late, and Reid said, "Saskia is looking for you." It was almost a command. Then I heard it again, and again. Those words hadn't rung my ears since I was twelve, and they still made my heart tingle. I'd heard she was in town, and although there were tons of people there that I was thrilled to see—none of them mattered like Saskia did. I wondered *if I could still make her laugh till she cried? If she'd remember the first day we'd met? If she was still flat-chested?*

The second she found me, she shrieked out, "De-eb-bie" exactly like she inflected my name all those years ago. It was laughter to my ears. The passing of decades had apparently made me cool again. We threw our arms around each other for an over the top hug, the kind that comes with laughter and screams. We sat down, matched memories, and melted into the mutual affection we'd had in 1962. We'd never taken our beautiful friendship for granted, we knew it was a miracle that we'd met each other. Out of all those kids who filled all those tiki-taki-houses around us, we found each other, and together we invented love.

Although we live thousands of miles apart, we stay in touch now, and occasionally even *eak-spay a little ig-pay-atin-lay*. I had lunch with Saskia recently, and she vaguely remembered the curious incident of the padded swimsuit bra which has stayed with me like a knife wound. We still giggle like schoolgirls at a mere gesture, a look, the sudden utterance of Barbara Glenn, or particularly the word "virginia."

Saskia continues to laugh with infectious abandon when we're together. She's finally grown into that confident laugh she'd improvised all those years ago as a child—a laugh which decides for everyone what's funny—a sound which holds a place among my very favorite in the whole world, for the sheer audacity of it. And just for the record, I'm pretty sure I can still make her wet her pants, and honestly, it just doesn't get much better than that.

Let The Boys Win, Or You'll End Up A Bitter Old Maid And Die Alone

There was nothing worse in Dad's eyes than being a geographic idiot—not stealing, cheating on a test, or even taking out a neighbor's eye with a slingshot. My father was a history and geography elitist, forever cursing about the, "Morons in the country who couldn't pull Iowa out of their asses, let along pick it out on a map. You wanna see how stupid people are? Just ask them where Iowa is. Unless they live there, they won't know, and even then..." If you wanted him to like you, you'd better have some state facts on hand.

My father began bullying me geographically almost the minute I slid out of the womb. "Welcome to America. We have fifty states here and I look forward to making you recite them all until you cry," were some of his first words to me. I learned how to name my home state and its capital, while still in wet diapers. When I was three, he asked me where I lived—I took his big hand—walked him to my bedroom where the pink ballerinas danced on walls and said, "Here." That answer didn't fly. Right then and there, he taught me, "New

Jersey, capital: Trenton." Dad didn't want an ignoramus tainting his family name and pulling down the Kasper average. He'd teach us new words at the dinner table give out extra homework, assign us books to read. It was like living with a six-foot hairy nun, but strict.

By age five, all the Kasper kids had to memorize every state in the country, recite their capital and name the chief export of that state or else—threats of private sleep-away schools, would get whispered at full voice, right outside your bedroom door. We'd play this game until we all excelled at it. The next level—things got dicey. My father would flip over the colored wooden map puzzle from his childhood, hiding the state's names, and then make us identify them one by one from the blank backs. We'd have to name it, spell it, state the capital, and put it back in the puzzle frame where the state belonged. He called it the Map Puzzle Game, and yes, it was just as fun as it sounds. Dad made us play it until our little fingers were cut and bleeding from the sharp states—like Kentucky and Maryland. Then he'd pit us against each other stirring up a nasty competition between my older, smarter brother Reid and me. I'm pretty sure he was using his Marine Corps training techniques to jam geography down our throats. He'd encourage us to compete like our spot in the platoon depended on it.

With a good memory and a desperate need for love, I mastered the first level of the Map Puzzle Game by age four. I was one year ahead of the curve on that one. I may not have known what coal was, but I knew there was lots of it in West Virginia, which sat just to the left of Virginia in the puzzle scheme and right beneath Pennsylvania, capital: Harrisburg. I can do this all day long.

Rhode Island, capital: Providence.

Minnesota, capital: St. Paul.

Stop me if you're bored.

Idaho? help me, I can't stop!

Marine Dad merely took my achievement as a clue that the maneuver was too easy, so he raised the stakes and made me do it blindfolded, identifying the states by the touch. "Uhm, it's big and pointy," I'd say fondling the second largest state in the union. "Must be Texas, 'The Longhorn State,' capital? Austin." I'd recite proudly.

"Good girl," Dad would sing-song, practically patting my little head, rewarding me with a biscuit. If I ever stumbled on a capital—he had little hints, "I'll conk you in the head if you don't get the capital of New Hampshire."

"Concord?" By age six, I had learned enough to see the pattern— I was afraid to excel at the challenge du jour, fearing that the next stage would be me naming the states blindfolded, only allowed to use my big toe to identify them. I'd take off my sock and rub it blindly along the edge of Arkansas and say, "Ouch! I think I feel the razorback state." Then the next challenge: perhaps I'd have to do it blindfolded, standing one-legged on a ball!

"Good girl!" he'd reward, tossing me a fish from a bucket.

My parents were both intellectually snotty, even though neither of them were a bonafide intellectual. My father didn't smoke a pipe, studying Voltaire in the library—nor did we *have* a library—we had a bar room. Mom never once attended a book club that read *Finnegan's Wake* or *The Fountainhead*. But they could both run categories on *Jeopardy*, and they each did it with the sole intention of trying to beat the smirk off the other.

"Who were the Phoenicians?" Mom would belt.

"I already said Phoenicians, *goddamnit*!" Dad would top mom's volume.

Then Alex Trebek would say, "Oh, I'm sorry. It's the Berbers."

"Oh *goddamnit!* The *goddamn* Berbers. I knew that!" Mom would scream. "I knew the *goddamn* Berbers!"

"I said, the Berbers! You didn't say the Berbers— I said the Berbers!" Dad would yell loud enough for them to hear him across country in the actual *Jeopardy* studio. Night after night, category after category, it went on like that. They'd both gone to Middlebury College, an exceptionally impressive school, and Dad never let us forget it.

I don't know exactly when the school gave me the IQ test, but sometime around the first grade, there was a shift in the way everyone looked at me—like I was dying. One day I was the star kid in the family who had aced the Map Puzzle Game and the next thing I knew, I was getting pats on my head from everyone—teachers, parents, even Santa Claus at the mall, *"Hello young lady, I have the perfect gift for you ... how bout some nice flash cards?"*

IQ scores could follow you around for the rest of your life. They'd decide which teacher you got, what people expected out of you, how many cookies you got with your milk, and whether or not you would ever get asked the question: "What color was Washington's white horse?" If your score was embarrassing enough, the whole world could use them against you like you were on the "FBI's Most Stupid List." Expectations are lowered and dreams are dashed. Maybe going to college isn't encouraged anymore, replaced with suggestions of a career-path involving a hair net and a hole puncher.

Dad started calling me his "sweet pretty little girl." He'd refer to Reid in the same breath as "my little genius." Even mom would shake her head in sad compadre every time she saw me, which was often since we lived together. My history questions suddenly got easy.

"Show me where the Mason Dixon line is, Debbie." I 'd run my chubby little finger across the imaginary line he'd taught me on the map puzzle just the week before.

"Very good. What war was divided by this line?"

"Uhm. You know, Dad. That war.

"That's right, the Civil War."

"Okay. Can I have another Ding-Dong?"

"Who won the Civil War?"

"Uh, the civils?"

"That's okay—you're not very bright, but at least you're pretty, and that's going to work in your favor," lamented Dad.

"I don't want to be pretty! I want to be smart!"

"Well, you're *not* that pretty," said Mom, "so—congratulations!"

Those comments just made me try harder at everything. Dad had turned me into a fierce gladiator, like his three sons. We all hungrily eyed each other as "the competition" for everything: attention, games, and especially bacon. Every week, there were several opportunities to win at something, leaving the other three in your dust, so we'd all jump in every game with that intention, hoping to get some sort of a nod from Dad. One nod could feed my hungry heart for a week.

One day Dad pulled out Risk: The Game of World Domination. He figured it was time we learn about world geography, and more pressing—how to become a ruthless conqueror. Surely one can see the future need for a skill like this.

Sometimes, when it was Dad's turn, instead of rolling the dice, he'd squeeze them up into his palm—take a deep breath and lecture his four children about his favorite conquerors—Atilla the Hun, The Khans, and "that little prick Napoleon." (Dad never had one nice thing to say about Napoleon.) He'd trace the route the Barbarians took as they swung through Europe, acted out how the Vandals from the Teutonic states pillaged through The Holy Roman Empire like hoodlums, cleaning out Rome's treasures. Whenever my father was attacking someone from the Russian provinces, he'd whip up a cheesy Trotsky-esque accent. There was something about the way Dad said, "Eye-am eettacking Irkutsk from Kamchatka!" that made you want to smash his head into the board. He'd even resemble a comrade—eyebrows on fire—oozing the smell of vodka and fish, laughing demonically and rubbing his palms together as he took over the world. Dad was a worse winner than he was a loser. He'd rub it in, making sure you understood how substandard and left out you were at that moment. There was no other purpose of playing a game in our house, but to exalt winners and stomp losers.

One night, he and his shitty Russian accent just uttered one "usk" too many. He'd marched through all my continents triumphantly, as if smearing the board with a twelve-year-old girl was a badge of honor. I'd had enough. I quit the game, threw down the dice, left my territories completely unprotected from Ivan the Terrible who was advancing on me from Kamchatka.

"Quitters are losers" yelled Dad, watching me retreat to the slammed door sanctuary of my bedroom. I haven't quit a game, since. I've cheated—but never quit. Dad taught us to compete like the Vandals—crudely ripping through the place, knocking things over, leaving a wake of rubble in our paths. Winning stood for "respect," and it was also the best path to earning Dad's love.

Eventually, through the laws of attrition, I too, became a terrible winner and a horrible loser. I'd get operatic, sometimes throwing the Monopoly iron at one of my brothers' heads when I landed on their snazzy blue hotels, losing all my money. "You're a capitalist pig!" I'd scream. "I can't build back from this! I'm bankrupt—you cheat!" I'd tip over my Scrabble tray, revealing crap letters, "I've had nothing but vowels all night, and you all know it. What am I going to spell, e-i-e-i-o? You had the J, the X, and the Z! Come on! That's bullshit! Sure I got the "q" but that was after I'd used all of my "u's" spelling Uluru. Sometimes I'd make people stay up all night for rematches with me until I'd finally win, just like Dad the Conqueror had done before me.

My youngest brother Joe would play games by himself. We'd hear him from his room playing Monopoly on his bed—dice rolling, car racing around the board. We'd overhear him getting sent to jail, cursing—we'd hear him land on his own Boardwalk and then pay himself. He didn't even always win—like he was teaching himself how to lose. Talk about low self-esteem.

Games were not just games in our house and the stakes were way too high for them to be much fun. They were tests, rites of age, badges of honor. By the time you moved out of that house, you were a killer, a skill that didn't go over very well when I began dating. I challenged crushes, dates, and boyfriends to games of Scrabble, Trivial Pursuit, tennis, and chess. If a guy argued with something I said out on a date, I'd respond, "How much you wanna bet?" Usually, he'd say, "I'm not going to bet you."

"Because you know you're wrong! Bet me!" To me, this was foreplay.

Mom would pull me into her kitchen corner of the world—where she'd sit at the Formica table in front of her ashtray and portable TV, warning, "Debbie, girls don't beat boys—you know that, right?"

"What?" I'd answer annoyed. I didn't know and worse—I didn't *want to know.* Who made that rule? All I knew was how much I wanted to win. I had to win. "Let the boys win, or they won't like you. You'll end up a bitter old maid and die alone," Mom repeated for years. I never heard her, not really. I thought her advice was left over from the stone age, a time when men slayed the mastodons while cave women sat around bitching that their backs hurt until someone invented cushions. Didn't she know that we'd been "liberated?" When I moved out, I was in search of people whom I could beat at games.

"I'll find men who like to lose," I said. Winning made me feel powerful, important, and even thin.

When I moved to New York City and began the eternal hunt for men, I'd go to bars and play my family's favorite car game: list the states and their capitals, for money. Times were changing, and I thought that any man I'd be interested in would clearly want a woman who could recite the states and their capitals in a pinch, in a snowstorm, even with a gun to her head. It was my peculiar talent, and I'd worked hard on it. It would go something like this:

Bellied up to the bar, wedged in between a few guys—I'd ask someone where they were from. Then ... in the sexiest voice I could muster, "Oh, Maryland? Capital—Annapolis? Nice." Next, I'd casually mention loudly so the barflies nearby heard me, that I could name all the states and their capitals. Most people wouldn't give a damn, but eventually, someone would take the bait and doubt it. I'd say, "How much do you doubt it?" Then I'd get a pool going, and I'd go to work alphabetizing the states and their capitals on a clean napkin. I could make a pile of crumpled bar bucks that way. It was beautiful, until one night this geographic illiterate insisted that I was wrong, and Tucson was the capital of Arizona. He even bragged that he was from Arizona, so he "oughta know!" Then he gathered some support from the other bar yahoos, and no matter how right I was, the internet wouldn't come to my rescue for several decades, and I had to hand my money to the loser in the "I'm With Stupid" T-shirt, because everyone thought Tucson sounded right, not Phoenix. Idiots, boy was Dad right. People don't even know where they're from! How do they find their way home?

"I suppose Kansas City is the capital of Kansas?" I mocked in a superior tone—because I knew how to attract men to myself and find love—I had long blonde hair and plenty of state facts.

"Well, yeah," someone replied like *I was the dope.*

"No, Topeka. I know that because my father taught me. 'I'll let you peek at the answer if you don't know the capital of Kansas.' I've known that since I was four, you map moron! Tucson is a dusty border town overrun with illegal migrant workers and iguanas. It's a desert shit hole—I've been there—there's no capital! Know why? Because it's in Phoenix, rhymes with Kleenex, and you can put that on your tombstone—pun intended!" I slammed my ten bucks on the bar and headed to another tavern to find different, smarter men, ones that I hadn't annoyed ... yet.

Sometimes my mother would ask, "I don't understand why don't you ever have any dates? What am I supposed to tell my bridge club?"

One time I ran home to my Upper West Side apartment, a mere three-block jaunt from The Red Baron where I'd been drinking for several hours (several years, actually). I grabbed my almanac, the higher power to all Kaspers, and dragged it back to the bar to finish castrating the drunk I was arguing with over the capital of Oregon. "Portland? Are you fucking kidding me?" I couldn't help it. He was cute.

Sometimes my mother's warnings would pirouette across my mind. "Men don't like to be made to feel stupid, especially by a woman." I'd consider it for just a second, before I'd dismiss it, snickering at her silly notions. *My generation has been liberated, Mom, men don't mind being idiots, the ones I like don't, anyway!* Besides, I liked to win, I had to win!

I had my future all mapped out. I would become one of those old bar hags who ass up the same seat night after night, guarding the corner of the bar, where "regulars" reigned. I'd pick geography fights with visiting Martini drinkers, dreaming that eventually, some nice man would find it cute—even impressive, and he'd fall in love with me—rescue me from my stool, and my rent-controlled apartment, which was managed by a nation of cockroaches. I'd post myself there nightly from happy hour—until the bartender waved his hand in front of my milky cataracts and yelled into my hearing aid, "Stop, Debbie. He doesn't know the capital of Alaska! Nobody cares.

"Well, then he's just an idiot. I even gave him the hint! 'Juneau the capital of Alaska?' What a mo-ron!" I'd laugh—to nobody. Every now and then, someone would care just enough to engage with me and my little challenge, and I'd win a drink and a nod to feed my hungry beast which would keep my competitive flame flickering within my lonely, stupid soul.

You're Going To Get Old And Wrinkled One Day Too, Debbie!

As a family, we had driven to Florida several times before this trip. That's six people who didn't get along in a station wagon for three days, singing songs which we all had different melodies for. "The Sunshine State" was where they were keeping old people, and some of them had our family names. My mother had aunts and great aunts there, my father had his parents there—and they were all old. It was no secret that I didn't much like old people. To me, they all looked like they'd been doing hard time on a chain gang—extra taupe skin buckling, colorless hair thinning to nothing, hands polka-dotted with liver spots. And no matter what any of them wore, it never fit. Grandparents were great, as an idea—but seeing them just made me sad.

"Well, you're going to be old one day, too, Debbie," my mother said nodding towards me in the back seat. "If you want people to be nice to you when you're dry and wrinkled—you better be nice to them now while your skin is still tight."

"Yep, you'll leak where you didn't even know you had holes, your teeth will turn green and fall out, you'll have to get a new set that sits on your bed stand at night," added Dad.

"Your butt will drop down to meet your ankles, your boobs will head to bed before you do at night, your neck will grow its own drapes, your skin simply *will not* fit you anymore," added Mom, who then chuckled until Dad joined in. Sometimes, for just a moment, they made a great team.

I was already depressed when we called our seats and loaded into the pale blue station wagon that morning. I'd lost my miniature pet turtle from Woolworths a few days before, it had died, it was my first pet and my first death—I was only six. Death just hadn't come up yet, it wasn't a kindergarten subject, and it sure didn't sound like something to look forward to.

About a week before this day, for my birthday, Reid, Dad and I had gone to Woolworths and picked out two grass-green turtles from the huge wading pool of hundreds more turtles—turtles so teensy you could hide them in the palm of your hand. I asked if some other animals came in this miniature size—horses? monkeys? Dad gave me one of those long, sad looks at my question.

We picked out one plastic terrarium for our two turtles to share—then we upsold him to the deluxe model with the removable plastic palm tree, wading pool, and a little deck where the turtles could sunbathe. Reid named his Popeye, mine became Olive Oyl.

I loved my first pet so much that I picked her up every five minutes to kiss her and make sure she knew it. To be honest—I was never clear on which one was Olive Oyl and which was Popeye, so I'd grab the one nearest and give it a big smooch—even hold it to my cheek for a moment, to let her know, "All is well." Reid said that Olive was the one that looked like she was drowning when she tried to swim. I looked down—there she lay—always sunbathing. She was a dud. Sometimes I'd pick her up and shake her a little to make sure she was okay, holding her belly up to my ear as if I were a turtle doctor.

"Stop fondling that *goddamn* turtle, Debbie, you're going to kill it," warned Mom.

Honestly, she was never much fun—she came home from Woolworths a dullard—withdrawn, a complete social disaster. All she did was loll around in the water like a green rock. Sometimes I'd hold Olive Oyl by the edges of her shell to fly her around so she'd know what it was like to be a bird, or I'd tickle her under the belly—anything to get her to smile. Popeye was infinitely more active from the start, always doggie paddling in the pond, even trying to crawl out of the steep and slippery sides of his plastic cage, perhaps trying to escape back to South America.

One morning, I woke up to find one of the turtles was lying face up in the shallow pool, little eyes bulging but staring nowhere. I burst into tears and called to Reid, "Something's wrong with Popeye."

Reid took one quick look, "That's Olive Oyl." I knew it to be true because the turtle still alive was doing laps, like Mark Spitz. I started to wail.

My mother tried to muster up some empathy, but the best she could come up with was, "It's dead." I moved into a blubber.

"For *chrissakes*, it's only a turtle, Debbie. It cost twenty-nine cents. We'll get another. Have your father flush her down the toilet."

At that moment, Dad swooped her out of my open palm and flushed her down the toilet—in one move, before I could scream

"Noooooooooooo!" I covered my little eyes with my teeny hands, from inside the bathtub, "No, Daddy, no!" I watched in horror, while Dad flushed twice, and poor Olive Oyl swirled counter-clockwise down the toilet—her burial at sea. And she was gone! It all seemed so cruel, so I wept inconsolably from the basin of the bathtub. This was the day my life changed, forever.

It was incomprehensible to me what had happened. My parents and my brother all crowded into the bathroom, offering pathetic condolences. "For *chrissakes*, Debbie, it's only a turtle! You are making so much of this!" said mom, throwing up her hands.

"Everything dies, Debbie," said Dad, trying to make me feel better.

All I could do was look over at the plastic turtle condo, which was exactly one turtle short of a pair, and burst back into tears. Nobody understood me. It wasn't about Olive Oyl—she was a drag. It was the idea of death that was ruining my morning. After several hours of hysteria, they finally called in Aunt Janet to explain death to me. Janet was everybody's very own Mary Poppins, and she lived right up the street from us. She loved kids, and we loved her right back. Janet was a school teacher who knew how to communicate with everybody.

I was still squatted in the bathtub, blubbering away when my favorite Aunt came in and dropped down onto the toilet seat. She said she understood how sad I was. *Thank God someone did! Who are these heathens I live with?*

"The turtle had to go back to where it came from," my aunt said.

"To Woolworths?"

"No, silly, some place bigger and more magical than that."

"I tickled her, and she didn't feel good."

"That's right. She wasn't healthy, and when you don't feel good, sometimes it is better if you die," Janet said, waiting just the perfect amount of time for me to absorb it all. "Everything has to go back to where it came from at some point, Debbie. Everything dies."

That was bad news for me. I started calling people out by name, "Is Mommy going to die? Is Daddy going to die? You? My brother?" I named everybody I knew waiting for a "no," but so far, I was batting a thousand. I finally asked the most inconceivable, "Am I going to die?"

"Not for a very, very long time. It's so far into the future it will seem like it never gets here," she said with tenderness.

"So that's a yes?" my wet eyes must have asked.

"Everything gets old—even trees and leaves get old, and then they turn brown and die."

"Am I going to turn brown?"

"In a way, yes."

And my childhood was gone ... *forever.*

Part II
How'd You Like A Poke In The Eye
With A Sharp Stick?

No matter how many times our family made this same trek to Florida, my brothers and I would get excited whenever we crossed a state line. We'd see the ads, the teasers, the dangling carrots. "You're almost out of New Jersey—the Garden State" or "Fifty miles till the Virginia border, Buckoo!" and from that moment forward, I couldn't speak for everyone else, but I couldn't to *wait* to get to the Virginia border. Then, after the big two-state build-up, we'd pass the "Welcome to Virginia" sign and Dad would scream, "We're in Virginia, kids!" But I didn't see a border, where was the border? There was no line—and worse, I'd feel no different, there was no thrill at all. This was a big let down. I expected a change. Real change, the way the states looked on my map puzzle; different colors, different shapes, maybe dancing bears, the Good Humor man handing out ice cream bars, something...? On this particular trip, everything just looked ugly—North Carolina, South Carolina, Reid—life. So much bad news had been dropped on me that week that even my KitKat bar had lost its appeal—it might as well have been a hard boiled egg. First I meet death, and now I find out that I'm going to get old and ugly too? *Why live? Why bother? Why was I born? Why is the sky blue?*

We were coming up on "South of the Border," the World's Fair of pit stops in South Carolina where station wagons full of families would stop to buy legal firecrackers, which were generally illegal back in their own home states. Cherry bombs for the boys, sparklers for the girls, Valium for the parents. Somebody had built it into a whole tacky city and then smartly placed billboards starting way back in Virginia, inviting you in a way that you dared *not* stop there. When we pulled into the parking lot, I didn't even want to get out of the car. I was obsessing over the concept of aging and dying. Up until this week, I'd thought that some people were old—some people were young, and those were just the breaks. I never took it for granted—I felt very special that I got to be the pretty little girl with platinum hair and flawless skin. I even managed to whip up some empathy for those less fortunate than I: the wrinkled, the disheveled, the birth marked.

Later that day when we crossed the invisible line that divides Florida from Georgia, I got some more bad news. I overheard that my mother's great grand something was going to be visiting the cousin we were staying with that night.

"Your Great Grandmother!?" I squealed. "Ew!?"

"She's my Great Great Aunt Willard. She's ninety-four. Everybody calls her 'Nana.'"

"What does that make her to you, Debbie?" Dad asked while checking me out in his personal microscope: the rear view mirror.

"Na-na-na," Reid answered. Everybody laughed, except for me.

"I'm not kissing her!" This was shaping up to be one shitty week.

"Oh, that's all right. You can sleep in the car tonight—you don't even have to come in the house. I doubt the alligators can get in the car, but I can't be sure of the water moccasins," said Dad, still watching me in his rear view.

"And I guess you don't want to come with us to Weeki-Wachi the live mermaid springs?" Mom piped in.

"They're not real mermaids," Reid said to make sure I had all the facts before I made my decision. He was two years older and twelve books smarter.

I didn't feel like visiting any old people that day, or any other day by the way! I particularly hated going to visit my grandparents' houses—either set, it didn't matter. Whenever I mentioned something like that, my father would say, "Would you rather stay home and get poked in the eye with a sharp stick?" Sometimes it was a toss-up.

I was content with a greeting card relationship with old people, a birthday or Easter card that had a duck on the front, saying, "You're a quack of a granddaughter." When I opened the card upside down—five beautiful bucks would float zigzag to the ground. How I loved those five-dollar cards, I even came to expect them every birthday. I loved the ones from my father's parents a little more because their cards had more like twenty-five bucks in them—they were the wealthy grandparents. I'd rip the card out of the envelope and snap it open in one move, never even reading their personal message. Grabbing my money, I'd flap it around in a bragging way like I was rich. I was under the impression that I was an heiress since I had wealthy grandparents.

Whenever we went to my mother's parents' house in Arizona it smelled like old people lived there. We'd walk up the driveway, and that old smell wafted our way, never the apple pie you were supposed to smell—more like musty pie.

Grandma and Grandpa Root, lived in a small tract home in Sun City, Arizona, which was ironically dark and depressing inside. Blinds were drawn, curtains practically stapled together, purposely shutting out Arizona's famous sunshine. And awnings were posted around the house in case any ambitious afternoon rays tried to break in.

Grandma Root was thin and pale, the color of band aids. She was so tiny I couldn't figure out how my mother could even have gotten inside of her to come out, as that's how I heard birth happened. Every time we visited, there was less of her than before—like she was disappearing. She always sat on her stained sofa and said, "Debbie, come sit next to your old grandma and let me kiss you!" I was a well-behaved child, trained like a baby seal, with the promise of snacks (or go without, depending on how I performed). I could always muster up a cheek or two for her to kiss. After all, she was a sweet old lady, but she had the family mole in the middle of her cheek, which looked like a flesh pearl hanging onto her blush face. I couldn't bear to kiss that cheek for fear of bumping into it with my lips, so I'd close my eyes and hold my nose.

My mother's father, Grandpa Root, would stand by the kitchen cupboard, nipping his whiskey all day until he finally burst into a sloppy song, trying to make a party out of our visits. He'd belch out Mexican folk songs, usually shooting spit on everyone while bouncing us on his bony knee. "La Cucaracha, la Cucaracha, ya no puede caminar," a song he told us, was about a cockroach that couldn't travel anymore since it had no marijuana to smoke. I could hear my mother's rolling eyes rattle from across the room, over Grandpa's choice of song. It was wildly inappropriate, and it didn't make sense to me, but he was never happier than spraying this song on his grandchildren. He'd run out of breath between stanzas and cough often, but he'd always bounce us on his knee (often two of us at once) till the last verse. Apparently, it was the only song he knew because sometimes, he'd start the whole thing again, nudging us to sing with him this time. My mother's family had spent eight years in Mexico City when she was a kid, so this was apparently the cultural remains of that experience—that and Mom's occasional outburst of remedial Spanish, "Buenos dias, Senorita! Donde esta la ... oh what do you call a library *goddamnit!*"

I bounced on Grandpa's lap because my mother willed it with bug eyes that said, "He's my father, *goddamnit!*" He was the hardest of the four for me to kiss. His nose was melting into his face like a candle and he constantly had bloodshot eyes which looked to be trying to make a getaway from his face. It broke my little heart and worried me. *One more thing to worry about! Getting a candle nose, and a melted face.*

My Grandmother Kasper was a tough old grand dame—a lady who'd been through hell—and came out on the other side with the "you have no idea," attitude. My parents ran around like ants on crack, whenever she came to visit, trying to make our house look better than was humanly possible—like a bald man wearing a hat—we still know! Once she got there, she'd judge, then showcase her disapproving looks at everything from a lamp to uneven ankle socks. Grandma's hair was borderline lavender, the color of the wealthy and the substitute teacher. Her arthritic hands had bulging knuckles with each joint in every finger overloaded and bursting with pain, like she was carrying pebbles in them. Her fingers looked more like gnarly carrots than fingers, but that didn't stop her from wearing her nails long, pointed and bright red, while her wrists were strangled by gold, diamonds, rubies—all begging attention to her hands. I never understood why. Maybe it was her way of saying, "Yes, my fingers are twisted ugly turnips, but I am still filthy rich, and whom might *you* be?"

Helen Kasper frightened all eight of her grandchildren, and all of the in-laws as well, with her cutting comments and her money. Her motto, "Children should be seen and not heard," was voiced often and loudly.

Grandpa Kasper generally followed close behind, like a butler, cleaning up her wreckage. "Oh, Helen—she doesn't mean that!" he'd say, offering a sweet but spotted cheek for us to kiss, a cheek that had seen a lot of sun and warded off many cancers. The seven cousins would all skedaddle the minute Grandma got sick of us, which was about five minutes into the visit.

One afternoon during the great hungry-eyed child migration of Thanksgiving, 1965, Grandma Kasper had cleared the room of all kids everywhere, except I, who rebelliously lingered behind. Grandma immediately asked me to leave the room as well. Figuring that this was my parents' place, I said, "You're not the boss of me." I may have even stuck my tongue out to emphasize the point.

"Oh!? You don't think so?" asked Grandma. She wasn't the least bit frightened, which surprised me.

But neither was I, knowing that my father wouldn't let anybody hurt us, *except him.* "Nooooooo!" I taunted.

"You're a very rude little girl,"

Without pause I said, "I think it's rude to tell people they're rude."

She smirked and nodded in a "match and game" kind of way. Grandma smiled at me from behind her society mask and motioned for me to skedaddle, which I then did. I'd made my point. We had an understanding from that time on. I said the same thing to Grandma and Grandpa Root the next time I saw them, too. It was time. "You are not the boss of me."

That kiss in Florida with my mother's old Aunt Williard was the lowlight of that life-changing trip during that crappy, endless summer—the one which killed off my youth. A summer that highlighted death and skin flaps as its main attraction. But just in case the memory ever does try to fade, there's a family photo to commemorate the event and keep it alive for me, forever. There she sits, an ancient, distant relative in a straight-backed chair, her sunken eyes shielded by rimless glasses, the sparse hair pulled into a loose bun, like a skein of wool, yellowed gnawed-down teeth, and the big floral dress that would have been more appropriate on a pioneer. Next to this eyesore of a relative stands adorable, but sad, six-year-old me, with the slightest upturn of my little nose, as I am about to go in for the dreaded kiss. I was most likely dreaming of the live mermaids that I'd see later that week, or the snacks my parents had dangled.

In the Chevy station-wagon on our way home from Florida, my mother thanked me for kissing her dinosaur and doled out some M&Ms. "You know, Debbie, one kiss from a young pretty girl like you might help her live a little longer.

"I don't care."

"You don't want her to die, do you?"

While I was thinking about that, my father reminded, "You're going to get old, too.

"I don't want to."

"Well, welcome to the club, young lady. But wouldn't you rather get old and wrinkled than die?" asked Dad.

I teared up over the two unbelievably crappy choices.

"We're going to go visit my Aunt Alice, Aunt Louise and Uncle Harold next week. Three elderly people who will want a kiss from you.

"No!"

"Life is about choices, Debbie. You don't have to ... you can always stay home and I'll get someone to come over and poke you in the eye with a sharp stick."

We drove through North Carolina mostly in silence, there was nothing to see, it looked exactly like South Carolina, which looked exactly like Virginia. I had plenty of time to ponder some of life's choices, and wonder from all sorts of vantage points ... how bad could it really be to get poked in the eye?

It's None Of Your Business
Where The Kaspers Came From

Most everyone I know has "people" always going on about where their "people" are from and how their "people" got to America. My friends the Bergs, brag, "Our people came from Russia. We're Russian Jews." That's very specific and certainly conjures up a snow-globe image of a small village, roasting chestnuts, and balalaikas being strummed by roaming, bearded village elders. I imagine random folk songs erupting in the street, words and melodies later bleeding their way onto Broadway—*Fiddle-diddle deedle-diddle-deedle-diddle-dum*—and I'm jealous.

I've never been a joiner. I generally start my own groups so I'm already in the club when the membership drive begins. Perhaps it's because I don't know where I'm from or where my family's from. I know what I've heard, but something's not right. Growing up, my ancestry was always shrouded in mystery—like we were part of some foreign bloodline witness protection program—and nobody was talking. There's just always been this sense of not belonging—the goose in the duck-duck-goose game.

My college friend, Paul Flanagan always boasts that he's 100% Irish, and I wasn't about to argue. He seems Irish—he has a hearty laugh and enjoys a cocktail or three. His wife bought him a subscription to Ancestry.com. "Guess what I am?" he asked in his leading way.

"Chinese?"

"Irish—one hundred percent!" He threw up his hands in a "What are you gonna do?" pose. I was jealous—not jealous of him being Irish—anyone can be Irish. They came over wholesale, in bulk. It was his proud clarity that irked me. There are bars in every major American city named after him for God's sake. Grabbing a Heineken, Paul asked, "What are you again? Aren't you something?"

I did my usual song and dance. "I'm a mutt—Scottish, German, Czechoslovakian, Hungarian, Polish, Mormon, alcoholic, atheist, Cherokee Indian—or maybe none of that. Nobody seems to really know. It's a secret—a need-to-know basis."

All I ever knew about my mother's bloodline was that her father's people were heavy drinkers from Scotland, making my mother half scotch—the other half was bitter. The family name was Root, even though no one had a clue what ours were. Mom's maternal side seemed to be from Scotland too, but nobody knew what part or who came over when. Dad's crew left one country and showed up in America a completely different nationality.

One day, out of the blue, when I was in grammar school, my mother announced that we were descendants of James II from Scotland. No idea what prompted her to even bring it up. It's not like someone had asked, "Are you perchance of the Stewart bloodline? Did you know Mary, or just in passing? Sad what she had to endure."

"Am I a princess?" I asked with my pale voice in case it was a family secret.

"If you like, sweetie-pie." Then I looked up James "The Who Cares?" in our huge Encyclopedia Britannica—he was from the 1400s. *Big deal, they probably didn't even have forks yet! Here, he was a king, yet, forced to eat his king's food face down in his plate because of the year it was.* I wasn't sure—*maybe they ate with twigs, sharp rocks, or even pointy elbows. Sad, really.* That same week, one of my schoolmates announced that she was related to Thomas Jefferson, he was her great great great something or other. *Now that's a name to bring up at a gathering,* I thought. Why would anybody start throwing around James II of Scotland to try and impress a crowd? Whereas classmates lined up in rows to congratulate Donna and her Thomas Jefferson connection, and I joined.

It's a moot point anyway since there's no corroboration on the James II story. Years later, and I still can't find a single brother who even ever heard that bit of ancestral scuttlebutt. So, either I dreamt it, or Mom made it up, not wanting me going to school on Family Tree Day only to have someone figure out that our ancestors were actually wild turkeys.

My father's side of the aisle gusted up a tornado of rumors throughout the years. One blew around the family, that we were descendants of Alexander Hamilton. This made sense—several men in the family had the middle name Hamilton, and I love musicals. I looked him up, and I was proud that he was a colonial overachiever; he created the treasury system, wrote "The Federalist Papers," and still found time to get shot by Aaron Burr. He wrote the federalist papers ... I write jokes. My family tree is clearly growing into the ground. This rumor erupted after my father and his father were both gone, but I got curious and went to Texas to ask my father's sister,

Aunt Janet. "No, that's not true," she said with a laugh, disappointing everyone. I felt sick. All my cousins and brothers started pointing fingers at each other. Who started this rumor? No one knew! We couldn't even trace hearsay back.

I was told that the Kaspers (Dad and Janet's family) came from Western Europe. Germany. Not the Germany of today, but from Bohemia, the part that couldn't hold onto its borders. It used to be Czechoslovakia, then Austro-Hungary—even Poland for a long weekend. The borders over there changed more often than I've changed underwear. We argued about the borders at a family gathering once, pulling out encyclopedias, almanacs, birth certificates. Joe started crying, "I don't want to be hungry!"

Dad abruptly ended our family border war, "We're better than German. We're BoHunks." (Bohemian/Hungarian—basically Polish, Hungarian, Czech, and German).We were getting nowhere. But it gets more mysterious because the name Kasper is always Jewish, except for my dad's family, who were Presbyterians (save my standalone dad, who was an atheist—orthodox, atheist). "God is for weak people. Religion is for sad people. It's a crutch!" he'd say with a laugh while throwing back his Canadian Club.

Mom's family got involved with a little start-up religion called Mormonism and headed west. "The women gave birth on the trails. They wouldn't even stop, sometimes the kid got left where he fell, we probably have some kin in Nebraska." Mom imparted to me late one night around too many cocktails.

"Really?" I asked, riveted.

"Maybe," she replied. "I could've read that in a book. It was so long ago—I just don't remember." My mother's parents were excommunicated from the LDS, they'd rather have cocktails anyway, so it was a win-win for all. Then Mom became an atheist, too. I was brought up with no religion and lots of alcohol. "Atheaholism." Our Sundays were for hangovers, we worshiped Bloody Marys. We crossed each other—not ourselves.

But here's the strange part—on her deathbed, my father's Aunt Alice, my grandfather's sister, pulled my half-sister Susan into her, confiding, "The Kaspers are really Jews!!" And she dropped dead. True story. That made sense to me because I'm a "Hebophile." I have always wanted to be a Jew. My best friends are all Jewish, I love kreplach, and I saw "Schindler's List" on New Years Day. There weren't a lot of goyum in that theatre! But my sister—she was crazy, and I use the term in the strictest way. She was insane. Bonafide. They say that if you shake your family tree, a few nuts will fall out, and Susan was ours. So ... did my Great Aunt Alice say that? Or did Susan hallucinate it? Jew? Not Jew?

On that same trip to Dallas, visiting Aunt Janet (the last gatekeeper of Kasper alternate history, aka "bullshit"), I asked. "Of course, we're Jews!" she yelled in front of her extended family of devout Presbyterians. I was thrilled, but her kids and her kids' kids all looked confused and depressed. I knew how they felt. I said "Shalom" and flew home, but pretty soon after that, my aunt was diagnosed with Alzheimer's. So ... back to square one.

I read somewhere that the earliest form of human life is believed to be bacteria. We evolved from bacteria out of the primordial ooze. Perhaps my ancestors didn't come over in the Mayflower, but they came over *on* it—as barnacles? And if we have evolved from bacteria, my great great great great grandmother could have been strep throat for all I know. So ... all I know for certain is that my heritage is nothing but a goulash of confused hearsay, my ancestry mired in the murk, and worse—my Judaism is but a mere pipe dream. Oy. I guess it's time to do some research. I'm slightly paralyzed by the fear that the real story would pale in comparison to the one I tell and, honestly, I just want to be a Jew. I hear that Mormons have stellar genealogy records and lists, but then again—the only list of theirs we'd be on would be their shit list. One day I will contact the Latter Day Saints, and I hope their report will mention the Cherokee rumor because only I even ever heard that one. If that one is true, then it would help explain my aversion to camping. Maybe I am a Cherokee Princess—or did I dream that?

The Day Dad Threw Us
A Surprise Half-Sister

One morning in 1967, when I was a pre-teen, my father left the house early, warning my three brothers and me that he was bringing us back a big surprise. "Big surprise," Mom chanted, blowing some used Kool smoke in our faces to emphasize the point. Convinced that we were finally getting the dog we'd been bugging them for, we all began to fantasize.

I wanted a puppy so badly, I would cry myself to sleep at night. It was on my Christmas list and my birthday list. I'd beg my parents anytime I had nothing else to do—then I started lobbying my three brothers to join my dog crusade.

Being the only girl in a house with three brothers—was like being a balloon in a nail factory—danger lurked everywhere I turned. My parents were uptight Anglos. Dad treated us like he was still in the Marine Corps, and we were the crappiest platoon that ever marched. Most mornings, he'd blare obnoxiously, "Reveille" at the top of his whistle to wake us up. Mom's thoughts on love were passed down through her Scottish people who believed "affection was like roast beef—only for special occasions, and even then, it might be tough and there probably won't be enough to go around." Her hugs were quick and to the point, like being held by a cactus. Usually, there was a cigarette dangling from her lips, so it was your job to make sure you didn't get burned. Yes, I'd dream of a cuddly puppy loving me the way puppies do—unconditionally, softly, sweetly licking me to sleep at night.

At precisely 5:00 my three brothers and I lined up at the front door like the Von Trapps, in wait for our puppy, arguing about whose room it would sleep in that night.

"You kids are crazy if you think you're getting a puppy. Who's gonna take care of it?" my mom laughed.

"I will!" we all yelled.

"Yeah, for about a week, just like the mice, the hamsters, the *goddamned* fish, and that stinky baby raccoon, for *chrissakes*. We kill one more animal in this house, the ASPCA is going to drag me to pet prison!"

But there was to be no puppy. Instead, my father walked in with a sixteen-year-old hippie! Even though I'd never actually seen a hippie, I was pretty sure this was one because she was wearing dangling earrings and a loosely-woven poncho. Her blackish-brown hair was divided straight down the middle, waving wildly down her back, almost chanting, "I'm free ... free!" The hippie smiled at me from behind the most devilish brown eyes I'd ever seen. A smile that tilted to the side, almost a smirk—that said "Boy, you're gonna be glad you know me."

Who is this beatnik hippie? And why is she with MY father? Dad began his verbal tap-dance by mentioning that he'd been married before.

"Married before Mom? How?" I shrieked. I didn't like where this was going. *First of all, where the hell is my puppy, mister?*

"I was married to Susan's mother, Helen. They live in Massachusetts."

"Who's Susan?" I asked stupidly.

"This is Susan," said Dad, thumb-pointing to the long-haired stranger standing right there in my living room, whom I now hated.

I suddenly felt sick. "Does she have our puppy?"

He began again, "This is your sister."

"Then why doesn't she live here?" I wasn't getting it. I was not the smartest kid in the house. I wasn't even the smartest kid in my bedroom, and I slept alone.

"She's your half-sister. You have a big sister, now. She's your big sister," he kept repeating as if the drone of the chant would lull us into liking the idea. I panicked, knowing that there wasn't enough love to go around here, already.

A six-pack of questions shot out of my brothers' mouths, "Why haven't we met her before? Does everyone have a half-sister? Are there more coming? What does 'half' mean? Does Mom know?"

"I'm standing right here, aren't I?" said Mom, deadpan. I couldn't help but notice that she didn't seem to be "in" on this surprise half-sister party Dad was throwing. Maybe she was wishing (like we all were,) that Dad had dragged a smaller mammal into the house that day: a guinea pig, a baby goat, a young Jehovah's Witness, anything but a sister, you can't just forget to feed sisters until they die. This will require much closer attention.

My youngest brother Joe, stomped off to his bedroom, screaming, "We already have a sister! and we don't like that one!"

"She's your half-sister because you share one parent. You have different mothers," said Dad.

"Can you do that?" I asked. "Who's her father, then?"

Susan straightened her smile, put her arms around me, and whispered in the most soothing voice, "Debbie, he's my pop, too. We'll share him, okay? I'm so happy to finally meet you. I've always wanted a little sister—this will be great."

I couldn't believe she was already hugging me. Boy was she fast. Susan was a Kasper all right—the spitting image of Aunt Phoebe, who died the year before of pneumonia (at least that's what they told us, more to be revealed!) Phoebe's and Susan's resemblance was eerie.

"You're my little Sissy-boo!" she said with more affection than I'd gotten—maybe ever! I smiled in my lying way. It was all so strange.

"Okay, but he's more *my* father, right?"

"Well technically, he's been my father for longer than he's been yours," said Susan."

"But he's *my* father," I insisted. "Mine." I'd always wanted a sister, too—I had to admit, but I wanted a *whole* sister. I didn't want one just dropped over like a fruitcake.

The Kasper weekend dinners were legendary—a roast of some sort, creamy mashed potatoes, asparagus with hollandaise, and for dessert: the family fight. During this awkward dinner, everyone was more jacked up than usual. Mom was tossing bourbons back like there was contest going. Dad was chain-smoking his beloved Lucky Strikes, and I was busy ogling and touching my new sister. There sat Susan blathering away about how fabulous we all were. She had something nice to say about everyone. Nobody knew how to react, so we all just sat there stupidly nodding. Compliments were rare around this joint. I'd learned to go without. If someone ever did accidentally compliment me, I'd get suspicious, like I was about to get swatted, or assigned more chores, or even tied down and forced into one of mom's bad hair cuts. Susan's joy was pure and infectious. Her spirit was already wafting around the house like incense and by the end of the meal, everyone started loosening up.

After I cleared the dishes, as I served up Mom's homemade New Jersey strawberry shortcake (which was smothered in whipped cream), an idea percolated from some mischievous spot buried deep within my unloved heart. In a quickly constructed moment, I piled extra whip cream onto Susan's strawberries, scuttled over to her new place at my family's table, held the plate in front of her, but instead of serving it ... I smooshed it into her face!

"Now you're a Kasper!"

After a shocked few seconds, from behind the dripping mask of white, my brand-new sister started cackling, and then we all joined in, laughing as one. "Oh, Deborah, I already love you!" she screamed. I fell hard for my sister at that moment. She had the kind of laugh that could chase the crumbs off a table. But then she kept erupting with that laugh, over and over until it began to sound a little unhinged.

"Welcome to the family," I said. My sister was the first person to love me out loud. She visited throughout that summer, and eventually, she started blurting out how much she loved me whenever it occurred to her, which was often. At first, it was pretty shocking the way she just threw the word "love" around like it was free. It was a little embarrassing, but it was also strangely soothing.

There we'd be in the middle of our meal, nurturing an argument, when she'd haul off and scream out something inappropriate, like "I love you, Pop! You're the best!" It would take us all a moment to recover. She didn't know you didn't "love somebody" in the middle of dinner, the poor thing, not in this house you didn't. Nobody in my family ever said the "L" word unless there was alcohol involved. And we hadn't ever called our father "Pop."

Eventually, my father started responding with something equally deranged, like, "I love you, too, Susie." I couldn't believe what she was starting here. Love was spreading like a rash. Then I started throwing it around freely, too, and most members of the family joined in eventually—slowly, slowly, but nevertheless.

Susie quilted me with a crazy patchwork of sisterly love that I'd only read about in Louisa May Alcott books. I was twelve years old when I learned how to say, "I love you, too." She was being raised in Massachusetts by my father's first wife, Helen, who my mother fingered as "ca-ray-zee." Mom pronounced it with several extra syllables like a beatnik might before banging on his bongo drums: "ca-ray-zee-ee." I was young, but I knew it wasn't good when your mother was ca-ray-zee-ee. Crazy was one of those things that could catch on, or so I'd overheard.

There was already some crazy on the Kasper side of the family. My father's youngest sister, Aunt Phoebe, was also "a bit nuts," something you could hear my parents often remark—if you were eavesdropping from around the right corner. Even I could see that Phoebe was different. When she laughed, she sort of snorted and shook her shoulders like a threatened hog. You couldn't miss the physical resemblance between Susan and Phoebe—which was baffling to me, since they'd never even met. It was crazy, man.

Our family would leak out secrets as you age, like a government agency raising your clearance at different levels. I had to wait until I hit forty before I heard some of the big ones. Scuttlebutt started dribbling out at a little gathering with brothers and cousins. My older cousin, Jeff began, "Aunt Phoebe didn't die of pneumonia, you know." Everyone started adding a tile of the mosaic.

"She committed suicide," said Reid.

"She was a lesbian too, so ..." added Joe.

"That's why Grandma and Grandpa sent her to psychiatrists and gave her shock treatments—because she liked girls." Reid said.

"She got thrown out of boarding school when she was twelve," said my cousin Chris.

"Yeah, she and another little girl were found naked," added Kathy.

My head almost twirled around on my neck. "What? Was I, adopted? How come I don't know this? Why didn't anybody ever tell me! Then why did she marry Uncle Hans?" Everyone looked at me as if I should answer that question myself. This was worse than the day I found out there was no Santa Claus—and by the hand of the same two spoilsports: the oldest of the seven—Jeff and Reid. Then cousin Chris put the nail in the coffin, "Just look at all her sculptures, they're all of naked women," she said, adding a knowing nod.

"Oh my God," I whimpered, just like the moment when I got the final clue about Santa.

Jeff had asked, "How could one fat man possibly travel around the whole world in one night? Don't you think he'd get hungry?"

"And why the red?" asked Reid, his small eyes slit, and judging me like I was an idiot.

My poor Aunt Phoebe—so tortured, living a false life, I thought. *Forced to marry a man to conform to a society that she probably abhorred—and it killed her.*

But it wasn't until many years after that first time I met Susan that I would find out that my mother had actually stolen my father from her best friend, Helen, one summer in Dayton, Ohio. Dad and Helen were newlyweds when Robert and Shirley ran off together and started a new life and a new family. Dad tried to get custody of Susan away from her troubled mother, but I'll never really know how hard he tried.

Susan continued to visit us in New Jersey in "the blurbs" as she'd called it since she thought we were all bourgeois. Before she arrived, my life was so carefully guarded and *coiffed*, just like our lawn that I didn't even know I lived in a suburb and certainly had no clue I was "bourgeois," nor was I clear on what it was. But like my sister, the thought of it outraged me, anyway. Susan was an exotic busker who brought music, poetry, sculpture, and unfiltered love into our suburban trance. She nurtured the gypsy in me and nicknamed me her little "Sissy-boo." I'd sit and listen for hours about her off-beat friends: Moses and Party Patty. She had a friend in Springfield who had flipped out. She knew people who were writing novels in Paris. I was mesmerized.

"Make sure you use birth control when you get laid. You don't wanna get knocked up by some moron in Cherry Hill, New Jersey. That'll be the end of your dreams. You'll be sixteen, changing shitty diapers," warned my new sister. "You're too good for that, Deborah. You gotta watch your ass, my poor little Sissy-boo. Don't get stuck in this shitty, bourgeois town," she said, snapping her big fingers right before my eyes. I still wasn't positive what "bourgeois" meant, but shitty diapers were pretty clear, so ... *No thank you to both.*

"Everyone just *baas* along with Mary, like sheep. Don't follow them, Debbie—make the sheep follow you."

One weekend, Susan took the bus down from college in Boston and insisted the family sit in our living room in a little circle while she read a poem, she'd eked out on the Greyhound. She began, "*The woman with the black hair, blacker than night, wronger than right.*" We were trying to be polite, which was not a family forte, so there were fits and groans from the peanut gallery of brothers. My mother stared them down with that "This will all be over soon" nod. Dad told them to sit the hell down and act like they were in this family. If ever you didn't want to participate in family activities, my father would accuse you of not being a member of the family. "You don't want to watch *Bonanza* with the rest of your family? Are you not in the family now?" He'd ask innocently like he really wasn't sure. If you said "no" to that off-handed threat, he'd go on, "Well, then you better find somewhere else to live, and good luck finding a family that doesn't watch *Bonanza*—it's the #1 TV show in America. Need help packing? I'll be up right after Ben Cartwright gets his stolen Impala back."

Dad was proud when Susan dazzled us with her artsy projects. She made mobiles out of feathers and antique beads. She painted, sang, took photographs—when I called them "pictures," she corrected me. Her photographs were of depressed people, forlorn train stations, a wrinkled old woman on a bench. Nobody in our house ever made anything more complex than a potholder, and mine were always riddled with holes, at that. My mother kept burning her hands when she used them. One week at crafts camp, I made her a napkin holder entirely out of Popsicle sticks, with some plastic jewels glued to it for decoration, only to be followed up with painted rocks, necklaces made out of daisies, and a ceramic ashtray that I painted a face on. Mom could put her butts out right on someone's face, which was something I think she secretly wanted to do.

My mom had mentioned the C-word in the same sentence with

Susan's name one night after she left. I was eavesdropping around the corner, twirling my baton. I was barely without my baton in those years, always twirling, tossing, passing through my legs, faster, like a mad majorette, I'd twirl in the living room, the kitchen, the yard, on my bed, I didn't care—it kept people at an arm's distance from me, and I was determined to make the school squad.

"Susan's different—not crazy. Believe you me, I know crazy, and this isn't it. You're just bourgeois, Shirley," Dad defended, trying to convince himself.

"She's different all right. I'll tell you something, Bob, poetry is something you read to people who want to hear it. You don't force it on them like a hot dog casserole! Some people like hamburgers. That's all I'm saying. This isn't Greenwich Village, and that poem didn't even rhyme. What the hell kind of poem doesn't rhyme? Coffin does not rhyme with laughing—no matter how you slice it."

Susan was always over the top with her exuberance about everything. "Deborah!! Your hair is beautiful! Pop! This is the best steak!" She had this cackle that lingered far longer than anyone else's, and she'd throw in a long breath releasing an "ahhhhh" at the end of it. But her joy had this twinkle in its eye as if to say we were the joke; we were the poor working squares of the world who didn't get it, and were missing the whole point.

When she left, she'd write me letters stuffed with more poetry. I held onto each stanza like it was evidence in a trial. I'd tack them onto my bulletin board that hung above my bedroom desk, right below my picture of Patty Duke. One day, after she went abroad to Paris for a semester, a postcard arrived from Paris bearing this message:

And the rain of eyes cries out buckets of vomit, falling on to the heads of idiots.

Even fourteen-year-old Debbie could notice that Susan's joy had turned, and there was something sad and weird on this postcard. I showed it to Mom, who said, "Well, the nut didn't fall too far from that tree. Her mother's a full-baked loaf of banana bread, I oughta know—she was my best friend."

Part II
Shock Treatments

Susan was twenty-one the first time she "flipped out," as we had come to call it. It had a kinder ring to it than "went crazy." Our pop had to fly to California to bring her home. It was the early seventies, and she had driven across country only to freak out on some bad acid in Colorado. Some guy she "shacked up with," as Dad put it, broke her heart, and by the time she got to Frisco, she was at the beginning of what we later found out was a manic-depressive episode.

My father filled us in on his harrowing trip. On the plane back from San Francisco, she rang the stewardess and when she arrived, blasted her, "Listen, Stewie, you have way too much rouge on—this isn't Kabuki theatre here—it's a plane, and you're scaring people." When the stewardess dropped off the drinks, my sister hissed, "Don't let the bad men make you be their whore." She usually did have a point somewhere in the back of her mind, blinking out a twisted Morse code of a message.

Back east, Susan was quickly diagnosed as manic-depressive, (what they used to call "bipolar" before the marketing people got involved). Her joy had found its soul mate—pain. Susan embarked on a lifetime of medications, psychotherapy, shock treatments, and a string of very private mental institutions only to be followed up with many state institutions. It was hauntingly like Aunt Phoebe who was also manic-depressive and had been in and out of mental institutions for most of her young life until one day, at 45, she took herself from that life, leaving no note, not even a "no, thank you!" This disorder is hereditary, so I began to worry about my own sanity. *Was I the next to blow?* I'd monitor my thoughts to self-diagnose, make sure I was having normal ones, whatever normal thoughts were, (I wouldn't have known a normal thought if it moved in and started twirling my baton.) I'd look at myself straight on in the mirror, and say, "Hi, how are you today?" And if no gargoyles crawled out of my eyes, I'd figure I was good until the next check-in. Dad foresaw the deja vus ahead of him: the therapists, the institutions, the shock treatments, the note.

In between Susan's initial diagnosis and her first official lock up, my parents moved her into my girlhood bedroom, since I was at college in Vermont. My father's idea was to offer Susan the normal life she never had, let her mingle with a couple of little brothers and eat more red meat. "She just needs more family time. We'll play games," said Dad. "We'll throw some steaks on the grill, and play Risk every night. She'll be fine." Somehow, my father thought that challenging his Bohemian daughter to an endless game of world domination over some charred cow, would spark her back to reality—or at the very least, awaken her inner conqueror—and then she'd have territories to invade, which would give her a reason to keep going on.

Two months into this normal life, Susan went stark raving mad and had to be institutionalized. It happened during a violent game of Risk, while Dad was attacking her from Irkutsk and it made perfect sense to me—he was a bully at this game—he'd pretend like he was really a ruthless conqueror and he had no problem killing off his own children and their entire nations. He'd wipe you off your continents and say, in the most unsympathetic way, "Bye, bye. You can go make me another drink now that you have no countries to protect." Sometimes he'd even use a Russian or German accent to say it. I completely understood how that could've been her last straw. When he did that to *me*, it drove me to go mix him a drink, and then one for myself (by age twelve).

My parents drove Susan to the suburbs of Philadelphia and checked her into a psychiatric hospital called Fairmont Farms. My parents' best friend Nancy Hatfield had gone there when she had her "episode"—so that's who my parents called for a reference. My mother was worried the neighborhood would find out. That always concerned her as much as anything, "What will people think?" She wouldn't dare ask for another reference, which she figured doubled the chances of neighbors finding out.

I came home for Christmas to my redecorated girlhood room. Susan had converted it into a sort of beatnik garage sale. Psychedelic hippie mobiles dangled from the ceilings, and poetry had been written on my private things. She'd written in the margins of my diary, defaced pictures of me, wrote across my face on one photo: *"Carlsbad Caverns, Dig Mistakes Underground."* I laid in bed that night, wondering if I was still in the line of fire to get the family insanity. I did a spot-check inventory on my fleeting thoughts, making sure they were normal. They seemed to be, *but how would I really know?* I wondered. Then I wondered if *that thought was normal. And then THAT thought. I'd be up all night (making me wonder the next morning if THAT was normal).*

When I visited Susan, I whispered how very sorry I was that she was locked up. She smiled that crooked smile, "We're all locked up, but only some of us know it," which gave me something deep to ponder that night in my bed. My parents told me that she'd been given shock treatments. Like mental bug zappers—they killed off her memory and stole her off-beat thoughts. This seemed drastic to me, as medieval as a bloodletting—something that they only gave to Kennedys or killers. They followed it up with a steady electric stream of more zaps, finally breaking her spirit, muddling her memory, and erasing precious memories of me, her Sissy-boo. She and I both begged my father to stop with the treatments, but the doctors had their way with her and continued the process of taking the "Susan" out of Susan.

Over the next years, she was in and out of Fairmont Farms a few times, attempted suicide a few times, and threatened it a few more. Sometimes she just wrote the note but wouldn't actually go through with the suicide. My sister was ambitionless from the shock treatments, and committing suicide was clearly a project with a goal at the end. The minute she was released from wherever we were holding her at the time, she'd run back to San Francisco again—and again—and Dad would have to go get her. Like Steve McQueen in *The Great Escape*, she couldn't stop trying to break free from wherever they were keeping her at the time. Then she'd get pumped with some different medication and dragged through some different therapy so she'd calm down for a while, keeping her nutty thoughts and outrageous ideas to herself.

Susan tired of San Francisco like she eventually tired of everything and moved to Vermont. She had a few distant relatives on her mother's side who were apple farmers there, so she began to carve out a simple life that didn't make her sick. Susan was relatively under control on a drug called lithium (the panacea of the manic) and although far from normal, she wasn't breaking down anymore. Like an old car, she could make it around town as long as you didn't throw too many peaks or valleys her way. She didn't always stop at red lights either, but she was hanging in there. I was still in college in Vermont, and I'd drive up to see her from time to time, and she'd always say, "Ah, Deborah, it warms the cockles of my heart just to see you."

I'd try to see her often—I liked warming her cockles—whatever they were. She still nurtured the gypsy in me, raining me with gifts of mobiles, paintings, or handmade jewelry. Nobody loved me the way my sister did. Somehow, I had transcended the bourgeois—she had picked me out of the family line-up and made me special. I became artsy, too. I knitted, crocheted, embroidered, wrote plays, and of course eventually became as anti-bourgeois as I possibly could—I moved to New York and became an actress (at several restaurants).

After our Pop died, Susan became a bit of a family project that the rest of the family had sadly neglected—like a worm-farm rotting on the windowsill of a fourth-grade classroom. I was living in New York at the time, so I'd call her occasionally, crossing my fingers that I'd find her using central ideas in her sentences. I'd tell her I loved her and ask her how the cockles of her heart were doing. She'd cackle and say something like, "I'm NOT insane, Deborah. Everyone else is." One night she said, "Hey, I need a new kidney—I'm going to be borrowing one of yours, so think about which one you might want to let go of. Left? Right? The one in the middle? Is there one you like better that you'd like to hold on to?"

I tried to make a joke, "My kidney? You never returned the Mamas and the Papas album I lent you!"

"Well, that's just not right," Mom empathized with me on the phone that night, "you can't go giving up one of your kidneys. Who's going to marry you with one kidney? Why is she picking on you? Why doesn't she hit up one of the boys for their kidneys?"

"I think you and me ought to go up there and see what's what," I said.

"You and I," my mother chastised, "you and I." My mother was a grammar snob. It was bad enough that there was manic-depression in our family, but she'd be damned if anybody was going to start substituting subjective pronouns for objective ones as well.

The next week, the state of Vermont also decided that Susan had slid out of her mind, and they committed her to The Vermont State Hospital. She called to tell me they were keeping her there against her will, the staff was wearing her jewelry and secretly performing experiments on her and they were pulling out her long hair to make wigs to give out to the other inmates. I assured her that I would investigate Wig-gate when I got there and encouraged her to take notes.

A few days later, June came. Mom and I headed to Montpelier, Vermont where the state hospital sat amidst the green mountains. Vermont has always held a special place in the heart of our family's history, and to this day, I'm seduced by its verdant serenity. It's a state that makes you feel like you're home, even the first time you go. My grandparents had gone to college there; my parents had gone to college there; I had gone to college there, and we were all privately jealous that Susan had managed to make her life there.

The institution that held my sister was a white-walled building with too many signs telling you where you could or couldn't go and why. When we got to where they were keeping her, I was faint from the smell of insanity. I hadn't seen her in a year, and a lot had changed. She was barely forty, but she was starting to look like Granny Clampett. Her previously luscious hair seemed to have been chopped off in random places with something not precise—like a socket wrench. She'd lost so much weight that her skin was hanging off her like beige fringe. Her teeth were coming undone, and her gums were gray and speckled. She had been a beauty in her day, but now she just looked forgotten, and she smelled like Bactine.

There were no private rooms in the Vermont State Hospital, there was nowhere that we could convene without a visit from any nut who wanted to join our family portrait (that is if Chas Addams had drawn it). It was Ethyl who butted in first. Susan made some formal introductions. "Ethyl, this is my boring sister Debbie—this is my wicked step mom, Shirl. A bit bourgeois, but she's someone who can make it work, polyester suits and all—so tread nicely. I didn't like her at first did you know that, Shirl? You're a home wrecker, but you know what, Shirl? You ain't so bad. You stole my mom's man. Did you know that, Deborah? Your mom stole Pop from my mom—hard to believe two women fighting over that fat old bag of hot air. So, Ethyl, my family drove up from New Jersey in a big olds-people mobile." Susan had passed the point of decorum and lost her filter. She blurted out whatever she wanted—no matter whose feelings got mowed over by her unkind words.

We nodded guiltily together like two kids who'd been caught stealing candy. She continued, "They came to see me because they think I'm crazy. That's what pulled them out of their little lives. They don't realize that they're the crazy ones—they're the ones locked up, not me. I can leave whenever I want, but they're stuck. I can walk right the hell out and never even know that I left. What are you gonna do, Debbie? Where you gonna go? I can go anywhere, can you?"

"It warms the cockles of my heart to see you," I said, trying to shake her back to reality. Susan smiled a broad one, showing me her grey gums; then she changed the subject and turned to her step mom. She didn't seem to remember that I was the one that warmed her cockles. She didn't even remember that I was her Sissy-boo.

"How is old Jersey, Shirl? A shit hole of a place to live, that Jersey! It's okay, I know. Shirl, I know how much of a bitter disappointment your life turned out to be," said Sue, winking at my mom. "We all can't be lucky like me. I got it made. I get to live in Vermont! Ethyl and I got it made."

Old Ethyl gave me the creeps. She was a lifer in a mental wing at the hospital. Her makeup was ghoulish—like rhubarb pie had been tattooed on her cheeks. Her hair was wrapped around the front of her head like a hairy cinnamon bun. Ethyl had insisted on getting very close to me and breathing on me like a dragon. Her breath didn't just stink—her whole insides stunk. She stroked my arm and said, "You have lovely skin. May I pinch you? You're a lovely girl. Your hair is so straight, like wheat. You remind me of me, we're the same."

"Thank you," I whispered. Old Ethyl was missing some teeth, and the ones she had managed to hold onto were black and sharp. I pictured her filing them down at night.

"I bet she could open a can with her teeth," I said to Mom as we drove away that night, trying to lighten the mood of the day.

"Why would she want to?" Mom asked, completely missing the point. Nobody was connecting with anybody on this trip. Everyone was on their own.

I went home to New York, convinced that my appearance had made a significant impact on my half-sister's life, so I could sleep freely at night. Soon afterward, Susan was discharged, but only to be set free in the green pastures of Vermont for a very short while. She had a few incidents that involved some car wrecks and some bad behavior. Pretty soon, the state of Vermont decided my Sissy-boo was in their way, and they legally suggested that she move into a half-way house. By that time, she only owned a shopping bag of stuff, so the move happened fast.

During more lucid times and behind everybody's backs, including her shrink's, Susan became active in mental patients' rights and had gone to court in Vermont, filled out some forms, making sure that nobody could ever make her take her medications unless she wanted to. When she found out that her kidneys were failing from the years of lithium, she took herself off her meds.

The doctor had told her that she'd blown out her kidneys, like two speakers on a stereo, and that she needed dialysis, or she'd be dead in five years—so she whited out the doctor's number from her book and quietly descended further into the amusement park in her head. She hit the manic-depressive skids, becoming one of those unsightly people who you cross the street to avoid.

A few days after receiving a very disturbing phone call from an unrecognizable Susan, her half brother on her mother's side, Mark and I drove the six hours to central Vermont to visit her in the half-way house where she lived. The century-old Victorian house sat on a sad street of a shabby mill town. It was the kind of town you'd bypass when you took the foliage tour in October. The house was filled with recovering drug addicts, alcoholics, and poor, unwanted Susan. The short house mother hugged me when I walked in and warned me that she was, "long off her meds, so beware—she doesn't make sense." The house mother quickly enlisted us into the ring of people trying to talk Susan into getting back onto her medications. I assumed that when she saw me, her Sissy-boo, she'd snap to reality quickly.

As I cracked open the door to get the first glimpse of my Susan, her back was to me and she was sitting on a hard chair in the middle of the stark room, with her fingers plugged into her ears, like she was fending off noise. She turned and looked up at me, smiling as if all was well. "Guess what! My fingers touch in the middle!" Then she cackled. I recognized her cackle, but nothing else was familiar. I couldn't talk her into anything. I couldn't even convince her to take her fingers out of her ears. That was the last time I saw my sister conscious.

A few months later, Mark and I drove to Vermont one last time to say our "goodbyes." Susan was dying of renal failure from all those promiscuous years of lithium. Spending the rest of her life on a dialysis machine seemed much more insane to her than insanity—and even death, which she settled for. I thought about the time she asked to borrow a kidney, and I made a joke. I wished I could give her mine now—all three of them.

My poor Sissy-boo had taken on the brunt of the family disease, keeping me warm, safe, and free of it. I was now well past the age that the gene would've shown up. I was safely stark raving sane, for what it was worth. She was the underground mistake—she was Carlsbad Caverns. She left this life with no particular fanfare and no family members at her bedside. I thank Susan every day for releasing the artist in me and saving my life. I loved my sister as best I could, which was never as much as she loved me. We had indeed warmed the cockles of each other's hearts, whatever that meant.

What Color Was Washington's White Horse?

Dad was a hulking six-foot-five ex-Marine who could whistle the entire "Marine Corps Hymn" in one breath while chain-smoking Lucky Strikes. And if ever he needed to whack one of his four kids in the back seat of his station wagon at the same time, he had the stretch and the talent. You were required to memorize the words to "The Marine Corps Hymn" and sing along if you wanted to stay in the family or even ride in his car.

"I can't HEAR YOU!" he'd bellow toward the back seats of his station wagon.

"From the halls of Montezuma ..." I'd belt out. "We will fight our country's battles ..."

Dad's key would go into the ignition and an American history lecture would rev up before we were even out of the driveway. Whether you were going to 7-11 for milk, or driving to Argentina to mine for emeralds, you were indentured into his IQ-improvement program. Dad's '66 station wagon became a pop-quiz-mobile, and I was always the kid who hadn't been paying attention in class.

If there was one thing my father despised, it was ignorance. He continually shoved information down our gullets and then made us regurgitate it—forever fearful one of his four kids had gotten short changed in the smarts department. So far, it was looking like it was going to be me. My older brother Reid was very bright, and everyone always mentioned it. My younger brothers were still baking, but boy did they seem smart, or so my father commented every time they'd crawl by. Perhaps it was the way Robbie would hit Joe over the head with a twinkie. Or the manner in which Joe pulled his diapers off and ran around naked in front of company, peeing on furniture.

How Dad loved to lecture, hands flying off the steering wheel to make his points. He'd borrow accents and blather on about history, particularly American history, which he made the centerpiece of our titillating road trips. Each time I got in his car during the entire decade of the '60s, I'd begin to sweat—which was not pretty on a prepubescent.

"If you don't know where you came from, you won't know where you're going!" he'd remind us, then he'd whistle "Yankee Doodle" like he was in the fife and pipe corps. My father was obsessed with history and loved to lecture to the sea of indifference that lurked in the backseats of his Chevy. Sometimes he'd wander historically to his favorite conquerors, Alexander the Great, and then something about the Berbers and the Celts and the Romans. Every lecture would be followed up with a tough review quiz while my mom rolled her eyes in the shotgun seat, blowing smoke at the closed window so it would double back and caress her again. Sometimes, once the quizzes started, she'd slip me an answer under her breath just to keep me from crying and help me save a little face.

My father took us to every historical point and battleground within a thousand miles of our hometown in South Jersey. "There she is! Gettysburg—the bloodiest battle of the Civil War!" he'd lecture. On another trip, "This is Valley Forge, the coldest winter of Washington's life." I'm sure he went on and on, but I wasn't really listening. I was busy counting tires on passing cars. Four. Four. Four. Four. We didn't have to go on these trips with Dad—he taught us early on that there were always choices in life. "No, you don't have to come to Fort Sumter, where General Robert E. Lee surrendered—you can stay home and paint the house."

When the quizzes rolled out, Reid was always reluctant to play. He knew he was smart, so it bored him to be tested on it. I, on the other hand, was too stupid not to play, so I'd try to answer questions, desperately seeking my father's approval, which he had very little of.

Once, on our Revolutionary War tour, I asked my father a question that haunted us both until the end of his life. I asked if the war was the reason why we had to pay for our cleaning lady. I remember posing the question proudly, like a champion at a spelling bee, hoping he'd turn around and say, "Why, Deborah! What an insightful question!" Instead, his head jerked around in a circle on his shoulders, a few times. Mom turned away pretending she hadn't given birth to me—cracking her window—perhaps wanting to evaporate through the space along with her smoke.

I doubled down. "Why not just fire all the slaves instead of having a war?" My father held his chest, trying to fend off a heart attack, then pulled over on the shoulder of the road right there in Virginia to take one of those long, disapproving looks at me. We had just left Monticello, Thomas Jefferson's home, so Dad began with Revolutionary War questions. "Who do you think we fought the Revolutionary War against?" he baited.

"Uhm, which Revolutionary War?" I asked, stalling.

"There was only one!" Dad screamed.

"Robert, calm down," said my mother. "You're scaring her. She's eight years old!"

"I'm pretty sure there were two, Dad."

"Reid knew this stuff when he was five! What are they teaching you about in that school—cookies?"

"I don't know," I said, which rattled him so much that the hairs inside his large nose began to shake.

"Who did we fight the war against?" he badgered. "And I warn you right now, you better know the answer to this. We were just in Williamsburg, for God's sake."

"The pilgrims? Um, Indians? Um, revolutioners?"

Dad sighed very sadly, a sigh that sucked all the life out of the car, "Who was in red?" he asked quietly.

"Um, the other people with guns?"

There was a really long pause before Dad asked quietly, "Here's one you can answer. Who's buried in Grant's tomb?"

I contorted my face and tried to work it out in my head. "I'm thinking."

"Yeah, I can smell the wood burning," was Dad's pat answer when anybody claimed to be thinking. "Your time's up."

Like Lee, I surrendered, "I dunno."

"You don't know? Grant! General Grant was buried in Grant's tomb! Jesus Christ!"

"I thought Grant's tomb was the name of a town," I whined. My father laughed one of those mocking laughs that said, "You are about to get sent to boarding school."

"Leave her alone," said Mom.

I looked over at Reid who had it all; looks, brains, and a Tootsie-Pop. "Can I have a Tootsie-Pop?" Reid smiled sadly at me, a smile that said "I'm sorry I got all the brains."

"Is that all you can say?" my father demanded.

"Uh ..."

"Robert, stop it!" said Mom.

"We'd better take her to the doctor and find out why she's not bright," Dad whispered so everyone could hear. Then, after he had sufficiently humiliated me in front of the only people I really knew (my mom and my brothers), he asked me the question that would always make me cry—the lowest of the lowest, the easiest of the easy. It was question that was actually designed *to* make you cry. "What color was Washington's white horse?" His tone was a mix-of disgust with a dash of pity.

At this point, I suspected the whole family was calling me the village idiot in their minds. I remembered from my father's lectures that idiots were stoned in town squares. Or was that witches? I suddenly couldn't remember anything, and I was sweating from all my orifices, even my ears. I figured that the next thing Dad would say was that I had better pack my bags and get ready to go away to school. Sometimes he'd even threaten to send me to Catholic school (just for effect, since both my parents were atheists). They really did not want ignorant children. The only thing worse to them than having ignorant children was having ignorant children that other people knew about.

I began to sob, and I kept it up all the way up to Washington, D.C. Reid gave me some chocolate, and I continued sobbing, but at least now, my tears fell down towards a happy mouth. My father looked in the rear view mirror after a bit and said, "You know I love you, Deborah."

"Uh-huh."

"You're my favorite little girl!" (I was his only girl—little or otherwise.) That was Dad's favorite thing to tell us all. "You're my favorite son named Robbie; you're my favorite daughter named Debbie."

We compared notes after he died and uncovered his scandalous practice—he had actually told each of his four children that we were his absolute favorite. We all kind of laughed once the secret was out, but eventually, we started eyeing one another like there were three donuts for four people, and nobody had eaten in days. I secretly knew that I was really his favorite. But then Robbie said the same thing out loud. Reid laughed, knowing it was really him. Joe said that Dad had told him, that the three of us were his favorite. We all laughed. The Kasper kids basked in self-deprecating humor.

When my father was dying, I rushed to his bedside, and I sat with him week after week while he withered down to half his size. I sat holding his hand each day, watching his bravado disappear into fear. I held his hand until it couldn't hold back anymore. I had an ulterior motive. I needed him to take it all back. It was 1984, and I had been carrying around a chip on my shoulder since I was still in undershirts. I had spent decades over-achieving just so my father would take the time to say, "Wow, did I misjudge YOU! You are one smart little lady." But he hadn't, yet. I loved my father plenty, but he had definitely helped erode my self-esteem.

"Dad, I need you to tell me that I'm smart," I whispered. "You always told me I wasn't very bright," I said one day toward the end.

"That was to encourage you to do better," he said, matter-of-fact, "and it worked."

"Tell me I'm smart!" I insisted.

He smiled up at me through all the tubes and the fear and the wall of shame he'd built around me. "Of course you're smart. You're a Kasper. There are no stupid Kaspers. We're bright. You were just the dimmest of the brightest. That's all I meant," he said with a laugh. My father was sad for me, I could see it in his dying eyes. He knew at that moment what he had done to me, and I knew that he knew.

"I'll tell you what," said Dad, almost sitting up. "Not only are you smarter than each of your brothers, but you've got more balls than all three of them, combined."

I started to cry. "Really? Really?"

"Yes. Really."

"Will you tell my brothers that?"

"Hell no—you're the one with the balls—you tell them." My father smiled up at me and winked. "You know you're my favorite." Then he sat up, and from behind the grip of complete kidney failure, he pulled his scattered, toxic thoughts together.

"Who were the Berbers?" he whispered.

I was pretty sure they were second century barbarians who conquered Europe. Or were they the ones who built the Cherry Hill Mall? I wondered silently before opening my mouth.

"I know this answer."

"I know you do, sweetheart. I know."

If I Sit On One More Hamster

I have always been a breaker of stuff, a ruiner. I can rip, drop, shatter, smear, crumble, burst, unravel, bang-up, disintegrate or splatter *anything you hand me*—from a Buick to mom's pot roast. Pat, my long-time partner, was always telling me to "SLOW DOWN," annoyed every time I opened a juice or milk carton—it would be mangled like a muskrat had broken in and taken a swig of our Tropicana. "Why do you open things like a serial killer?" he once asked, shaking his head. "There's a road map on all items giving you step-by-step clues how to get in there—you don't have to break in, I swear."

It hasn't fallen away through the ages either, in fact it's almost improved with time, and perfected itself into a science. I'm a victim, really. I come from a long line of careless clodhoppers, so using things has just never run a smooth course for me. Opening items? well that's a challenge all its own. For what reason, I do not know, I am always harried to open things, and then panicked over all the other things I might have to open, next.

My parents used to call me "Hurricane Debbie." Mom later

imparted that she always knew when I'd been in the cookie drawer. A package would be savagely severed down the middle, and there'd be crumbs leading from the half-open drawer right up to my bed. I'd try to lie my way out, whenever Mom showed me a crushed donut box (which looked to have been stomped on), or a mutilated bag of candy (clearly opened with a nail clipper), or potato chips—slashed down the middle with what could only have been a mouth.

"Maybe Joe's gerbil did that?" I'd offer feebly.

"From his cage? Let's get that rat in the circus, Bob—we're sitting on a million dollars."

My biggest crime was lying. I'd be so filled with shame that' I'd blame anybody or anything that had been within yards of our house that year. And that was the crime that got me punished. To my parents, lying was the worst thing a kid could do (except be stupid). They'd made it clear that they didn't want any stupid liars for children—*good luck with that!*

Carolin Hatfield, whom I've known all my life, recently reminded me of a tragic Christmas in the mid-sixties—a day I'd just about managed to forget. On that morning, I galloped up the winding block to the Hatfield's house, proudly wearing my new cowgirl outfit—spurs on, little rubber boots, plastic guns in their holster, fringe flying like a horse's mane behind me. I couldn't wait to show off my favorite present to Carolin and her older sister, Nanette. I just loved the Hatfields—they were my parents' best friends, and the families had bought houses right up the street from one another to prove it.

Bunk and Nancy were the coolest parents around. First of all, you got to call them "Bunk" and "Nancy," and boy did they love to laugh. Bunk was a descendant of the "Hatfields" from West Virginia, which completely impressed me as a youngster since he was the most famous person I knew—his family lineage was practically American royalty. Little did I know at that time, that his ancestors ate gophers and lizards, and yanked out their own teeth with coat hangers. The Hatfield's house was exactly like ours, except flip-flopped in its layout. I was allowed to knock and walk right in—that was everyone's understanding at both homes. Their large living room with the cathedral ceilings had been rearranged to welcome the Christmas tree which lorded over way too many opened gifts still on display in their boxes. Tissue paper and new clothes were strewn everywhere, while their two nasty Siamese cats sat guard. Cats which were beautiful but mean, and nobody could stand them except the Hatfields. Both cats had an equally shrill meow, which sounded more like a drunk old hag dying than a cat. "Meeeeeeeeeeeee-owwwwwwwwwwwwww," they'd let out, hitting dozens of sour notes and taking out a few eardrums. And when both of them meowed at the same time—it sounded like two drunk old hags dying, which was twice as bad.

That morning, the family was finishing their pancake breakfast, so Bunk sent me up to Carolin's bedroom to wait for just a minute. (I never did understand why I couldn't just sit down and have a pancake or two.) Nevertheless, I climbed the stairs quickly, opened her bedroom door, and my eyes widened. I couldn't believe my luck—there splayed—all of Carolin's and Nanette's Christmas loot! I figured nobody would mind if I played with some of the toys—after all, we were practically cousins. So ... I began to open things in my special way.

"Minutes later," as Carolin tells it, "you ran down the stairs, faster than anyone's ever seen your chubby legs move, with a look of horror on your face. You darted past us, barely looking our way, screaming, 'I have to go home! My mother wants me!'"

"How did I know? Did she send up a smoke signal?" We both laughed like kids on the phone that day, at my bad fib. Yet at the time, it was traumatic for both of us. I can still hear those judgemental cats screaming as I ran out the door, like Nazi sirens. Carolin quickly dashed upstairs to find every single item had been touched by a clodhopper. Everything was opened, and most of it already broken, ripped, or disfigured. Her Tressy doll's hair was pulled out past its stretch, never to "grow and grow" again. Nanette's Clue game box was crushed—Colonel Mustard's card mauled while being torn out of its plastic wrapper, so you could count him out as the murderer—*forever.* The yellow cake batter for the Easy-Bake Oven was splattered across the royal blue carpet, like a distant galaxy. I managed all that in five minutes—quite a talent, actually. They should have just fed me some pancakes.

"Then the hurricane struck again," Carolin said, still chuckling. "We were eating dinner on my birthday when you showed up, so Bunk sent you down the stairs to the game room to play. What seemed like even less time, you ran back up the stairs and flew out the front door, screaming, 'I just remembered I have to go to the bathroom.' I went down to the game room, and there ... my brand-new Barbie's head was off, just sitting next to the body. Her emerald taffeta evening gown was ripped—hanging off her shoulder like Ken just had his way with her."

After we laughed at my antics, it quieted, and I said, "I'm so sorry," clumsily trying to apologize for something that happened forty-nine years ago.

Why they left me alone with the toys again, I'll never know. Didn't these Hatfields learn their lesson the first time? And why did

I always show up during meals? Weren't my people feeding me? Seemed to me there were a few people to blame here.

Carolin had called me up crying, that tragic Christmas morning, "You broke my toys."

"No, I didn't—they were broken when I got there."

"It was all brand new!"

I hung the phone up and sobbed out of complete humiliation and decided I never wanted to see Carolin, *again.*

Whenever I'd get caught in one of my honed fabrications, I'd be banished to my room where my demons lived and ballerinas danced on the walls. Usually because I had smashed something and then denied it. I'd try to blame it on the dog or a brother—once I even blamed it on my hands, whining, "They just weren't working very well and maybe I needed to go to the doctor." It wasn't unusual for me to ask to see a doctor whenever I was in trouble.

I couldn't help it, things constantly slipped through my fingers shattering into piles of *what the hell was that?* I even broke my mother's heirloom vase which had been sitting in its place, on my mother's buffet, not bothering anybody for years. That is, until the day it suddenly beckoned, even double dared me to touch it from atop my mother's dining buffet ... "Come on, do it, I won't tell." These were the items that children weren't even allowed to walk by, let alone fondle. But my fingers were just so curious, like they had minds of their own.

I'd cry in shame on my squeaky trundle bed, wishing I was a graceful ballerina like the ones doing squats on my walls. Some nights I'd ponder going to charm school like Donna McBride had. Ever since—her hair was always arranged in a neat little pageboy, and she could seat herself at her sixth-grade desk without even bending at her now trim waist. It was very impressive.

My three brothers were no better, they ran through our poor house like lost angry bulls from Pamplona. Robbie and Joe had a fifteen-year feud that could burst into action with a look or a sneer, it didn't take much. Fist fights broke out in the living room almost daily—lamps jumped off their tables—dirty ashtrays flew to the floor for cover. They'd even wake up fighting—chasing each other from room to room in their underpants, down the stairs through the living room, down more stairs to the game room, screaming out the door like they were in a play, and this was rehearsal. One day, it would be Robbie after Joe, "I'm going to kill you, you little asshole!"

The next day, Joe would tear after Robbie, "You're going to die, you big asshole!" Joe was one tough little baby—the neighborhood bully by age three. He punched a hole in his bedroom door while still in diapers. Not sure what went wrong that day—maybe his mashed carrots were cold? He also flung a ten-pound toy metal dump truck at me, but I ducked, letting the truck hit our father's twenty-gallon tropical fish tank, cracking a hole big enough for the dozens of bright fish to be forced through the glass hole out onto the carpet. After our chorus of "uh-ohs," we dashed around, catching the fish as they flew through the hole. They'd squirm in our palms—for the second before we'd chuck them into a pot of water which Reid had improvised. Reid always saved the day.

Twenty gallons of fishy-sea-weedy-fish-pooped-in water flooded onto my parents' living room floor that day, then seeped deep into the new carpet—on through to the floorboards. When my parents got home that night, they didn't even yell at Joe. "Because it was an accident." We all kind of came to Joe's defense, which was Reid's idea, not mine. I was ready to turn him over to the dogs—I was so sick of this brother. He was not normal—like something out of a Stephen King novel: "Joe, Baby Monster."

We managed to save most of the fish although they had to rough it for a few days in Mom's pots and pails until Dad could go out and buy them a new home.

Later that summer Reid was smoking a cigarette in my parents' bedroom while baby sitting the rest of us, and their bed caught on fire. Then the flames began moving around the house. My parents called him a "hero" for evacuating his brothers and sister in a calm and timely manner. He even remembered the hamster cages and Sam the dog.

"He saved his family's life," the newspaper article said. A bit of an overstatement, if you were to ask me—nothing burnt except the master bedroom, which *he* lit on fire.

Robbie had ADD before anybody had labeled it that and was known around the house best as the kid who would leave his animal cages or buckets open because he'd take the creature out to play and then forget, turning on *Batman*. We had constant sightings of confused mice, lost hamsters, and slow-moving turtles in various spots around the house. They'd make cameo appearances just long enough to help turn my mother's hair thin and prematurely grey.

Mom and I would shriek, terrorized while Robbie dragged in snakes, frogs, salamanders, snapping turtles—all dangling in his muddy hands behind his back like he was a magician.

"Mom, can I keep it? Can I keep it? Huh? Huh?"

She'd usually say, "Yes," without looking. "In the garage!" She never wanted to see what Robbie held behind his back that he'd "rescued" out of the creek behind our house, she preferred to take a sip of her bourbon. But she knew it wasn't a butterfly or a bunny.

Robbie's home away from home was the creek—he'd spend hours, days there, maybe he was a salamander in his past life, and he was just bringing some family members home. I had to check my bed every night, like we were camping, eternally. And on occasion, there would be a white salamander, or a gerbil sitting on my pillow. I was grey by age fifteen.

Robbie's hamster disappeared one day. It was early December when he mentioned that the creature had escaped while he was cleaning the cage. There were about two lies in his sentence, but we all started scouting for the hamster so he never got called on his fibs. One: Robbie never cleaned a hamster cage in his life, and Two: The hamster didn't escape—it was far too pudgy—almost chubby enough to be a guinea pig. So Rob had to have let it out. Everyone was on alert for the suburban rat, afraid to sit anywhere, lest it be nestled under a cushion. This went on all day, and whenever Mom was about to relax on the couch, Rob would scream, "Mom!"

She'd barely catch her balance swooping back up, "*Goddamnit*, Robbie! You wait until your father gets home, young man! I swear, if I sit on ONE MORE HAMSTER! This is it with the little rodent pets with the *goddamn* squeak of the hamster wheel all night long. Doesn't that thing have anything else to do but ride the Ferris wheel? And you have cedar chips all over your desk—go clean that up before I call your father! No more animals! they're all rats—chameleons are just rats that change colors, baby raccoons? rats with striped tails, broken-winged birds—rats that you feel sorry for! This is not a petting zoo!"

When the furnace came on later that night, a putrid smell wafted out of the heating vents. The longer the heat warmed up, the worse the smell got. My father quickly figured out where the hamster had gone—to the bowels of the heating ducts. The poor little thing had left its cedar-chip world behind in search of a better life—and failed miserably, like so many of us do. He fell down into the heating conduits. By midnight, the hamster began to slow-cook, making smoked rotting rodent carcass our breathing air. Fried flesh was the potpourri at the Kasper house that Christmas. And as the heat boomed on, the smell of the sizzling creature was carried out to every room in the entire house. There was no escape.

The hamster died in the middle of the duct system, finding its final resting place where no one could get to it without costing my father a "damn fortune" to remove the disintegrating hamster. Dad opted to wait till it was through cooking—completely burnt to ashes, which took about six weeks. You could barely breathe without gagging. Everything we ate tasted like rodents. Breakfast: pancakes with hamster sausage. Roast beef dinner: rat au jus. Everyone felt so sorry for Robbie, that he didn't even get punished.

That Christmas dinner, I was doing the dishes, as I always did by myself (life was so hard, I was the only girl in the house), and I dropped one of my mother's good Wentworth china gravy boats, which promptly shattered all over the linoleum floor. I glanced into the dining room to see if anybody had noticed, and they were all laughing over some story Dad had just told, so I swept it up quickly and threw the pieces away, knowing that my parents wouldn't have minded if I'd just told them. Accidents do happen, especially around this joint. *No reason to interrupt their moment*, I thought, besides, there were still those three brothers I could blame it on, and they deserved it—they never got what was coming to them for their idiot shenanigans.

I recently had the occasion to speak to a very successful octogenarian on the phone. At the end of the call, I asked quickly (of course), "Hey if you could give me the most precious piece of advice, just one thing that you've learned in your long life, what would it be?"

Without pause, "Haste makes waste," he said.

I couldn't believe my ears and could barely contain my disappointment. I wanted something helpful. Eighty years old, and that's all you got? Haste makes waste? Isn't that a sampler? How about a stitch in time?I thanked him and threw my phone recklessly to the side of the couch. I walked to my snack cabinet to grab a cracker, muttering aloud, "How about, 'to thine own self be true?' How about, 'live and let live?' How about, "*Spend all your money before you die, they don't take cash in hell?*"

The top of my Triscuit box was ripped, even hanging open, and yes…there were crumbs around it. "SO WHAT?" I yelled at the box, "I can live a very happy life, moving through it quickly," I bragged, cracker pieces flying out of my mouth. "Yeah, this is what 'to thine own self…' looks like." Besides, I am a victim, this is practically a disease—a family disease.

Pat screamed from the other side of the house, "Hey can you two keep it down in there? I'm watching TV."

I continued my conversation to myself, *to myself.* "I won't be shamed, anymore, this is 'mine own sel'" I'm a Kasper and we break shit.

The Day Herman's Hermits Stood Me Up At My Birthday Party

The days of my gullible youth when I took everyone at their word and my world was full of wonder are sorely missed. I believed in magic, miracles, and catching moonbeams in your hands, fireflies were fairies if you hoped hard enough, and a wish on a dandelion could certainly make dreams come true. So, when I was told that Herman's Hermits was coming to my thirteenth birthday party on my parent's back porch, in Cherry Hill, New Jersey ... of course, I believed it. Believing things was what made life worth mentioning.

I was throwing myself a party, and the enviable centerpiece would be my new plastic stereo, bought by Mom with S&H green stamps. I only had three albums but really only needed the one. My plan was simple, although it took me weeks to devise. I would play my Herman's Hermits album, and when "The End of The World" came on, I would slow dance with Kurt. It was my party; he would have to dance with me. I willed it, so it shall be. Even as a kid, somehow, I knew about the magical power of positive thinking—sure you may call it delusion, but to me, it was hope.

I had what seemed to be an unrequited love for Kurt, who went to Catholic school. He probably didn't know that I had never been kissed, that I had never even been held by anyone outside my grandmother who hugged me a little too often and too hard. Yes, I was in little girl love with Kurt, and also Herman's Hermits—actually, his name was Peter Noone (the lead singer of Herman's Hermits), whom I loved. I couldn't have picked the others out of a line-up, so I called Peter "Herman." Somehow, from my corner of suburbia, I believed that one day, he would be mine.

These teen idols had that talent to make every girl in the world think they were singing only to her. Somehow, Herman could see out from *The Ed Sullivan Show*, through my tiny portable TV, into my pink bedroom of dancing ballerinas and woo me with his songs until I fell on my bed. He'd look around and see pictures of himself above my desk, then wink and say, "Soon, Debbie, soon." When he crooned out, "Don't know much about history ..." through his crooked teeth and dirty blonde Beatle bangs, I'd get tingly feelings that I wouldn't be able to name for years.

That morning, my cousin Kathy and I decided to walk around the neighborhood—high entertainment in those days. On really special occasions, we'd head to 7/11 to buy some gum. Scattered up and down the streets were uniform homes all stuffed with kids we knew. I'd lived in this neighborhood for years and knew almost every family in each tract home. We'd slow down past the cute boys' houses, hoping they'd just coincidentally walk out the front door at that moment, and often they did. Life was dreamy.

We cut up Weathervane Lane for no real reason, and there stood a few older-looking girls hanging out in front of a house which I didn't know. One had boobs and a mod hat; the other had Twiggy's cut. We crossed the street, and I said "Hi."

The girl with the Twiggy do said, "Alo," with a British accent!

"Are you from England?" I asked like she was a celebrity. "You sound like Ringo."

"Righto," she said with the most adorable cadence.

"I've never met anyone from England," I gushed. "It must be cool to be from England."

"Jolly good, righto, carry on." Then her friend with the hat that flopped around her ears spoke with an accent too!

"Alo, loves."

What were the chances of meeting mod chicks from England on Weathervane? Monica lit a cigarette and asked if I wanted one.

"Do you want to come to my birthday party today?"

"What are you doing here?" my cousin blurted a little suspiciously.

"Visitin' my auntie, she lives there," she said, nodding toward the unfamiliar house.

Kathy and I nodded "oh" at one another. It made sense to us. "Do you know Herman's Hermits?" burst out of me like someone had just given me the Heimlich maneuver.

"Of course, Love," she said.

"REALLY!?" Kathy and I both shrieked at the same time. We only knew a few Brits: The Beatles, Herman's Hermits, and now these two hip girls standing right here ... *of course they all knew each other!* I thought. My milkman knew my postman; my seventh-grade teacher knew my sixth-grade teacher; and the liquor store owner knew everyone in the Kasper family. My concept of the world was that it was as big as I could wander, and only as wonderful as I could dream.

"He's here, in Cherry Hill, coincidentally," said the girl with the boobs.

I didn't ask "why," since it all seemed plausible. This was the center of my universe, and miracles happened, why wouldn't he be here? Gasping for air, I asked if he were staying at The Rickshaw Inn (a schmancy hotel on route 70, with an Asian theme). That's where my rich grandparents stayed when they visited. The lettering on the hotel's sign looked like chopsticks, and in front of the hotel sat an oversized iron rickshaw with geraniums climbing out of it.

"OK, if I bring him to your party tonight?" More of a statement than a question.

I almost had my first orgasm. "Yes! What kind of soda does he drink? I have Coke, Tab, Fresca, and Orange Crush."

Kathy and I floated home, ecstatic over what the other kids would think when Herman walked into my party. "I love his crooked teeth! His hair is always too messy. I love that—his bangs—kind of greasy and cute."

"What about Kurt?" asked Kathy.

"What?"

"We are going to be so popular," Kathy said. We gushed all the way back to my house, trying on the popularity we'd soon enjoy, going through every friend who was coming and what they would say.

Then we ran into my older brother, Reid the sensible, the wrecker of all daydreams. "I give up," he said with no tone when I made him guess who was coming to my party. My brother was a few years older and was beginning to show signs of disdain over my positive thinking (which he called naivete).

He laughed in my face and said, "Deborah, why would he come to our back porch? Think."

"Because Monica is from England, and she knows him!" I said in the "duh" tone. I couldn't believe what a bummer he was being. "They're probably from Philadelphia, or Camden, *love*," he said with a really bad and exaggerated English accent (which I had to admit wasn't that different than the mod girls' cadence). Kathy and I stopped in our tracks since we hadn't even considered this.

"Debbie, your problem is ... never mind ... we don't have that kind of time now," laughed Mom. "For one thing, you're very gullible. Here's a tip: If it's really good news ... it's probably B.S. Don't believe anything until you see it with your own eyes, and even then ..." I wasn't convinced. "People in the suburbs lie, because we're bored ... *to death*. Yesterday, I even told the gas station attendant that I was on my way to Hawaii, when he asked 'how far are you going.' Apparently he didn't know his geography, he didn't even ask how I would get there." She said when I asked why they would've made that up?

"You're thirteen for *chrissakes*, use your head for something besides tilting it when someone asks you a question."

The sun limbo danced all the way down as my party guests arrived, each one walking around the side of our house to our back porch. About half-way through a fun party, at which I was the center of attention, the two Brits arrived, alone. I was heartbroken. Crestfallen. Humiliated. My life was ruined until Monica presented me with a note in front of everyone. "Peter is so sad he couldn't come!" she grandstanded around the party. I flapped the note a little to make sure everyone got the gravity of the moment. There, scribbled on a small sheet of white paper, was the most artistic handwriting I'd ever seen.

I read aloud:

Dear Debbie, I am so sorry to miss your party. Love Peter.
It was so neatly written! It was from him! I showed the note around to my friends. We all cried with joy, a little. I kept that note stuffed in my diary until I was too old to still believe in it. Then I got sloppy, and the note slipped away along with my dreams of marrying a teen idol—I was forty.

The party was still near perfect since my dream came true. I had my first slow dance with Kurt. We danced to "The End of the World," of course, and he held me very close. I forgot all about poor Herman.

Thirty years later, I was with my in-laws in Hershey, PA, staying at The Hershey Hotel, a gorgeous luxury inn on the national historic registry. We were right at the mouth of the world-famous amusement park, where an "Oldies but Goodies" show in the Amphitheatre starred Gary Puckett and Peter Noone! I told my sister-in-law, Pam and the others, the story. Everyone laughed at my childhood naivete, perhaps a little too hard.

The next morning, Pam found herself in the elevator with an aging Peter Noone and quickly told him my story, asking for an autograph. He graciously wrote a note: *Dear Debbie, I am sorry I missed your party. Love, Peter*

Pam rushed to find me at lunch to deliver the note, which I have cherished to this day. I put my Hershey burger down, dabbed my hands on a linen napkin and fondled the note. It was verbatim! The handwriting was even similar. When everyone stopped laughing, I said, "Did you happen to ask Herman *why* he couldn't make my party?" Everyone laughed again, perhaps a little too hard.

You Just Can't Get Enough Of Yourself, Debbie, And We Can

I'd broken a cardinal rule. I'd called Mom during *Jeopardy*. I had called to tell her I'd decided to write a one-woman show. During the commercial, she finally asked, "Who's it going to be about?"

I couldn't believe the stupid question. "Molly Pitcher, Ma."

"The rest area on the Jersey Turnpike?" she mocked, "that Molly Pitcher? Or do you mean the one who brought water to the soldiers in the Civil War? Or was that the Revolutionary war? Well, if you ask me, you'd be better off doing a show about Sarah Lee. She was a trailblazer, too, and you could give out cheesecake after the show." Mom had the best deadpan sarcasm.

"The show will be about me, Mom. That's what one-person shows are. They are generally about the one person who writes them!"

Her objections, thinly disguised as questions, began to flurry—

"It sounds long—Who's gonna wanna see that? I suppose if your father were alive, he'd come. Who am I gonna sit with? My bridge club won't come, I can tell you that right now. You embarrassed me in front of them the last time. They came as my guests when you did your shtick at that cheesy comedy club. There were mice in the bathroom! I've never been so humiliated in my life, you said 'fuck' a hundred and five times," she pressed on with no encouragement from me.

I knew how hard it was for my mother to say "fuck" to tell me that I shouldn't say "fuck." I wasn't even sure I'd ever heard her say it. It told me that she was on at least bourbon four.

"I still can't look Ruth in the eye," Mom continued. "I looked over at her halfway through your little skit, and she was crying. Is that the effect you want to have on people? Isn't the goal to make people laugh, not weep?"

"I doubt it was a hundred and five times. I wouldn't have had time to say it a hundred and five times, it was only a forty-minute set, for fuck's sake."

"I counted," she croaked out, losing her breath.

"Well, that must've been exhausting."

"It was! Why do you think I had to leave right after the show?" she laughed. "I went home and passed out." My mother was always a little sarcastic, and hyperbolic, but buried under all the disguise her truths laid out like a wooded path, obscured but always heading to a point. "I think you are insecure," she threw in.

"Gee, I wonder how that happened! You people put me on a diet when I was seven! Telling everyone I was so chubby when I was born that you had to breast feed me skim milk! Then my whole life everyone told me I wasn't very bright, in a thousand different ways: jokes, riddles, stories. How would *you* like to grow up thinking you're fat and stupid?"

"Oh, stop complaining. Some children don't have shoes, you

know. I had to give Doris Sharpe's money back for your show. She had nightmares, she has Lupus, you know, she doesn't need that kind of talk. My generation doesn't care for the F-word. You never heard that word when we were growing up—unless you lived on the docks. Everything was much more gentile then."

"Bullshit! Where do you think I learned these words?"

"I don't care for that word either," she mentioned casually, like a queen ordering more tea.

"Dad used the F-word all the time, Mom! And he said 'bullshit' even more!"

"Well, nobody had to pay him to hear it! He used it for free. You can't charge people and then just stand on a stage and say 'fuck, fuck, fuck, fuck.' What's funny about that?" Mom's glass clinked against the phone as she raised it to her mouth. It was time for a drink and butt break. She sucked in unfiltered smoke and huffed. "Oh, well," she said finally, "whatever you want, sweetie-pie." When push came to shove, Mom was my biggest fan. She enjoyed my career vicariously.

I knew she was indulging in one of her favorite tics, patting the top of her head, to make sure she still had her hair. Her hair had been thinning down the past several years, and she had taken to blaming it on her kids, always telling us we were driving her crazy.

"That's not a drive, Shirley—it's a short walk around the block," Dad would say. She used to blame her drinking on us too: "You kids are driving me to drink!" Until we realized that she'd drank long before she knew us. She drank all the way through her four pregnancies and then drank more while breast feeding. All this helped explain my deep affection for cocktails made with milk: White Russians, Brandy Alexanders, and Kahlua and cream. She also doubled up on her smoking during her pregnancy with me. Years later when I confronted her about that, she said, "Well, I was smoking for two!"

I also knew that she was sitting in her muumuu, either the purple with the pink flowers or the pink with the purple flowers. She'd wear one, while the other lay exhausted in her drawer openly praying she'd get some more muumuus. Mom was as loyal to her house wear as she was to her children.

She was very queasy around some words. She really hit the roof if a girl said, "I have to go pee," which my generation always said. She'd literally cringe. One time at dinner, just the two of us, she tried to tell me all the words she'd prefer I didn't use. She said, "The F-word, the BS word, and the other one I can't say."

"Well, then, how will I know what not to use?" I continued slurping my vodka cranberry juice.

"I can't say it."

"Just tell me the first letter."

"I can't."

I had no idea what the fuck she was talking about. So, I said, "What the fuck are you talking about?"

"If I say the first letter, you will hear me say the complete word."

I couldn't figure out her cryptogram, so I drank the end of my Cape Cod and said, "Take your time and figure it out. I have to go pee."

"That! That right there!!"

"Pee?"

"Stop saying that! You sound uncouth," she screamed, covering up her ears.

"We all say that, Mom."

"It makes me literally sick. It's disgusting. You sound like a hillbilly."

"I'm going to powder my nose," I said and stumbled away,

chuckling over the stupidity of that 'excuse.'"

"Why are you doing a one-woman show, anyway?" Before I could answer, she blurted to her TV, "What is a crustacean?"

Five nights a week, from 7:00 PM until 7: 30 PM, Mom was usually unreachable. She was just not available for comment, criticism, or caring. She might as well have been in a sensory deprivation tank or performing brain surgery. If you were clueless enough to call her, Mom was not above answering the phone with, "Well, somebody better be dead, or at least feeling very ill." And if no one *was* dead, she'd hang up and continue playing her at-home *Jeopardy* game, which involved a pack of cigarettes, a glass of bourbon, and the remote control. Hunched over in her floral gown, she worked that remote like a show buzzer. Right there in 1982, my mother had created the first interactive game show, blurting out answers to the show like she was the fourth contestant.

"What is a spore?" she yelled at her TV.

My mother was in my stand-up comedy act, which is why she brought all her girlfriends to watch me. To this day, I cannot quote my mother without lowering my voice an octave and dragging on an invisible cigarette, sounding like Harvey Fierstein had swallowed Bea Arthur.

On stage: I'd smoke an imaginary cigarette, croak out her scratchy smoker's voice, coughing at the same time I'd deliver my punch line. Mom was such a big hit that I ended up writing more for her to do. Eventually, she became the star of my act, which delighted her. If I'd bring her back for a 'callback,' just rolling my eyes and miming a puff of the cigarette would get me another laugh. My mother had a fantastic sense of humor—she'd laugh until her smoker's cough kicked in. She gave me permission to use her in any way I saw fit in my shows, or otherwise. And, I have.

"What about you?" Mom had been down on me my whole life about not loving myself enough. She's the one who first noticed I had low self-esteem. She once called me up in New York and left this message on my answering machine: *"Debbie, I just took a self-esteem test in Reader's Digest, and well—you failed. Thank God your father's dead, this would just break his goddamn heart. He died with a broken heart, your poor father worried sick about you and your career. His dying words were about you. He said, 'Tell Debbie she's getting fat.' Well, happy birthday, sweetie."*

"It's a journey to self-discovery," I defended. "It's about me learning to love myself."

"When are you kids gonna get that there's nothing to discover? This is it. Put away your map and get on with your life, Magellan."

I was born with the "look at me, please, someone, look!" gene, always performing for my friends, in front of classes, but I got my first professional gig when I was ten—it was a self-booking; my cousin Kathy and I put on an act to the song "Nothing Could Be Finer."

We got two umbrellas—choreographed a song and soft shoe routine to be debuted on the balcony overlooking our living room for the entire family. We began in a squat behind the open umbrella in bathing suits, jumping out to sing, "Nothing could be finer than to be in Carolina in the moooooooorning," pointing our little toes, punctuating every other syllable. The crowd cheered—and it gave me goose bumps. I wanted more. Clearly, I had real talent, and maybe Kathy did, too, but I was a star. My father told me so later when he slipped me a few dollars, making me a professional dancer. I loved the feeling that making people happy stirred in me. I got the urge right then to always entertain, and bring joy to an otherwise nothing kind of a day. (In other words, I craved attention.)

I had the perfect house to become a star in. It was a split level with six stairs, protected by an iron railing, that led up to a large landing. The landing overlooked the living room, like a stage, putting our audience in the orchestra pit or the peanut gallery. The stair railing was perfect to slide down to make grander "ta-da!" entrances.

Kathy and I eventually took our act on the road. We'd tap in backyards, basements, cars—whenever and wherever anyone requested, *or not*. We kept honing the act, tightening up the choreography, and growing our fan base.

We also put on car skits, riding in the back seat of a car: Dad's, Aunt Janet's, we didn't discriminate. We'd sing silly songs that drove people nuts. In fact, we sang them *to* drive people nuts. We could just look at each other, nod, and that erupted a performance right there, guerilla style—in a car, or a mall, or a restaurant. Innovative, edgy, annoying.

Then Kathy and I started writing—pounding out little preteen skits. Our first one was about our family. Somehow, we innately knew to write what we knew. We exaggerated everyone's flaws, oblivious that this was called "parody," and we performed our scathing skits on our overhanging wannabe stage in my parents' house. This entire creative spurt had been inspired by the new tape recorder my cousin got for Christmas. It was the most liberating doohickey I'd ever seen. We'd record ourselves being funny (hilarious, really, if you were to ask us). In fact, we could barely finish our writing, we'd be on the floor, laughing. We'd rewind the tape, hearing that nails on blackboard screech, and play it back, and then again. We'd nod when it was good, shake our heads in disgust when something needed work; then we'd perfect it until it was ready. I was the director, the head writer, and of course, the star. That's the only way I would even participate, having total artistic control.

Once we rehearsed the parody, Kathy and I performed it in front of our entire family, making fun of all. Everyone roared with laughter to see themselves on stage, except my father, who was hurt. We were court jesters who'd crossed the line, betraying the king. His character was the least exaggerated in the skit, since his flaws didn't really need us—they were already buffoonish on their own. For one thing, he could not be wrong, and he had to have the last word. He was notorious for continuously asking one of his four kids to, "Go get me *The Almanac!*" to prove himself correct. Every argument with anybody (which was everybody), ended with Dad proving his fact in *The Almanac*, opening it with tender intent, "aha!" he'd cite, plopping his pointer finger on a spot. "I was right, of course! The per capita income of Sudan is lower than Egypt's, just like I said." Usually, he'd snap the book shut to help punctuate his intelligence, a nano-second before any of us could even check his facts. My father literally and physically could not be wrong—he was not capable. One time when he was proven wrong by his beloved almanac, he had to leave the room. When he returned, he challenged Joe to a game of chess, something he knew he could win, and then slaughtered the seven-year-old just to get his mojo back.

The most outrageous episode was when I'd returned from seeing my best friend, Sue Bluestein, in York, Pennsylvania. I casually mentioned they had a Baskin Robbins there—this was a revelation to me that fooderies had chains. Dad famously answered, "Why—there's no Baskin Robbins in York!" He loved contradicting people, and he was usually right, but this time, he'd overstepped, hanging himself far out on a thin branch, and he couldn't walk his way back because the tree was on fire. *I had been inside of it.*

"But Dad, I went there!"

"You're wrong."

"I ate a chocolate chip mint ice cream cone."

He finally asked for *The Almanac*, but he couldn't find an ice cream category. "Well then, I'm right."

In Kathy's and my skit, every time I impersonated Dad, I'd yell out, "There's no Baskin Robbins in York. Are you stupid!? Joe, go get me my almanac!" And then we'd "call it back," no matter what anyone else said, my impression of Dad would bark, "That's not true, Joe, go get me my almanac. Where's Joe? Where's Rob? ROBJOE! Someone, get me my almanac!" The entire family was laughing their asses off, except for Dad, the six foot five Marine, whose feelings were hurt.

My father always picked on Robbie and Joe to run his errands since they were the youngest. He'd taken to calling them "ROBJOE," and whichever one was stupid enough to appear would always have to go and get something for him. "Oh, there you are!" We weren't even sure he knew the difference between the two. "Go get me my slippers!"

"Dad! I'm not your personal slave, you know?" Joe one time yelled.

"Well, there's where you're wrong, RobJoe!"

That night at the dinner table, my father tried to defend himself, saying, "I still say there's no Baskin Robbins in York." He couldn't let go.

I went to college and majored in theatre, then on to graduate school, eventually moving to New York, each step making me a much smaller fish in a much larger pond. There I found my way to the comedy clubs. Now, I'd decided to combine all my talents and do a one-woman show. It all began with an umbrella and a couple of goose bumps.

"Are you still talking, sweetie pie?"

I said, "it's the ultimate self-reflection, a theatrical exploration. I have things in me I want to express, Mom." I continued, seeking some validation.

"I mean I think it's great, sweetie, but I'm just curious. Where do you get this from—this do-re-mi-mi-mi-mi thing you have? Be careful, there's a very thin line between self-absorption and men. Maybe you were born with too much testosterone and way too many brothers—sorry about that, kid. Clearly we did not pay enough attention to you as a child. We're all paying for that now. You just don't seem to be able to get enough of *you*, and the rest of us can. Some of us have, already. Well, I thought we gave airtime to all three of you, equally."

"Four."

"That's right. Oh well, we are very proud of you, even if you don't make it, you are trying, that's all that matters. You have such a pretty face."

"Mom, do you know how insulting that is?"

"Why? Homely girls would kill for a face like yours."

"I didn't have anything to do with my face, now did I? So it's really more of a compliment to my gene pool. And what you're saying, is 'you have a good head, but we need to find somewhere better to keep it.'"

"Is that going to be in your show?"

"Maybe."

"Will I be in your little show?"

"Definitely."

"Then I'll take some tickets. Oh well. Have fun, that's all I mean. You keep looking for YOU. The mystery of where you are and who "dunnit." If you solve the crime, let me know."

Before I could say, "I already know who dunnit ... "

"I have to go, Jeopardy's back on. 'WHO WAS SIGMUND FREUD?'" she screamed at her TV, and then, 'Who was Dr. Spock?' The baby doctor. I never did read that dumb book." And she dropped the phone onto its cradle, but not before letting out a slight victory cry.

Does Running Through The Streets Naked Sound Fun To You, Debbie?

Just about immediately after "The Anita Hill Hearings" erupted on television in 1991, my budding feminism swelled into full-blown outrage. This was the first time they televised hearings like this, and they were holding the country hostage. As a nation, we were enthralled—as a woman, I was ready to march, except that I couldn't pull myself away from the hoopla long enough to even *bathe*. A salacious national debate took place while America's women were coming together. "Everything is going to be different now," I'd said to my best friend Janette on the phone that first night. All my girl-friends were constantly on the horn, throwing around the phrases "Long Dong Silver, Pig, Women Unite!" It was an exciting time to be pissed off.

My phone rang in my apartment in New York City about two days into the hearings, and it was my mother. It was an odd call—she got right down to business. She usually dialed the phone, and while I'd be saying "Hel-lo?" she'd be taking a hit off her cigarette, followed by a sip of her cocktail—then clash her highball glass accidentally into the phone, and breathe heavily while I'd start the conversation, "Hi, Mom."

Sometimes she'd say, "How did you know it was me?" And Sometimes she'd add, "Which one did I call again?"

Pretty quickly, it became apparent that she was acting as a delegate from her bridge club in the Jersey suburbs. She had two tables full of best bridge friends she'd been playing cards with for over thirty years. They played bridge, had lunch with cocktails, chatting all the while. Occasionally, the bridge club had questions about real life, and apparently, I was the kid who was having the realest, so I'd get the call. One time my mother called, "The girls and I were wondering if a lot of young women, you know, like your age, are getting that IUD thing inserted?"

"Yes," I said, closing out the conversation. I had one and didn't want the bridge club knowing about it, so I cut the call short, keeping my metal form of birth control to myself and the airport security scans.

This time: "The girls and I were wondering, were you ever sexually harassed by a boss, Debbie?" she asked with the innocence of a person raised by rabbits.

"Just bosses, or do teachers count, too?" I asked, mirroring her innocent tone.

Mom's bridge club was made up of women who had raised dozens of baby boomers between them—they were the generation of pre-lib women who went to college to find husbands. Most of them didn't work, but they were bright, well-informed ladies who ran the PTA and formed auxiliaries raising hundreds of thousands of dollars for local hospitals every year. They tried to keep themselves relevant through one another, their children, and *Time Magazine,* which was the bible of the suburban culturally and politically hip.

My mother kept up on every single trend and historical pivot point going on in the world. She always knew what was happening. When I was ten and Reid was twelve, she'd called us downstairs, waving *Time* as if it were a report card that one of us had tanked and said, "You don't smoke marijuana, do you?"

Reid said, "Not yet. But you know I'm the kind of kid that's going to try it—I think we all know that." She frowned at her oldest child and then looked to me for a response.

"I don't think so, Mommy. Can I go back to my room now?" She called me down the same steps to the same living room on that immortal Sunday night in 1964 when The Beatles rocked the world on *The Ed Sullivan Show.*

"Debbie, come down here—you'll want to see this!"

I stumbled down the stairs twirling my baton, "What? See what!?" I was the only pre-teen in America too cool to watch The Beatles change the world of music and the world itself—forever. Thirty million tuned in that night—but not Debbie. I didn't even think they were cute; it looked to me like they were wearing wigs, which just seemed creepy. "Can I go to my room?" I always had to be back upstairs in my bedroom. One would think I was training a dragon up there.

During The Summer of Love, my mother watched from her kitchen, on her 18" portable black and white TV, while the "free hippies" danced around Golden Gate Park in a frenzy. "Debbie, come look at the free hippies. My God! What is the country coming to? Look at the hippies with no bras! You can't tell the boys from the girls. They're probably all high on dope! Weed, they call it. They also call it hooch, mary jane, pot, dope, stash. They smoke it in a joint—they take off their clothes and run around naked. That's what marijuana leads to—nudity. Such a strange generation, you kids. You don't want to run nude through the streets of San Francisco, do you?" Reid disappeared quickly—I think Mom might have given him some ideas. She turned her Spanish Inquisition on me. "I'm just curious if that sounds fun to you, Debbie?"

"Ew!" I didn't even like to be naked in front of myself. Can I go now, Ma?" I was twirling batons with Carolin Hatfield in the backyard.

The next year, we had a Moon landing party. We were all required to sit on the living room floor, watching the new huge 26" black and white TV, saying things like, "wow! jeepers!"

"Debbie!!!" she'd screamed up the stairs.

"What? I don't care! Why do I have to come?" I yelled back thru my closed door.

"This is history, Deborah. Get down here!"

"It's all history!" I screamed back. "It's history up here too!" I finally sauntered down, holding onto the stair railing as if I were a movie star making a quick publicity appearance.

I had been in front of my bedroom mirror taking stock of my teenage acne, and I was waiting for Jeff to call. I remember this because I wrote about it in my diary. There was no mention of the Moon landing, but whoever Jeff was—I'm still waiting for the call.

Yes, Mom was in the national loop, but it was sadly apparent at this point in American zeitgeist that my mother and her bridge club were oblivious to what was really going on in the workforce. The bridge club had sent my mom out on another reconnaissance mission to report back to the seven others.

"Has anybody ever sexually harassed you?" she'd asked bluntly.

I laughed for effect. "Seriously—are you kidding? Mom, I've never had a boss that didn't sexually harass me." I went on, using a tone that said: "Exaggeration is required in times like this!"

She sighed. I sighed. I could hear her sadness from across the Hudson River.

"I had no idea." I heard a hint of compassion in her response which she generally only doled out during really horrible incidents. After a pause which my mother filled with a puff of her cigarette, I lit into her. I was honestly a little annoyed that these bright women could be so clueless.

"It's a man's world? What did you and your 'little friends" think'" I enjoyed calling her friends "little," it was a bit of payback from my childhood.

"I thought maybe decorum prevailed, and that maybe my daughter was safe." I think she was doubly sad that she'd missed it, she hadn't picked up on the country's dirty little secret.

"Yeah, well, no." I could tell she was baiting her breath for me to impart some stories. She wanted to get back to her card club with something juicy, so I tore into a few of my suddenly relevant tales, all of which paled in comparison to Anita Hill's.

"Well, remember that movie I got cast in which I never actually did? Ever wonder why? Well, the pig (a famous comedian, who I cannot name) who wrote it—fired me. He called me day and night, making semi-lewd comments, inviting me over to his apartment to rehearse. I wasn't sure what to do, so I went."

"Ooooh," Mom warned—several years too late.

"He told me there'd be others there, and after all, he wasn't Jack the Ripper, Ma—he was a comedian. I was going to star in it, so I had a lot at stake."

"Isn't he old?" Mom asked.

"No, he was old three decades ago, at this point, he was dead but nobody let him know. His skin was greasy and splotchy—and his hair plugs had hair plugs. When I got to his condo, some guy was leaving, so Jackie (oops!) says to him, 'Can you believe I have this gorgeous woman I get all to myself?' and he started making cooing sounds at me, like we were a couple of pigeons sitting on the window shelf. Then the other guy left, and we were alone. He made me sit right up against him on his sticky black leather couch, and by the way, he had gold flamingo statues in his condo as decoration! You would've hated it, Ma."

"Tacky," my mother said. I even heard her gasp a little.

"And when I finally got up the nerve to ask when we'd sign the contract and how much I was going to be paid, blah, blah, blah, he grabbed me, distorted his face into what he thought was a sexier one and said in his horrible Brooklyn accent, 'Well, it'll be a lot more money if you sleep wit me, I can tell youse that.'"

"Jesus! What did you say?" Mom asked, probably from the edge of her couch.

"I laughed right in his face, 'You gotta be kidding. You and me? Oh that's just NEVER gonna happen, get a grip!' I grabbed my purse and ran out the door."

"Why didn't you tell anybody?"

"I told everybody."

"Why didn't anybody do anything?"

"Well, I wasn't sure whether to file my complaint with the comedy ethics board or the Upper East Side morality monitors."

"I'm so sorry. I had no idea. I don't know what to say."

"I was a kid, I had no clue what to do. You may not have taught me how to balance a check book, but you also never taught me that I had to sleep with someone if I didn't want to."

"That's correct. Unless he's rich, and then you should try to want to," she replied, half-kidding.

Then I told her about a college professor who literally chased me around a desk like we were in a Doris Day movie. We ran around a few times until I dashed out the door into the hall.

"What did you do?" Mom asked.

"Well, I showed up very late for his class later that day since I was in the ladies' room crying, and when I walked in, he said, 'You're late, Miss Kasper,' I couldn't believe his nerve, so I shot back, 'I don't really think that's a problem, do you? I ended up getting an A in his stupid class."

"Good," she remarked. "I don't know why you never told us."

I was on a roll now, the memories flashing back too rapidly to even hold them all.

"Then there was the hideous restaurateurs who grabbed my face in his hairy palm and licked my mouth with his swollen grey tongue when I asked if we had Eggs Benedict. Right there in the kitchen."

"Didn't any good-looking men ever harass you?" she asked, trying to lighten the tone.

"No, I harassed them!" After we chuckled for a minute, I continued. "Anyway, it was my second day at a waitressing job that I desperately needed. It was Sunday brunch in the '80s in NY—practically a religious experience—and there was a full room of annoyed customers who had been waiting. The restaurant was brand new, and things were very rocky. I was the only waitress working, and the place was packed. I rushed back out to the dining room from the kitchen, disgusted from the grey tongue incident. I wanted to walk out. But instead, I started taking tables' orders like a mad robot. I went from two-top to four-top, took over twenty tables of brunch orders, and instead of putting the orders in the kitchen (so they'd get made by the chef), I walked out the front door just like Norma Rae! I marched out with my apron pocket overstuffed with orders of pancakes and over easies that would never be made. I just kept heading north on the Upper West Side of Manhattan, and neither Norma nor I ever looked back. Those people are probably still waiting for their brunch."

"I guess I don't have to worry too much about you, Deborah."

After a strained quiet, I said, "So ... do you and the bridge club think he did it?"

"Who?"

"Long Dong Silver."

"Hell yes. Hell yes, he did it. That asshole." A word my mother rarely used, if ever. But the world was becoming the type of place where you had to reach deep and maybe even break your own rules to express your outrage.

"Pig," we both said at almost the same time.

I hung up the phone—but not before telling my mom that I loved her. I felt closer to her than I had in a while and weirdly safer now that the Cherry Hill, New Jersey, bridge club, was waking up.

We're Nice People, We Don't Poke Holes In Our Face

A woman I knew slightly—a friend of a friend in high school in the late sixties and early seventies—recently Facebooked me that I had pierced her ears when she was thirteen. "You're welcome, but no memory of that," I wrote back hastily. "I hope you asked me to!" I added quickly, and I meant it. I honestly didn't remember at all. I hoped I hadn't just chased her down and stuck her earlobes with a pin while she screamed for the police. It could've been so, after all it was the time when ear piercing was all the rage, and I was running carefree those days. I did many things people didn't want me to.

At first, I really was blank on the whole incident, but then it started to come into focus. If you sit quietly for a spell and squint your eyes, memories will come into focus, like tuning into a radio station before you've quite hit the vicinity. The truth is out there. My ear-piercing resume came back to me with a startle. "Oh my. I was quite a poker," I mused.

As it turns out, I had actually pierced many teenagers' ears.

Some were friends—some not. In fact, I had even pierced my own. It seems I was a serial piercer. Sure, we're all pierced now all over hell and back again, but at that time, the mere thought of a pierced ear was rather avant-garde. Tongues, bellybuttons, noses, eyelids, genitals? We'll, we'd have to wait decades for that ground breaking movement.

The only people who had pierced ears before the Summer of Love were the immigrants—foreigners and their brew of kids, or to quote my father: "Gypsies!" After 1967, earrings were the de-rigueur amongst teenage girls, particularly the ones that dangled (the earrings, not the girls).

I come from a WASPY background, and at that point in time, not one member of either side of my family had any holes in their bodies that a doctor hadn't poked. I was thirteen or so when I asked my parents if I could get my ears pierced. I always prefaced questions like these with something like this: "Sharon and Katy have pierced ears, and it looks really nice. They're very popular now. I'd like to be popular. I mean, they're just earlobes. They don't do much, really." Neither parent even bothered to look up from *The Philadelphia Inquirer* to dignify my request with a response. I think I detected an eyebrow raise on my dad, which was kind of like an acknowl-edgment. I waited a minute in case my mother wanted to say what I'd heard her say so many times that decade, "We're nice people." Then perhaps she'd add, "Nice people don't drill holes in their flesh."

I probably blew a bubble with my wad of Bazooka and moved on with my meaningless day, asking my parents more things that they wouldn't respond to: *Can I go to Jamaica for a month with some other eighth graders? Do you mind if I convert to Judaism and have a bat mitzvah? I'm ready to go all the way with boys. Any objections?*

I am almost thirteen! (Truthfully, I wasn't even sure where "all the way" was or if you had to pack a bag to go there.)

But I was no quitter, and within a day, I was up at my wild friend Katy McGirl's house, who was one of the first to have hers pierced. I was admiring her beautiful holes and the gold studs she was modeling. We decided to dismantle a cheap pair of fake silver earrings from Woolworths and glue two peace signs to my earlobes with Elmer's, to simulate pierced ears. We snickered throughout the project, proud that we'd found a way to pull one over on my parents, and ultimately, hopefully, get my way. "Sweet Talkin' Guy" sang to us from the Philadelphia pop station which went everywhere with us via our transistor radios, underscoring our lives.

I planned to go home, sit at the dinner table, and if my parents freaked out, I could rip the peace signs off and laugh. "Haha! The joke's on you!" I'd say. "I would never desecrate my body like that! What am I? Hungarian?" There would be some harsh words before I could unveil the ruse. Dad would probably call me names and tell me he was disappointed in me. That was Dad's go-to. I'd heard it when I got caught cheating on my fourth-grade math test. I'd heard it when I pulled up all the flowers from my next-door neighbor's garden, and I would certainly hear it at the dinner table that night. I never got to tell my father what a disappointment he'd been to me. We had no pool in the backyard, we'd never been abroad. Disappointment's going around in our house, Dad.

My parents had strict ideas as to what looked cheap—tattoos, earrings, and Fords in your driveway were all on their list. "Tacky," my mother loved to say. "Just tacky." Of course, Mom's "tacky list" was top secret until you wanted permission to do something. Then she'd say, "That's tacky," which was a "no" with no discussion.

That evening, I pulled my long blonde hair back, so the peace sign earrings were in full view. I slunk down the stairs to the dinner table, took my life-long assigned chair and passed the green beans to my brother Joe, leaning over the table dramatically so everyone could see me. No one said "boo." In fact, they barely looked up from their meat. I got frisky and flung my long blonde hair back and forth, flopped my ears around like a dog. Nothing. The times were definitely changing, and I guess my parents had made a slice of peace with the earlobe movement. My glued-on peace sign earrings went unnoticed, or at least un-commented on, so now I could pierce them for real.

Around that period my fifteen-year-old brother, Reid came home wearing a headband around his forehead which slightly controlled his long dirty blonde hair. My father screamed, "Jesus Christ! Do you not own a mirror? Shirley, get Reid a mirror! Maybe he doesn't know he looks like a faggot. His hair's halfway down his ass, for Christ's sake. Do you know your hair is halfway down your ass? And now you're wearing your sister's headband! Are you a girl, now? Shirl! We have another daughter! Boy-oh-boy, you look like a *goddamned* Indian, for *chrissake*. You look like a faggoty Indian. Is that the look you're going for? Do chicks dig the faggoty Indian look?" Dad continued ranting as Reid jumped up, and headed up the stairs to his bedroom. "Where did we go wrong, Shirl?"

"All the kids are wearing their hair down their asses. It's the fad, Bob, get with the times. Boy are you square, Daddio."

A few months later, I flew to Dallas to visit my cousin Kathy, with whom I'd already made the great piercing pact of 1969. We had pledged long distance over the phone that we'd be piercing each other's ears in her bedroom behind closed doors, and that was that. We both drew blood off of the end of pins in our separate states to cement the deal. You couldn't have stopped us with a cease and desist order.

When I arrived in Dallas, we finished planning our pact. It was a pretty simple operation, really. You merely needed ice, a pack of matches, and a needle. Some people used a cork to catch the needle as it came through the other side, but we thought *corks were for sissies.* After much back and forth, and mind changing, we decided to do Kathy first. I would pierce hers, and then she would pierce mine, in kind. That was the pact we finally agreed on. Our talks about this lasted longer than Woodstock.

Kathy carefully locked her bathroom door to keep out non-piercing dissenters. Her younger sister Chris knocked, trying to join us, but we stood firm, not wanting anyone to know what nefarious deeds we were up to in the bathroom—as if we were drowning small animals in the sink. I began fondling the needle. I used a black magic marker to mark the spot, dead center of her lobes, checking them a hundred times in her bathroom mirror to make sure we were dead center. Kathy had already snuck into her parents' freezer and stolen some ice cubes, which I held on her lobes to get them numb. Then I lit the match to bask the needle in the flame, sterilizing it, and before anybody could changed their minds, I shoved it through in one thoughtless thrust. It went through like a fork goes through a tough filet mignon, with intent but not ease.

After the first hole was drilled, I quickly took a 24-karat gold stud that we'd bought at the mall that day and pushed it through the welcoming. Anything cheaper in the karat world, you risked infection. We cleaned it with alcohol, and I swiftly moved onto the second lobe. Kathy was doubly pierced before she could even register any pain. I was practically an ear surgeon—my hands were steady and my confidence was already legendary. Everyone in the room was impressed and we both said so.

But when it was my turn, with my ears marked, iced and ready to be lanced—my cousin Kathy started shaking and shrieking that she couldn't do it. As the elder and experienced piercer in the room, I placed my hand on her shoulder, looked her in the eyes, "Of course you can, young grasshopper. You can, it's just flesh." Kathy wasn't having it and started running in circles the way a four-year-old might on Christmas, then she began hyperventilating, "I can't! I can't. I'm sorry! I'm not that kind of girl!"

I couldn't imagine showing up in high school with no holes in my lobes. I would be the laughing stock. The fad had been spreading fast, like a "someone's pregnant" rumor, and I'd told everyone that mine would be pierced by the time I got home.

Without fear or care, I grabbed the needle out of her hand and shoved it into my own lobe. Before any pain bled through, I thrust it through the second as well. I put my studs in, cleaned them, and that was that. Like a soldier in the Civil War who had to cut his own leg off—I would be branded a brave hero, maybe even made an honorary doctor.

Back in New Jersey, word spread quickly that Debbie Kasper was tough and peerless at ear piercing. Pretty soon, I had a following. Girls lined up. Needles were sharpened; lobes were scared; parents were pissed. The cool girls at school suddenly nodded at me in the halls. They even started asking me if I could pierce their ears, too. I became a roving Piercing Pagoda (the mall kiosks which charged big bucks to pierce ears in the seventies). Sometimes I'd go to the mall, stroll past the Piercing Pagoda, and make "harrumph" sounds. I'd stop and watch their technique and shake my head. "No, no. That's not the way—it's all in the wrist—the wrist I tell you!"

I had my own little kit. I'd come to your house or you'd come to mine, I could perform my skill anywhere at any time. I'd even pierce ears in the girls' bathroom at school between classes if that's what was needed. No matter where we did it, my hands were steady, and your holes would be even to a fault. I think I may have even bullied a few reluctants into it, dangling my ever-ready needle toward them. I couldn't stop. Occasionally, I'd walk the halls of the school, admiring my work, and checking for infection. One infection could dampen my reputation and I knew it. Girls would wave their ear lobes toward me in the auditorium or the cafeteria—just their way of saying, "Thank you! All is well, Dr. Ear-poker!" I'd nod and move on to the next satisfied customer.

I am proud to say I have a spotless record—no lawsuits, no infections, and plenty of clean, even holes running around the world, with my name on them. Sadly, my own self-inflicted holes, aren't even. One of my hanging earrings always dangles lower than the other. Every time I look in the mirror at my off-kilter face, I have to tilt my head, slightly and lean toward the lower hole to even them out, and I curse my cousin, "Damn you, Kathy we had a pact!"

Isn't Your Best Friend's Father A Mafia Hit Man?

By the time I was heading into high school, I was desperately in need of a new best friend. It was time to shed the cousins and the daughters of my parents' friends and find my like kind, whatever that was. Our high school had over 6,000 kids in it since the other high school on the east side of town was still being built. The world was bursting with baby boomers, and we had to go to split session to make room for all the bloat. Coming in as a freshman was confusing and frightening—a bit like skateboarding onto the turnpike at rush hour; if the merge didn't kill you, the looks would.

Clearly, in this intimidating morass of a school, I would need someone to pass notes to in the hall, have lunch with in the vast, hall of humiliation they called a cafeteria, and blab endlessly with on my new princess phone. We would talk for hours every night about what Bobby wore to school that day, or whether or not "he" looked at me in the hall. (Fill in any name, my crushes changed weekly.)We would tell each other a thousand things, all starting with: "You can't tell a single soul! Cross your heart? Hope to die, stick a needle in your eye." We'd say the whole thing in unison—the pact of the thirteen-year-old American girl, which would stand up to any signed treaty. We may not have been annexing territories, or declaring wars, but we had honor.

My older brother Reid and I had our very own phone number, but only one phone to share. Two teenagers, one phone—a bit like throwing two sharks one severed leg. The private phone was not so much a gift, more of a survival tactic on my parents' part—they were "sick and goddamn tired of running up the stairs every ten minutes to knock on bedroom doors to get one of their teenagers to come to the phone!"

My father was annoyed by the constant ringing, he started answering the phone, "Fulton's fish market, we've got cod today!" or "Grand Central, where ya goin'?"

When they'd say, "Is Reid there?"

"Yes he is" and he'd hang up.

Reid and I had to trade the phone back and forth, plugging it into our room's wall jack all the while having an ongoing knock-down fall-out about whose call was more pressing. He'd be pulling the phone out of its jack in my room. I'd be yanking on the receiver, coiled chord stretched straight, Reid would be heading to his room, I'd be standing firmly in mine—we'd both be screaming, "It's my turn—it's my turn—it's my turn!" We'd taken to justifying whose call was more pressing.

"Gail's father caught us naked in her bedroom last night, and I had to jump out the second-floor bedroom window. He chased me down the street with a rifle, yelling, 'I'm gonna kill you! Stay away from my daughter, you little prick!' I left Mom's car there. I have to call Freddy to drive me to get the car before Dad gets home and asks where the hell it is," he said one night. Reid's life was way more mercurial than mine, I might as well have been sharing the phone with Mick Jagger.

"I don't know," I whined. "I have to call Sharon and see what she's wearing to school tomorrow. What if we wear the SAME THING?" I immediately began scouting my new best friend in the narrow halls of Cherry Hill West, waving to all, like I was already the homecoming queen. I fell in with Connie for a while. She'd just moved from Nebraska, which impressed me. "Nebraska?" I wrote to her in a note, "Lincoln? The capital? Did you eat a lot of corn? Ha-ha-ha!" I wrote, trying to dazzle her with my geographical prowess.

"Wanna go to the mall and steal some shit after school?" Connie asked in the return note she sent back using the nerdy girl sitting between us. Passing notes in school was the national pastime of the teenage girl—the original text. Notes which always traveled in danger of being intercepted by a teacher and read aloud, like a king intercepting a traitor's letter on the brink of war.

Connie snapped her gum at anyone who came near, and wore her long eyelashes curled and shellacked with Maybelline. I'd never seen eyelashes like that in person. She had real sass—fourteen going on *what the fuck are you looking at?* Connie was dark, her fun always turned sinister. She wasn't happy unless she was ruining someone else's day in the mix. Squeezing the word "shit" into any sentence was one of her few talents.

We'd meet up at the new Cherry Hill mall by the fountains where she'd smoke cigarettes, trying to urge me to try one, but that was something I drew a line in front of. My home was overwhelmed with Mom's and Dad's cigarette smoke from dawn till lights out. If

Mom wasn't lighting one up, Dad was. There were about five packs consumed in our house, daily. My parents rarely opened their mouth without a ray of smoke escaping. I wasn't just getting second-hand smoke but the nicotine delivery of an actual cigarette—they just saved me the trouble of lighting up. They'd smoke in the car with all the windows shut so the smoke would smack up against the glass and bounce back, enveloping the whole family. I once saw Dad light a cigarette on his way into the shower. He left it burning on the sink, and he no doubt grabbed it on his way out. Mom would've smoked *in* the shower, if she could've gotten the matches lit. My mother had the worst smoker's cough anybody had ever heard. She broke ribs with her cough, and she'd clear rooms, which inspired many of us to find another bad habit. For me it was cookies. Smoking sure didn't seem like fun to me. I didn't give a shit how cool it made you look, and I could've used a some "cool" at that point in my life, just ask Reid.

That first time we began my shoplifting internship, Connie led me into Woolworths, wiggling her small hips, with me trailing close behind, trying not to trip over my desert boots. She sharply turned down the first aisle, where the Woolworths kept the cheap jewelry. Without even glancing their way, she scooped up a fake ruby necklace and shoved it in her open purse, all the while snapping her Wrigley's. I was spinning like a searchlight, sure that the teased-hair cashier with the beauty mark was watching me, and we'd get dragged into the basement of the five and dime where a one-eyed dick would shine a light in our eyes to turn us against each other. "Connie made me!" I'd have to say, or he'd burn me with his cigar. Then we'd get sent to a reformatory where we'd have to scrub toilets on our knees while a hairy butch warden stood over us with a fly swatter. Reid made me watch *Dragnet*, so thank God I knew what could happen if ever we got caught. It was time to decide if I wanted a necklace that badly.

Connie continued wading up and down Woolworth's aisles, tossing makeup and unneeded hair ornaments into her gapingly open purse, like she was trick or treating. She thought the Mary Quant lipstick was already hers—she just hadn't picked out the color, yet. It dawned on me why the Mullers had to leave Omaha—Connie was probably the only thirteen-year-old wanted by the Feds.

My first grift was a tube of Maybelline mascara, which promised me black sticky eyes just like Connie had. I pulled it gently off its hook, palmed it in my hand like a con man in a three-card Monty game. I slid it up my sweater sleeve, and then slithered it quietly into my purse, all the while humming "The Marine Corps Hymn." I was smooth, almost expert, except that I immediately began to sweat. I suddenly felt the cold stare of that cashier lady on me, so I put it back quickly. Connie wiggled her little hips toward me, whispering, "Oh for shit's sake! What a *goddamn* sissy!" She snapped her gum, grabbed my purse and started throwing useless items into it, not caring at all who was watching. "Here, you'll need some of this shit. You need an eyelash curler if we're gonna be friends—take this eyeliner shit too," she whispered loudly. "What other shit do you need?" she screamed loud enough for them to have heard her back in the Corn Husker state. I wasn't cut out to be in Ma Barker's gang. My heart started beating out the *Dragnet* riff. Dun da dun dun-duuuuun.

Connie's family moved again within a year, but not before she taught me a ton of shit, like how to have the best lashes in school. I was secretly relieved when she moved away. I knew she'd talk me into more shit, and I'd probably get "sent up the river" before I was fourteen. Going up the river was something I'd heard them say on *Dragnet*, and I had no idea what it meant, but it didn't sound very good. I was a good girl before I met her—I had scruples, but Connie had left me with about one.

I met Lorraine Butano freshman year in math class. I let her cheat off of my geometry test. Honestly, you'd have to be really desperate or pretty stupid to copy *my* math quiz, but it turned out to be a great way for me to make a new best friend. We both got D's. She was proud—I got sentenced to nightly tutoring with Dad, ad infinitum. Lorraine was the perfect best friend—she laughed recklessly at all my jokes, she didn't shoplift, and she didn't "put out," which were my only criteria at that time.

Lorraine was a male magnet due to her premature size D boobs, which were sprouting so fast she practically burst through a bra a week. My brother always perked up whenever she was coming over, suddenly wanting to hang out with me. Dad said, "I like that Lorraine." Honestly, her breasts were practically a deformity, and I figured that the next bra size she'd work up to would be a forklift.

"You'll never get a date with her around. Don't they have any flat-chested girls at school?" my mother remarked without looking up from her *Readers Digest*. She was right. The boys would claw me out of the way, even knock me over just to stand in the shade of Lorraine's rack.

My new best friend and I laughed like crazy together, but beneath her laughter something lurked—it wasn't joyful—more like lava erupting. Now that I know the truth it all makes sense.

Lorraine's family would pack up and move to a new neighborhood every four months or so. We'd lived on Cherry Tree Lane for my entire life, so this was a little weird. Their houses were always the biggest on the block, but they all looked the same from the outside: lights dimmed, shades drawn, like the whole place was locked down, and tucked in. I was never invited inside the Butano's homes, so I could only imagine what was going on in there beyond the window dressing. Everyone always came to my house after school, because my parents were "cool" (French for *they didn't give a rat's ass what we did*).

One night, my mother took a sip of her bourbon and looked up from *Time Magazine*, "What does Mr. Butano do?"

"Nn-nnh." I said shrugging.

"Why do they move so much—they skipping out on their rent?"

"Nn-nnh."

"Something's strange," she concluded.

I did my goodbye shrug and grunt and left Mom blowing the smoke from her cigarette into an over-head bubble—like maybe it would form letters and answer her sudden concerns.

One day, I asked my new best friend, "What does your dad do?"

"I don't know. I hate his guts!" she screamed.

I was shocked—I didn't even know you were allowed to hate your father! It certainly hadn't ever come up on *The Patty Duke Show*.

"He's a fat pig. I hope he dies." Lorraine screamed—and she wasn't kidding.

Later that month, after some nudging, I was invited over the Butano's. When I got inside, it felt like Lorraine had to clear the visit with a panel of people somewhere, since it seemed "staged." Still, it was the grimmest place I'd walked into in all my fourteen years. The front door mat should have said, "Welcome, We Lied."

Her mom was cooking in her humongous kitchen. She stopped

stirring, blotted her hands on her rumpled apron and mouthed, "hello" with all the smile she could muster, which was just barely. She seemed sad—her clothes surrounded her body in a random way, and her bouffant was sliding off to one side. She could've been a great contestant on *Queen for a Day*. She looked like she deserved better than this, whatever *this* was. Lorraine's two sisters stuck their heads in the door to say "hi." They all had the same sad brown eyes, but then I realized that they weren't sad at all—they were scared, almost begging "help me." I already wanted to go home.

I glanced into the dark dining room, and there sat the source of their fear, Mr. Butano. Lorraine nailed it—he looked like a pig—fat, with bulbous lips that flopped over themselves, and he was sucking on a cigarette like it was his last meal. He was surrounded by an equally grotesque group of middle-aged men and they were all in black. I got the feeling that I wasn't supposed to look right at them, which was just fine for me since I'd already decided they were perverts—which I thought meant "creep". Lorraine said, "Dad…this is my friend…" He waved us away with his fat hairy hands, and turned back to the other perverts. *Why aren't they at work?* I wondered.

Lorraine and I ran down the hall, into her bedroom, slammed the door shut and collapsed on her bed, laughing.

"See?" she mugged.

"He seems nice. You made it sound like he was horrible. His friends seemed nice, too." I said, trying to be supportive.

Pretty soon, her sisters burst in and flopped down on the bed with us. There they were, three beauties, one prettier than the next: luscious hair, flawless complexions, big boobs. But then—I couldn't *believe* what started spewing out of their perfectly heart-shaped mouths.

"I hate his fucking guts," screamed the oldest.

"I hope he drops dead," the thirteen-year old added. While I'm taking this in, right there on Lorraine's pink bedspread, the whole conversation very quickly turned into a plot to… kill their father. Right in front of me! I didn't even know you were allowed to kill your father—never saw that on *Perry Mason*. And it didn't feel like this was the first time they'd discussed it, either. I was completely nonplussed (a word I didn't actually know then).

Yes, I should have piped in, "Golly, isn't murder wrong?" But I was way too intrigued. I was also a little scared that they might suddenly turn their rage on me, they all seemed very mad. After a few more seconds, I finally uttered something stupid like, "Shucks, you don't mean this—he's your father."

"We hate him. He's a pig. We're gonna kill him!" They chanted like a Greek chorus.

All I could eke out was, "Hhhhow?"

"Knife."

"Poison."

"Hire one of his ugly friends."

The thirteen-year old seethed, "I'd stab him in the eye with a fork and not look back." They were like little girl gangsters. I decided right then and there, best to keep on their good list.

Suddenly I blurted almost involuntarily, "I forgot, I have to go home, my mother needs me to … uhm … go there."

I escaped from the bed-room sit-down, called my mom on the hall phone to come pick me up, immediately. I was scared to death to walk past the posse of black in the dining room to dash out the front door. *What if Mr. Butano comes after me? What if the men in black grab me and throw me against the wall? What if the sisters start stabbing him while I'm still there? What if become an accessory to murder and get sent to the "big house?"*

When Mom honked her horn, I darted to the car like a rabid dog was biting at my ankles. I never asked Lorraine if I could go to her house, again.

For the first time since we'd met—I didn't want what she had—the boobs, the complexion, the boys, the sisters, or that big, dark house. I was grateful for my flat chest, my teenage acne, and especially for my family. We weren't the Cleavers, but no one was going to get stabbed at the Kasper's no matter how annoying you were.

The Butanos moved to the east side of town that summer. It became harder to maintain the friendship, and by junior year, much to my relief, it withered away like an un-watered flower. My new best friend was Sherry. She was perfect: our boobs were the same size.

When I went off to college, my mother sent a letter one day, with an article from *The Courier Post* about Joe Butano. He'd been killed, Mafia style—stuffed in a trunk in a South Jersey mall parking lot. Mom wrote a note:

Didn't I tell you they were strange!?

The article implied that the Mafia had him whacked, but I wasn't so convinced, since I knew there were other "whackers" lurking around wanting to take a stab at it. Seemed like several people wanted the man dead. Maybe the sisters did it? I never saw or spoke to Lorraine again, so I'll never really know, for sure. But I remain grateful that I managed to make it out of high school without annoying anyone so much that it got me killed.

Daddy Says You'll Need Money For Beer At College

When I told my mother I'd been molested by the dim-witted dish-washer in the basement of the Maple Shade Diner, she said, "Well, that's probably just because you're new. I doubt he can keep that up every night."

"Want me to go up and punch him?" asked Dad.

"No! I don't want to work there!" I cried.

"You'll get used to it," they both said at around the same time—one of the rare times I remember them agreeing on anything.

It was the summer before college, and I was one the first of the three waitress jobs I would work my way through in two months, putting me in every diner in town with a name tag, cork tray, and a bad attitude. My parents dropped the bombshell on me two days after graduation—barely recovered from all the parties—it was just so cruel. "You're going to want some spending money to buy things up at that expensive college of yours," Mom said on her way back from the basement picking up the bedsheets.

"What do you mean exactly?" I yelled as she descended the stairs. I had my first and last panic attack right then. Until this exact moment, I thought my summer would be free. This was the week I found out that I had gravely misunderstood my position in the world, and sadly, I was not an heiress. I was devastated, and worse, Mom just told me to get a summer job. "But it wasn't even my idea to go to college," I whined. "Now I have to go to college and get a job for the summer to help pay for it? That's not fair! I had plans!"

"I had plans too! I was going to run away with John Wayne to Acapulco, but your brothers' socks were dirty."

Mom had such a thing for John Wayne, which just made me cringe. She'd make me watch *Red River* over and over until I finally admitted he wasn't hideous. She loved Montgomery Clift, too. "That Monty—yum!" He was pretty and all, but he was no Paul Newman, that was for sure.

"I thought I'd do some traveling this summer," I said, pulling it out of my ass.

"Where do you think you're traveling to?"

"Places where I've never been, you know *different*."

"There's a different place you can go right now—down to the basement and get the other load of laundry. You've never been there, and it'll be *very* different for you—people work there."

"That's not fair!" I shouted as I headed toward the basement, which was several floors from where we were, "I just graduated! I'm tired. Don't I get a vacation?"

"Your whole life is a vacation!" she laughed.

If I had a nickel for every time one of my parents said that to me, I wouldn't have needed a summer job. It sure felt like my parents had planned this whole thing out—discussing it behind my back, whispering in the shadows like French Resistant spies—because, at that exact moment, Dad walked by and threw a section of the paper at me. It seemed awfully coincidental.

"What are these?"

"Classified ads. A list of the places hiring in town."

"There's a list?" I was impressed with how organized America really was.

"There's lots of jobs hiring. I circled some ideas for you. You could work at the mall or a restaurant. I'd be happy to have a pretty girl like you bring me a hamburger. You can go get me my toast when it pops up right now, might as well start practicing." He lowered himself onto the couch methodically and held his most precious gadget toward his TV. The remote control was my father's favorite invention since the automobile because they both provided him with more time to spend sitting. "I figured you could probably save about $1,500 bucks this summer. That's not pocket change. You could buy an awful lot of beers up in Vermont with that."

I had never waited on anybody in my life, but of all the jobs I wasn't qualified for, this seemed like the one I was least not qualified for. I had cleared many a table in the Kasper household. Being the only girl, I washed all the dishes for all the meals for all the years. Suddenly, I felt so used, remembering all the non-paid waitressing I'd already been doing. I screamed to both my parents. "I've had to do all the dishes for everyone for always. I might as well been in the Peace Corps! What did Reid ever do?"

Reid had gone off to college the year before and was now treated like a guest when he showed up. He'd sweep in from college, toting his laundry. His golden hair was well past his waist, practically hiding the crack of his ass, which always hung out of his hip-huggers. Sometimes he'd have a few other hippies in tow, their T-shirts always making some crude and bold statement like, "I'd LOVE to Eat Your Peach." They'd swoop in—eat us out of house and home and split whenever they felt like it—like a rock band. And I'd have to do their dishes!

"He cleaned the garage, the basement; took out the garbage; mowed the lawn; and shoveled the snow. Those were weekly chores," said Dad.

"Well, what about those other two, Robbie and Joe? They don't do a thing!"

"Joe's twelve and Robbie's thirteen. We're happy they can dress themselves. We'll find positions for them after you leave."

"You guys shouldn't have had kids—you shoulda had a pit crew! This whole thing is so unfair. It's not right. Some of my friends got cars for graduation, you know."

"Some of your friends got straight A's, scholarships, and were admitted to real colleges," my father said.

I actually didn't know anybody personally like that, but I supposed it could've been true. I didn't get into a good college. I had decent enough grades, okay college boards, but when it came to getting recommendations from three teachers? Nobody wanted to write one for me. "The one I'd write won't get you into the type of institution you're hoping for," said my science teacher, citing the time I smuggled frog eyeballs from the biology lab, and bounced them up and down the hallways. (I couldn't help it, they were otherworldly bouncy, which I discovered quite accidentally when I dropped one while dissecting a frog in lab, and the damn thing zipped around the room bouncing off of walls and ceiling for many minutes before it was finished.) Flubber had nothing on frog eyeballs. Then she suggested I find someone who didn't know me at all and ask them, like the boy's gym teacher.

The morning I went to get a job, I walked toward the front door dramatically but slowly, giving my parents the time to say, *oh never mind, silly! Run, play, travel if you like. We were just trying to make you a stronger person, but we've made our point. Come on back in let's have French toast!*

My mother saw me dawdling in the foyer from the living room balcony, a perfect peak over her world, like the rock the Grinch ogled Whoville from. "Smile and tell them you're a hard worker," she chuckled, rolling the wheel on her lighter to bring up a flame for her cigarette, and then waving me out the door with her lit Kool.

I got into my mother's turquoise and white convertible Oldsmobile—which I had annexed senior year and made the rounds to every diner in town.

The Maple Shade Diner was the only structure that hadn't been stripped to the dirt on the old Maple Shade circle when the township built the massive overpass that overpassed it by. It was hard to get to this leftover diner which stood alone on one of the loops. Most never bothered to try anymore, except those who worked there or lost drivers looking for a mall, or the shore, and simply got frustrated, so they'd stop in for some pie. This was my fourth and final stop, getting "we're not hiring" from all the other hostesses.

When I walked into the tarnished aluminum joint, a Greek woman named Leila, who stood about 4'11" in heels, shook my hand and sat me down in a ripped vinyl booth. I sat on some stuffing as it was escaping, wiggling my butt to get comfortable. The jukebox was playing "Hey, Did You Happen To See The Most Beautiful Girl

In The World?" (which turned out to be the hippest song on that jukebox). She asked me if I had any experience at all, holding her head to the side while I stumbled over my answer. I was winging it since I hadn't decided if I was going to lie or not. Leila seemed kind, so I hit her with the truth glancing around the empty diner. "No, but I do have three brothers ... so ... I had to clear all the dinner dishes, which I think was very unfair."

"You're hired," she said.

"Really?" I asked, disappointed. I wondered who I would wait on.

"You'll have *za* best shift there is, 11 PM. to 7AM," lied Leila with her Greek-glish. At first it sounded kind of perfect; *I could have all my days free and still go out and party, every night,* I figured. *I wouldn't miss a thing.*

Leila introduced me to the only other waitress who worked there, Betty, a lifer who immediately pulled me aside and said, "Stay out of the basement," then she nodded ominously.

I showed up at 11:00 PM at the Maple Shade Diner for my first ever summer job. By 11:05, I wanted to quit. I was already tired, and decided that I needed a different job. I would *never* be able to go out at night to *any* party or hang-out. I'd have to leave at ten, go home, get into my uniform. Then I'd work all night like a dog, I'd get home at 7:30 AM, go to sleep ... sleep all day, work all night, eleven to seven. *That's not a life,* I thought, *that's a country-western song. Nope, this will not work!*

That first night, I waited on nothing but drunks and their mentors—sloppier drunks. When we ran out of ice cream in the big tan colored drum, I yelled to Leila, "We need more ice cream!" It was a small place, and I was the only one on duty, except Leila, who said she was just hanging around to make sure I was "okay." Starting tomorrow, I'd be running the place, she said. I was eighteen, and I was about to be running the midnight shift of a broken-down diner.

"Do you *sink* I'm going to go get ice cream? It's downstairs in the *beeg* freezer. Go!"

I remembered Betty, "Stay out of the basement." I started rehearsing my "I quit" speech as I climbed down very steep ladder-like stairs to a black room which certainly had mice. I sat my big white waitress shoe on the floor, waiting a second before I put the second one down, like I was wading into a creek. There in the corner sat the dishwasher—Ray—with his picker finger shoved mostly into his left nostril. He didn't even pull it out when he heard me coming and left it there when he saw me. *Wow, that's confidence*, I thought.

"Hi, I'm Debbie. This is my first night. Ice cream over this way?" I said, nodding toward what looked like something that would have ice cream in it—a freezer or something.

Ray didn't speak. So, I continued over to the freezer, which was waist high, and I bent over to pull the ice cream drum out of its cold spot, when Ray quietly came up behind me and stuck his hand up my short dress and pulled on my bikini underwear. "Are you kidding me?" I screamed, spinning around.

"Ray! Stop molesting the girls!" Leila yelled down the stairs. "I'll send you back." I never asked her back where. My mind considered some possibilities. *Back to Greece? Back to the looney bin? Back to the womb?*

The second night was when things went downhill. A group of child-drinkers came in. A kid who didn't even look old enough to be out without his parents blew his cookies—retainer and all—all over the front foyer in front of the cigarette machine. You couldn't get into the place without being welcomed by his pile of puke. Leila had just left, leaving me alone with Ray, the cash register, the cook, the vomit and the whole dilapidated diner. I went to get Ray with his mop and his bucket—I wasn't cleaning it up—that was most definitely a job for someone who lived in a basement and picked their nose—no, not me—I was going to college, excuse me very much.

By the end of the first week, I'd honed my craft, getting myself in shape to move up the waitress ladder. I was practically a pro. Even Betty said I looked pretty darn good as she left at eleven one night. I could slap an order on the spindle, call it at the same time, "Eggs over on the easy, little bit of pig on the side," tell Ray to stop staring at my boobs, all the while buttering table two's toast. I lined platters up and down my arms like an Ed Sullivan plate spinner. I was already growing a beehive hairdo and a starter moustache. I told my family I was considering changing my name to Delores.

Every morning, I came home and counted my quarters, nickels, dimes, dollars, and if I were really lucky, a five or two. I was bringing in an average of $25.00 a night. My dad said, "I'm proud of you. $25.00 a night? Let's see, times five days a week, times two and a half months. That's $1,250. You can almost make your goal, kid. That's a lot of beer!"

"Your goal, Dad, mine are very, very different, and they involve other people paying for me."

About a month in, I went to Olga's, a shiny silver diner on the shore circle. It was a little further away, but I heard from Betty that you could make $50 a night there, and I wouldn't have to work the shit shift. "Fifty?" I shrieked. "I'll work one night and quit!" I practically left in the middle of the conversation to run over to Olga's. I'd already put in an application, but they weren't hiring at that moment. Timing was everything with these jobs.

Olga's was the stop to make on the main road to the Jersey Shore from points west, like Pennsylvania. It was packed and classy, except for the Pennsylvanians, whom the Jersey people disliked and they didn't like us right back. There's something about bordering states, that always encourages a rivalry. We wished they'd stay on their side of the river, and some even wished it loudly, knowing they were just using us to get to *our* shore.

There were no overpasses hiding Olga's entrance; the circle there still stood proud and difficult to round—particularly if you were from Pennsylvania. But everyone could and did pull into Olga's Diner on their way to the Jersey Shore. Olga's pies were tri-state famous and were on display like diamonds, always spinning around in their glass home, inviting you to pick out the one you'd like to try.

I'd gotten busted at Olga's by a truant officer just a few months earlier that year. I cut school, wearing my Cherry Hill High School West majorette jacket with my name embroidered proudly across the breast. Mary DePolis and I sat at Olga's counter at 11:00 Tuesday morning, eating pie. We were heading down the shore like all the high school kids did during the spring months, when they cut. The truant officer (basically a policeman who flunked too many tests to have a gun) escorted us out—me by my elbow—like a scene from *West Side Story*. I shot my mouth off, "I didn't finish my coconut custard pie. That's not fair!"

The truant officer assured me I had bigger problems than pie. He took us back to school, and we both got suspended. My father picked me up that day, "It takes a special kind of stupid to cut school wearing a school jacket, Debbie."

I couldn't argue but to say that it was Mary's idea. She told her parents that it was my idea.

Tina, who was Olga's daughter and the diner's boss, hired me on the spot. She was Greek, too, but her English was polished, really just missing slang, jokes and a reason for speaking. I was beginning to see the trend of these diners—nobody worked there for any extended amount of time, except for the lifers. There was always one shitty section (usually near the bathrooms) that none of the waitresses with upswing hairdos and sassy mouths would work. Nobody but rowdy teens, families with children in highchairs, and town drunks wanted to sit there either—so they'd hire young college bounds to work the crappy section. Tina sat me down in the last booth in the back of the new room and glared at me over her wire-rim glasses—her eyes the steely color of a Magnum. Tina's boobs were so overstated that when she leaned forward, she cleaned the table with them. I was already afraid of her, and she hadn't spoken yet. "You look familiar to me," she said suspiciously.

"Nope," I lied.

Then I remembered she'd run out after us, breasts flapping in the wind, the unpaid check clenched in her righteous fist, "Who's paying for the pie? Someone owes Olga eighty-five cents!" I remember thinking, *lady, I might get thrown off the majorette squad today, and you're worried about eighty-five cents? You are one selfish witch!* Tina told me that she could train me, but it's really best to just jump right in and learn on the fly since I had experience. I don't think her English knew the phrase "on the fly," but I agreed. She kept shaking her hands around, saying, "You should just jump into the pond." She assured me that all the waitresses were quite lovely and would be "happy" to show me the ropes.

There were about nine lifers that worked at Olga's. These women were professional Jersey waitresses—teased hair, cork trays glued to the palms of their hands, and the strongest legs you've seen out-side of the javelin throwers at the Summer Olympics. Their name tags said things like "Marge," "Peg," and "None of Your Bees Wax." No matter what anybody said to them, the pat answer was "what, hon?" Except they dropped the "t" so it was "whahon?" they'd ask, squinting like something was hurting them while trying to make sense of what the hell you were talking about.

Part II
Tips From Eloise With The One Eyebrow

Eloise was the self-appointed head waitress. She looked me up and down and then went back over her tracks, stared me straight in the eye. "You're not so much." I agreed with her and ran into the kitchen. I think she'd been working there before the diner even opened. I figured she ran the tractor that leveled the land, poured the cement, built the booths with her own two claws, screaming, "Finally, Jersey can eat Moussaka!" Eloise was probably only sixty, but she looked eighty, with her facial expression frozen on nasty. Maybe she'd tried on a few other faces—like one would test a lipstick color—you wear it a few times, see how people react, then you settle on which tone to wear for the rest of your miserable days. She'd lost her eyebrows in a mishap somewhere and didn't care enough to go find them. Now she'd taken to drawing them back on with what could only have been the new black felt tip pen. Some days she'd even fill in little fake hairlines, like we were to think that the brows were growing back on their own after a hard winter. But they never arched cor-rectly—they looked more like moustaches, expect that there were two of them, and sort of above her eyes. Her brown hair was teased and stacked in a complicated three-layered beehive that would've looked better as a wedding cake. There was so much Aqua Net on her stack it formed a smelly, shiny sheath of hair. I imagined bugs often circled her head, on hot days, looking for dessert. She followed me into the kitchen and said, "Hey, you, new girl!"

"Debbie," I said quietly.

"Don't bother. I ain't never callin' you by no name. I seen your kind, and I don't like you. I didn't like her, and I don't like you. You so much as look at one of my customers; I'll stab you with a cork screw. You got that?"

I smiled and said, "I'm going to college in the fall," trying to talk her into liking me since it would only be for a few months. I mistakenly thought that anyone could be nice for six weeks.

"I don't give a shit about you and no college. You can go to brain surgeon school for all I give a rat's shit. You could leave yesterday, and it ain't soon enough for Eloise. I seen lotsa girls like you with the long blonde hair, you think you're something else, but you're no better than me, you snotty bitch. "

"Well ..."

"I'll tell youse one thing, watch yourself, summer blonde. There's some broads here who ain't as nice as me, and I ain't training you. Tina can go fuck herself with a bottle of Worcestershire sauce. Why should I? when you're just going off to some fucking college in the fall? Huh? I ain't goin' nowhere. I'm supposed to train you? Teach you my tricks? What kind of stupid jerk-off would even do that! And don't watch me neither. I catch you even lookin' my way, I'll stab you in the ass with a steak knife, you got it?"

"Thank you," I said, scampering out of the kitchen through the swinging doors to the diner floor where Tina grabbed my arm, eyes slit in anger.

"I remember you now. I'm deducting one coconut pie from your first paycheck. Don't make me sorry I hired you." It was like I was in a horror movie, and Bela Lugosi was about to jump out of the phone booth to bite my neck.

I was scared every time I walked into the diner to work my shitty little section. Whenever I passed one of the posse, each and every one of them looked me up and down, and made the face that I'd come to recognize as disgust. They all had eye-glasses dangling on chains scraping their collar bones, tiny calculators in their apron pockets, and pens that their insurance agent had given them. Everyone's hair was wrapped around itself in a twist or beehive, or some kind of swirly thing I'd never even seen before. If you ever walked by one of their tables and accidentally let your eyes drop onto the white Formica, or on their customer's food, they'd push you along, "This don't concern you—get to the back." Eloise threw me a look if I even wandered through her section, which I had to do to get to the pie case. Usually, I'd talk people out of ordering pie—just to avoid the night sweats. I was nothing more than a loss in tips to these lifers, plus my legs were smooth and strong, free of varicose veins, and my bunions were many years in the future.

Every day I showed up and got the *Godawful* station—the one by the bathroom and about a football field's distance from the kitchen. If Tina ever assigned me a teeny upgrade of a better station (like the one caddy-corner to the latrines, as opposed to the one that opened up onto them like a terrace), either Eloise or Maria from Paraguay would yell, "bullshit!"

Eloise would push on, "Put her in the shit section like the other idiot girl!"

So, every shift, I was stuck in the shit section that reeked of urine. I came to get used to the smell. If a customer said, "Whoa, it smells like a bathroom here!"

I'd say, "At least it doesn't smell like vomit." Then nod as if they lucked out.

All the waitresses had to eat their meals together at a table in the back of the kitchen either before or after your eight-hour shift. After a few weeks, things seemed to be going pretty well—no one had physically hurt me, yet. The tips were even more than fifty a night, so it was all okay for now. Marlene was actually pretty nice— she was probably only forty, so when you separated her from the badgers sharpening their claws in the corner, she'd at least talk to me. I even fantasized that she'd probably take my side if everyone jumped me one night. At least she wouldn't dive in too, I thought.

Then a miracle happened. Tina had a meeting with all her wait and busboy staff one Tuesday between shifts, announcing that there were so many mistakes on the checks, that the diner lost $500 last week. I figured they were all mine, I was so bad at math.

Eloise yelled out, "Ain't none on my fuckin' checks. Mine are perfect, and anybody who says otherwise can take it outside." She pointed her finger in a clockwise direction at every waitress there, one at a time.

Tina continued, "So, from now on, you are all going to have to pay for any mistakes you do make—addition, wrong tax, forgetting the pie, not charging for coffee. At the end of the week, I'll add them all up and give you the amount, and you will pay me out of your aprons before you walk out the door. Every Sunday."

There were general groans and grunts, but nobody stood up to her, except me (on the inside) and Eloise. "You won't be seeing me on Sunday, Tina." I won't owe you one thin goddamn dime."

Tina looked at Eloise in that way that battered wives look at their husbands.

We all filed into the kitchen to get ready for the dinner rush, and everyone was pissed off. I wasn't too bothered since I knew I'd just walk out if she tried to take money from me. She was a millionaire; I was a hundredaire. *You ain't takin shit from me, bitch. You put your hand in my apron, I'll stab you with a Bic pen!* But to the lifers, this was huge, and they all started squawking like drowning dolphins, about everything that no one ever had the balls to say to Tina.

When there was a clearing in the rumble, I quietly said, "I think that's illegal."

They all turned toward their very own college girl, and someone said, "How do you know?"

Of course, I didn't know. I was just trying to fit in, but it could've been true. "I'm going to college in a month. You just have to know these things. It's illegal to make waitresses pay for their mistakes, right, Eloise? She can't do that. Right? Eloise?"

Eloise then said something so nice to me I figured that maybe we were gonna go grab a drink together after shift. "The college twat might have something." I swear I saw a little smile and a nod toward me. We were immediately all bonded together against the common foe; we were a family and I was in, I was practically a second cousin, twice removed.

"So what do youse think we should do?" asked Dot.

"I'll tell youse what we do! We say 'no,'" I said. "Not today, Madam Mikonos! We say we're gonna take her to court! Maybe even call immigration. These guys in the kitchen ain't legal! But we gotta all stick together. Are we all together?" Everyone nodded emphatically.

"You do it," said Eloise, glaring at me. "You go tell her. You don't give a shit if she fires you, and we sure don't give a shit neither." They all laughed, and I even joined in. "You don't got any kids to feed, you don't even got a boyfriend or a car to keep up. You got nuthin' goin' for you. You got nuthin' to lose, and you don't mean nuthin' to nobody."

Everyone chimed in, validating how much nuthin' I had.

"Okay. I'll tell her on Sunday when she charges me for my mistakes. I know I'll have the most." Everyone agreed.

A few nights later, before my 5:30 shift, I was eating at the staff table when Ms. Congeniality took a seat across from me. "Hi, Eloise," I sang out like a dirge. She didn't even look up from her foiled wrapped baked potato. One of her eyebrows was half off, and I debated whether I should mention it. The other was scooping in an under arch, perhaps in some attempt to overcompensate? It's not like they were ever a matched pair, not even close, but this configuration was a new low. It didn't look like it had been a good day so far.

"Hhhow are you?" I continued, sucking up.

"Better than you, always will be—and you remember that, girl." She'd taken to calling me "girl." I pretended it was a compliment.

"I don't doubt that. You are an amazing waitress. I love watching you stack plates up your arm. How many can you do?"

"Six big, seven small," she said, still chewing, without looking up.

"Nobody's better, Eloise." I thought I detected a "thank-you" nod.

"Where are you from, Eloise?" I asked, pushing my luck.

The week before, she'd told me that when her son was a kid and got sick, she gave him a sugar cube soaked in kerosene. She told me to try it—it gets rid of anything that ails ya. I assured her I couldn't wait to get sick just so I could try her backwoods remedy.

"The Pines," she finally said, referring to the Pine Barrens—a stretch of state park thickly covered in pine trees, cedar creeks, and drunken suburban high school kids cutting school. It was like our little slice of West Virginia right here in South Jersey. Folklore had it that The Jersey Devil lived there (our local version of Sasquatch). The woods were thick, and it was certainly the home to scattered inbreds and other illiterate red necks—and now, our very own Eloise; part hawk, part creature from the black lagoon. Perhaps she *was* The Jersey Devil.

"Wow," I said.

"Wow what? You don't know what the hell you're talking about. It's a shithole."

"Do you have any brothers and sisters?" She looked at me over her half glasses, eyes burning right through mine, chewing a piece of roll with her mouth open, like a washing machine splashing around the butter and then dough, then butter ... teeth ... roll again.

"Yeah," she said smugly. "I got lots of them."

"Oh, I have three brothers," I said as if she gave a shit, which was my new tactic with these wolverines.

"I got seventeen," Eloise said with her chin out as if to say, *top that!*

"Seventeen brothers?" I gasped out.

"Yeah, and ten sisters." She shoved more of the roll in her mouth.

I dropped my spoon, splattering minestrone on Emily's roll. Her eyes fell to the bread while she took a moment to decide if she felt like taking the time out of her dinner break to hit me.

"Your mother had 27 children? That's a lot," was all I could think to say. I was appalled and I pictured her mother's poor uterus, stretched beyond it's shape like a deflated kiddie pool; shrunken, spent and full of holes. But I decided not to say that. The conversation slowed, so I asked, "Are you close?"

"Who?"

"You and your brothers and sisters."

"Yeah. You wanna know how close we are? Last week, some fat slob sits down in D-4, and I go to take his burger order—he says, 'Eloise, don't you recognize me? I'm your brother.' 'Yeah?' I says. 'Who isn't?' and I walked away. I made Margie wait on him. I'm sure he's a crappy tipper the cheap jerk-off. He's only got one ball, that one."

"No kidding," I said as I bussed both of our plates into the bus pan.

That Sunday, after my day shift, Tina called me over to give me my pay, which came in a small manila envelope with scribbles on the outside. As we sat at a table, she pulled out a banded stack of checks, with red marks and hieroglyphics all over them. "You owe me $101.05," she said, showing me the checks and all the addition mistakes I'd made.

I looked briefly at her evidence and blurted out, "Tina, its illegal. You can't charge your wait staff for mistakes—we could sue you." I had believed my own bullshit.

"Not here—it's not. This is Olga's law. Pay up. Come on!" She started smacking her palm impatiently, expecting me to dig into my black nylon apron and pull out my Sunday tips.

"I won't. I will not pay you! What am I gonna use for drinking money in college? These are *my* tips. I waited on assholes from Bellmawr—and cheap schmucks from South Philly to get them. I got threatened every single day by that Godzilla you call Eloise. You're not getting one penny from me. I'll fucking sue you! Ask Eloise—it's illegal. Eloise!" I yelled. Eloise walked by me like I was in somebody else's section.

"You're fired," said Tina. Eloise waved "*Bye-byeee.*"

"You can't fire me! This is America, we have laws!" I said, pulling it all out of my ass. I had no idea where my indignation came from. But I had developed one standing philosophy that summer: "Touch my tips, and I'll shave your moustache!"

"Well, you can stick around if you want, but you'll have nobody to wait on."

Now, as fate would offer, it *was* illegal for her to do that. The college girl who happened to replace me was someone I knew. And when Tina handed her the Sunday bad news, she took notes each week, and she went to Camden and filed a complaint with the Labor Board and got a hearing. She needed a witness, and of course, none of the lifers were going to testify. It was a good thing for everyone that I'd be available to do just that. Good thing for everyone but Tina, that is. It was just after Labor Day, and I hadn't left for school, yet. The court ruled in our favor, and Little Olga had to pay my friend back all the money she collected from her and she couldn't fire her! It was beautiful. Tina was so furious, I thought I saw fire shooting out of her nostrils.

With only a few weeks left, which represented another $500 bucks to me, I got hired at the crown jewel of diner jobs, PONZIOS. I'd been thrown out of there several times during my rowdy high school days, but it didn't occur to me that I shouldn't walk in and ask for a job. I'm not sure what drove me—denial? Stupidity? Greed?

Ponzio's was the town's pride, a sprawling Greek diner specializing in Italian food and perched on the busiest circle in town. My high school friends and I hung out at Ponzio's after football games, or after drinking in McDonald's parking lot. We'd cause a ruckus or two: seven of us piled in a booth, squirting ketchup at each other, or we'd spill coke all over the table, if the spirit moved us. I'm sure we left no tips, or maybe we'd stack up five dimes like it was a tower of gold. But now I was an adult, with a job. Things were different.

Maria ran the place, and when she took me to the back room to sit me down and hire me on the spot (all in the timing, all in the timing), she sized me up and down with her very narrow, harsh eyes. "You got a lot of moxie, kid, walking in here, asking for a job. You think I don't remember you? You're a pain in the ass. In fact, you were the ringleader! You think I should hire you now? Why should I hire you?"

"I've grown up."

"Since June?" she asked, with cold doubt in her eyes.

"I'm a really good waitress," I shot back, now confident in my skills. "If you hired me, there'll be no trouble from any of my friends anymore. For one thing ... I won't be coming in. I'll send the others to Olga's." Marie looked interested in that proposal, as if I were some mob boss. I had severely overstated my influence, but she hired me, and she treated me fairly. I got kicked around like a dog, no more no less, than all the other waitresses in South Jersey. But the tips just kept getting better.

In one short summer, I had climbed the status ladder of diners. I reached the pinnacle, and I was proud. I hung up my hair net, put my apron away, and deposited my last roll of quarters into the bank account my father and I had opened in June. I'd overshot my dad's goal of $1,500 by a bit. I liked having my own "scratch," as the Jersey waitresses called it, and Dad said he was proud of me, which was more precious to me than the money.

I took my parents out for dinner to thank them for all the meals they'd fed me and to get rid of a stack of filthy ones that were so crumpled, the bank didn't even want them. I had lots of them.

When we sat down at the Steak and Brew's dimly lit table, I glanced around knowingly. Restaurants would never look the same to me, again. I would never be able to enjoy a meal without knowing what really goes on there. I'd seen cooks spit in food if you sent it back. Some waitresses would eat right off your plate before they brought it out to you (that was me, actually), and if food got dropped in the kitchen, you'd just pick it up and throw it back on the plate, anyway.

The hostess dropped off the menus, and I said, "thanks, hon." I told my parents, "Look, this waitress has ten tables. This whole section. Wow, she's good. I don't even see a busboy. Oh, there he is—see with the bin, he's the busboy. I wonder how much she makes a night. This place is packed." I was curious who had to fill the ketchups. "You wouldn't believe how many ketchups I had to 'marry' this summer." I told them how whenever I got the chore of 'marrying the ketchups,' I'd line all the half-full bottles up on the counter and start singing the wedding march "du-du-du dum!" My parents laughed—they were proud of me, and they enjoyed knowing the inside scoop of a restaurant, too. "See that section?" I pointed to the back one near the bathrooms. "That's where the new girl works. Furthest from the kitchen, smells like crap"

When the waitress came over, I told her that I was one with her, that I understood her pain, I'd been a waitress—for two long months. "I know how your feet feel every night. I get it—I'm eighteen years old, with a backache all the time, now." I told her I'd worked at Olga's and Ponzio's and left it at that.

"How is old Tina?" she asked, smirking.

"We took her to court and won. Restaurants aren't allowed to charge you for mistakes. Spread it around."

"Thanks. I started there, my first summer job, before college," our waitress admitted. That frightened me. I looked at her with the "Please go on face."

"I fell in love with the cook at the Diamond Diner. We got married and had our first baby, so I never made it to college, and here I am." My mother made a tsk sound, I kicked her under the table.

"Well, you're an excellent waitress," I said, impressed. "Make sure you give me the check, Ronnie."

She said, "Whahon?"

When she dashed away, my father said, "She got knocked up. That's what happened."

I gave my new peer a 30% tip, thanked her and then God that I was going to college, even though I was already missing the hustle, just a little. Mom, Dad and I walked out into the sweet smell of the September night. I took a deep breath—I huffed out yesterday, and breathed in tomorrow. I was relieved that I wouldn't have to be a waitress, *ever again*, like these poor, miserable women. Turns out I didn't know my ass from a piece of coconut custard pie.

Selling Your Blood Sounds Like A Great Idea!

Less than three weeks after I graduated from college with my BFA in theatre, it occurred to me that I was completely unemployable. Besides being able to roll a one-handed joint while singing the entire Mothers of Invention white album, I had no marketable skills. I'd majored in theatre, minored in high finance: I got high—my parents financed it.

"College is the best time of your life, so have a ball!" said Dad as he dropped me off at my freshman dorm four short years before. Not as much an opinion as a threat. He said it in the car on the way up the Jersey Turnpike, even demanding an "uh-huh" back up from the toll collector on exit 17W. He said it again as we crossed I-95 into New England, hammering the point home all through Connecticut, right on until we got to the green mountains of Vermont. He even yelled something like it out to several other freshman and their parents moving into the dorm the next day.

When we met up with a coed moving into my dorm with her

parents, my father said to me loudly for their benefit, "It's all a slide down a mountain of snot in a sled made of shit from here, kids, so have a ball on your old man's dough." The other parents looked at each other askance and moved on up the hall. He knew how to scare up some friends for me. My dad had been humiliating me most of my life with his big mouth and his crass ideas. "So, get loaded on us—because after you graduate, you'll have to pay for your own *goddamned* life!" he yelled out his window in the parking lot as he drove away that evening.

The night before I began college, we spent at the Putney Inn, a faux country hotel, less quaint than the name sounds, particularly this eve. It was run amuck with rich suburbanites from the lower states, all dropping their kids off in the morning for the first day of the rest of their lives. We drove up alone, just Dad and I. We were trying to cram in some last minute father-daughtering. Dad was trying to figure out where all the time went, while I confessed I thought this day would never get here! He tried to explain the concept of time passing much faster when you get older. How at his age, every year, July 4th comes right after Christmas, and just as soon as you pack away your flags, you're pulling out the Christmas decorations again. Then it's the 4th of July again. Then Christmas. Then you're fifty. He slammed back some double shots of CC and water, and more of the "sad truth," as he liked to call reality, seeped out. I slammed back my legal vodka for the first time in my eighteen years. (I knew which state to go to college in.) Vermont was one of two states that sported the 18-year-old drinking age. I had my future all mapped out, and I was barely nineteen.

"You don't know what the hell you're in for here, Debbie. I ain't gonna lie to ya. Life is not a balloon like it says on your psychedelic poster, it's more like chasing a truck full of refrigerators, but as soon as you catch up to the truck, someone hurls another *goddamned* refrigerator at you! In four short years, your little party will be over, and you will have to work for your money for the rest of your miserable life, just like the rest of us poor schmucks. And you know what's worse? The four years are gonna go like this," and he snapped his fingers. Dad emphasized the word "work" like I was gonna get stabbed. Then he shot back his fifth CC and water, rattling the shrunken ice in his glass toward the frizzy headed waitress in the calico pinafore. "Another."

This scared the shit out of me—the thought of working for a living drove me right to the theatre department. To me, nine to five were odds, not hours. I'll be a movie star, I decided right then and there, sopping the juice from my shrimp scampi up with a piece of sourdough bread at The Putney Inn.

The years flew by like an acid flashback, the fun was over while the open wound of reality was festering and needed to be dressed. I was back at "go" where it all began—New Jersey—and I needed a job so I could get the hell out of there. My actual degree was a Bachelor of Fine Arts, a B.F.A. or, as Dad liked to say, "What's that stand for? Bad Frigging Actress?"

"Oh, Robert!" my mom would always chide, flicking her cigarette. "Don't be such an asshole. You wonder why your kids all hate you so much! You put them all down all the time! Do you even know? Half your kids don't even come around anymore. I haven't seen Robbie since he climbed out his bedroom window on Father's Day. I heard he was living in the woods, somewhere. I'm sure Debbie will get a job.

Still, Dad was right, nobody was looking for actresses, not bad or otherwise, not in South Jersey, anyway. My father liked to rub in how much my expensive college had actually cost him. It was a personal challenge to see how many ways he could slip it into the conversation. "Debbie, pass me the hollandaise—I can't quite reach it. I paid my arm and a leg to that private college you went to." Or "Shirl, have you seen the child that sucked up our retirement fund? She's going to have to drive me to the donut shop to work my second job. Has anybody seen my hair net?"

One of the few things my parents had in common was a slice and dice sense of humor—always at someone else's expense. Their favorite past time was to pour a couple of high balls a few hours before sundown, relax into their easy chairs and wait for one of their four children to stop by so they could cut us up, aka, "the Kasper family shooting range." It was like a Dean Martin Roast by dinner hour.

My father's material was left over from some cheesy Vaudeville act. It was supremely funny-free, and it never changed at all. Dad liked to call my youngest brother Joe "Jo-Jo the Dog-Faced Boy," and he'd bark it like he was selling tickets to the sideshow. "Here he comes Jo-Jo the Dog-Faced Boy! He walks; he talks; he crawls on his belly like a reptile." Ask him where our mother was, "She went out to feed the pigs, and the dogs ate her." He'd constantly invite us to go out and play in traffic. If you asked him what time it was, he'd sing out, "Time all dogs were dead, don't you feel sick?" He'd laugh like hell—a laugh that laughed alone.

My long-haired older brother got the brunt of his abuse. "Hey, Reid, is that you? The Feds stopped by. I showed them where your pot was stashed. We rolled a joint, listened to some of your records—The Grateful Assholes. I hope that's okay with you, son. Ya know I was wrong about that song "Truckin'" it's not so bad … it's terrible."

Most my friends had gone to school in search of a husband—I was in search of wit to defend myself around these people. I'd been brought up by a pack of witty wolves with a mortgage. "You have one month to find a job, sweetie-pie," said Mom. "And then you're out on the street. We're not running a boarding house here."

"No," said Dad from his own throne, "We're running a half-way house, so either get a job or get a drug addiction."

My parents' threats used to be empty, but while I was away, they'd worked on their tough love, and things had changed. The first month I left for school, they sold my zebra shag carpet right out from under my Peter Max design hide-a-bed, stripped my autographed Paul Newman poster right off the wall, put my dog, Sam, to sleep, and hawked my award-winning rock collection at a garage sale—for five bucks!

"Five bucks! That Mica Crist was worth a buck fifty itself. You were ripped off! And that poster was autographed!" I screamed.

"By you! Let some of the helium out of your head, superstar. You signed that yourself." She was right. I had signed it myself. It was coming back to me now. I bought a Paul Newman in *Cool Hand Luke* poster at Spencer's Gifts and signed it: "*To Debbie, you're a doll! No, really! You're special—what a great girl—Love Paul. P.S. I really like you.*" I dragged new best friends home from school just to show it off, telling anyone who believed it that he'd gone to school with my parents, and he just so happened to stop by one night for dinner with a poster under his arm coincidentally, and there was this chemistry that was palpable between us. I wanted to be a movie star mostly just to meet him exactly as he looked in *Cool Hand Luke*.

Holding down a job was something I only knew about from watching *That Girl*. Marlo Thomas always had a job, every week a new one. In fact, *That Girl* tore through them every half hour. *I can do that*, I thought. I'd waited tables over the summer before college, but I swapped diners up every couple of weeks. Many of the kids I went to college with had trust funds. And there was some designer money there. There were DuPonts, and Simmon's Mattresses, and a Morgan (the rum and the banks). We even had a Boyardee ... as in "Chef." We called her "Uh-oh Spaghetti-o's" behind her back, and I have no doubt that behind my back, they called me "Little Miss No-Car." I wasn't quite sure what a trust fund was, but I pretended that I had one as well. I had called my parents from college and asked Mom, "Why hadn't anybody trusted me with a fund?" I pushed on through her laughter, "Is there any chance I had one somewhere behind my back? Waiting for me to turn 21? That I wasn't aware of? Maybe?"

"Yeah, sweetie pie," she said, lighting her Kool. "We're loaded—sssh! Let's just keep it between us. Your father doesn't even know. I come from a royal bloodline in Scotland—you're a Princess, sweetie pie. I was gonna throw you a surprise coronation, but you figured it out. Oh, well, that's what happens when you go to school and smarten up. Don't tell your brothers or your father. You and I are going to go back to Scotland and overthrow those murdering Windsors—just waiting for the right moment. Someone's gotta pay for Mary." She laughed so hard she coughed. "Who do you think would have set up a trust fund for you?" she asked.

"Grandpa?" My grandfather had been a millionaire back in the forties, when apparently it counted. "Perhaps he could have," I offered weakly. My father's retirement plan had always been for his dad to die, constantly asking Grandpa how he was feeling, in that tone you use when you're suspicious of someone. So far, Grandpa was healthier than Dad, but Dad hadn't given up hope, especially since my pricey private college had sucked up all his savings. Yes, my family was breeding down.

AVON offered me a job on the spot. My parents bought me the flowered turquoise sales case packed with all sorts of ceramic jars in various animal shapes filled with creams and perfumes, all working together toward the master plan of a softer, sweeter-smelling world. I immediately began to plan out my cosmetic empire. There was no stopping me. I was hopeful. I had the right product, and my hair was long, straight, and blonde. I'd read the brochures, and they pretty clearly stated that I was about to make a lot of money if I were a go-getter. "Oh, I'm a go-getter, all right," I assured the regional manager at the local Avon office. Whenever we needed a fake ID, I had been the one to get it. I could also miraculously appear with a bottle of Kahlua at two o'clock in the morning for late-night White Russians. The sales kit brochure went on and on about the cologne that came in ceramic train containers, and their biggest seller—the horse head filled with man's hand cream that could turn me into the next millionaire.

The first morning as an Avon Lady, I got in my mother's car, drove across the street, parked, and rang Mrs. Bittner's doorbell. The woman who opened the first door into my cosmetic empire wore a faded housecoat and last month's hair appointment on her head. Myrtle Bittner was a new neighbor, and I'd never met her.

"She moved in a few years back. In fact, she bought your diary at the garage sale, so she knows how much you weigh. She's strange, I took over a bottle of Early Times to welcome her to the neighborhood, she didn't even invite me in to drink it with her. It was after three, for *chrissakes*," Mom said.

Myrtle told me her husband would kill her if she bought any makeup. I looked over sadly at her eyebrows that she'd colored a tad too auburn and certainly too shiny. In fact, her whole face was too shiny. I knew this all for a fact because I was now an Avon Lady, and I'd received an hour of cosmetic training over the phone from a woman with a lisp, who kept saying, "Yeth, you are going to thell! Thell! Thell!" Myrtle needed my help. Her hair was too dull, her eyebrows were too red, and she could've shown a public service announcement on the glare of her forehead. If anybody needed makeup, it was Myrtle Bittner. In fact, it may have already been too late. I gave her my samples—she needed them.

I drove up the street, passing up house after house, as many were not "Debbie friendly." There was someone's house whose son I had pulled a chair out from under in eighth grade, and he broke his pelvis. Best not to bother them, they might still be holding a grudge. Someone else whose pansies I had unearthed when they didn't buy my Christmas cards in the sixth grade. By the time I knocked on the second door of the day, an old high school friend opened it, handed me a joint, and next thing I knew, we were watching a *Three Stooges* marathon. I gave him the horse head filled with moisturizer for men, leaving my turquoise suitcase empty.

On day two, I threw away my empty case of samples and used the tears my father had spent thousands of dollars training me to whip up. I talked Mom into staking me in a move to Boston. "Three of my girlfriends from school are moving to Cambridge, and their parents are paying for it. I have to go. I will literally die in this town," I told her. "Die! I will die here if you make me stay one more day. These are not my people."

"Only if you don't tell your dad," she said. "It's just that he spent a fortune on your college education already. Jesus Christ! That school was pricey—we all had to make sacrifices. Do you even know how many times we ate meatloaf?"

Dad gave me a few bucks too, but only if I promised not to tell my mom. "Your mother is pissed off at how much your *goddamned* college cost us. We've had to switch to Canadian Club." There were great advantages to having parents who didn't get along—they reveled in betraying each other. We often lived scenes right out of *Lion in Winter*.

I moved into a huge four-bedroom apartment in Cambridge with my three best friends from college, each of us less prepared to make rent than the next. Up until this point, our money-making schemes had been limited to mooching, begging, borrowing, canceling classes at the last minute and pocketing the class fee, or sharing textbooks but sending duplicate receipts to all our parents. Growing pot plants on our windowsills from seeds a classmate brought back from Guatemala had been a lucrative college enterprise, but no one had any clients in Cambridge—yet. Liz could macramé plant hangers, and I had learned how to hustle drinks at a bar. I'd discovered a neat little con quite accidentally one evening in a crowded bar on campus. As I was sucking down the last white out of my Russian, a drunken guy in front of me swung around carelessly, knocking my milky ice glass onto the floor. Before I could assure him the drink was empty, he was already buying me another, saying, "I'm sho shorry."

By the time I would graduate, I would've had over a hundred drinks "knocked" out of my hands and received countless apologies. I was practically a professional con man, and it wasn't until I made that fatal mistake—the same guy knocked my drink twice in one night, that I got busted. My scam had come to an end, and word spread fast. From that fatal night on, I had to either: A. pay for my own drinks, or B. sleep with someone for them, like the rest of the chicks. "What kind of girl do you think I am? I have my dignity."

I tried the dropped drink con (or the DDC) the first night out drinking in Cambridge, but the Harvard men were smart. "No way! That glass was empty!" the pre-law student scoffed. "You aint *that* pretty!

"Yah! I'm aware."

"Tell you what, babe, I'll buy you a drink if you come back to my frat house and do me and all my brothers." Boston was a cold hard city, and the price of a drink there was steeper than the price in Vermont. A whole frat house? I'd rather get a job.

There were weeks that would go by when we ate nothing but Kraft macaroni and pears. My roommate Liz's parents had a pear tree that had unexpectedly shed dozens of pounds of pears that fall, so we took her baby blue Volkswagen Bug to Connecticut to get several shopping bags full of them, chugging along the Old Boston Post Road. Like Pilgrims, we ate what was harvested that month, not one duck more. When the pears were gone, it was time to go back to work. After all, the cold hard New England winter was upon us. There were harsh winds coming and unfriendly strangers among us.

I put an ad in the paper that I was available to teach private baton lessons. *The Real Paper* was Boston's answer to *The Village Voice*, and it came out on Thursday. By noon, I got two responses:

"Yeah, ya know what you can do with your baton," the gruff voice said to me on the phone.

"I have a baton you can twirl, toots," said another one.

I was shocked. My roommates were shocked that I was shocked. *"Basic marching and strutting techniques offered in private,"* my ad bragged. But I had misspelled strutting, so it read "stutting." Truthfully, my twirling talents were only medium to rare, but I was tired of fried pears. I was a majorette in high school—but just barely. I was the last one picked for the squad, and that was only because someone got mononucleosis.

"Majorette? That's French for too flat-chested to be a cheerleader!" said my brother Reid, who by this time, was a world-class wit.

During my first pep rally as a twirler in high school, the baton flew out of my hand and knocked a freshman dumb. The fighting song came to a clean end, the pep rally halted, and I spent the rest of the afternoon at the nurse's office apologizing to his parents and promising to carry the lamed boy's books to classes for two weeks. Our family mutt, Sam, had been hit in the head by my baton so many times that he spent the last years of his dog life stumbling around, answering to Bob, which was also my father's name. They'd both come to eat dinner at the exact same time. If ever I wanted to clear a room or a pep rally or a funeral, I only had to show up with the baton.

But that cold fall in Cambridge, after ferreting out the obscene calls, the weirdos and the liars, I was left with a grand total of no one who wanted to give their child baton lessons. This was a narrow-minded city, this was. The '70s were drawing to a bitter middle; all the flowers were gone, and I was heartbroken, jobless, sick of pears and five dollars poorer. I hated Boston so far.

I signed up with a Temp Agency called ODDJOBS, but my thirteen words per minute typing score, with six mistakes, didn't impress the suited lady on the other side of my application.

"Give me a job, and I'll show up," I bragged, trying to dazzle her. I thought that was a bit of a selling point. What did I know that people were supposed to show up when they had a job? I then said something I'd heard Ann-Marie say on *That Girl*. "You won't be sorry."

She assured me that she already was and that in the future, I shouldn't use my own parents as a reference, particularly since when she called them, they laughed. I asked ODDJOBS to give me any strange job they got in. "I'm an actress. I'll do anything—I'm kooky!" I screamed as I flew out the door, certain I had energized my base.

The lady from the agency called pretty quickly, and one whirlwind Monday morning in October, I was on my way to my first assignment. They sent me to Gilchrist's Department Store on the outskirts of Cambridge dressed as a clown to celebrate its grand opening. Gilchrist's was kind of a low-rent Macy's with more bins and fewer sweaters. At the bottom of my resume, under special talents, right next to making faces, insulting people, and winning first prize at several pajama parties for lip-syncing "They're Coming to Take Me Away, Ha, Ha!" I also mentioned that I could juggle. Never mind that I could only juggle three balls—an over-achiever at the agency had read my whole resume, and she was moved.

So, I was off to Gilchrist's dressed in a clown outfit. I went for two solid weeks to cruise the aisles and juggle my three red balls. Even the four-year-olds weren't impressed. Some cried, others ducked—my juggling skills rivaled those of my baton twirling. My clown outfit was big and overlapped everywhere, so eventually, I started hiding the balls in my puffy arms to entertain the kids in strollers—now a magic clown. By the end of the first week, I was stuffing more than balls into my arm sleeves. I figured that nobody would ever suspect a clown. It wasn't the first time I'd shoplifted, it had always been a hobby of mine, and here bored, in this empty store, I thought righteously—they're practically challenging me to misbehave. And this new store was overflowing with bins of things they wouldn't miss—stuff I suddenly needed. I had to have it all. And

God how they were screwing me—paying *me*, a college graduate, an embarrassing $3.00 an hour! Yes, I'd been pushed to the edge of my self-righteous limit.

So, sometime during about the fourth day, I started shoving hair bands and Chia Pets and plastic vases and Paul Revere coffee mugs up my billowy sleeves. Then I'd transfer it to my purse in the locker room and take my loot home on the red line, smiling to myself how I'd cleverly given myself a raise.

By Monday on the second week of my temp job, miraculously, I'd gotten a second raise, and I needed my pant legs along with the arm sleeves to accommodate it. By the end of the day, I had knee socks, two boxes of Rice-a-Roni (the San Francisco treat), scarves, hats, plastic Kleenex holders, tie-dyed thing-a-ma jiggers, deely-bobs, and what-have-yous all stuffed into my pant legs. I waddled through the front door, telling the store security guard that I'd decided to wear the clown outfit home on the subway just for fun, as I crunched past him. There wasn't a purse big enough. Then it occurred to me that maybe I should steal one the next day.

My scam was brilliant—as they all are—until they aren't anymore. Around mid-morning on Tuesday, a nosey five-year-old girl saw me stuff a purse into my right pant leg. Children wept as the store security escorted the shoplifting clown into the locker room while cafeteria waitresses, salesgirls, and cleaning ladies watched me empty out towels, mood rings, and Summer Blonde hair lightener. They even stripped me of my clown outfit, as I would not be coming back to Gilchrist's the next day.

I got my first nine-to-fiver while standing in line at the Boston DMV, bragging about how unemployable I really was. I'd been standing there so long I started forging alliances with my neighbors, like,

"I'm going to the vending machine. Hold my place, and I'll get you some salted nuts and a Tab."

Barb had just graduated from Radcliffe and was going to Med school at Boston Children's Hospital. She was going to be a neuro-surgeon. "Right on, sister," I said. "I'm going to be a movie star," I mentioned casually.

Billy was about to fly Icelandic to Luxemburg and then onto Vienna, where he would teach German to Americans. It sounded suspiciously to me like they had all done their homework in school. I sighed quietly.

Lou, my future ex-boss, was standing there too, with an arm load of manila envelopes and a stack of license plates. I guessed that he was doing car registration business of some strange sort. His head was noticeably small, and he had a cheek-mole that looked enough like a fly that it made you want to swat his face. His gray-black hair was slicked back, greased to a sheen, like a hoodlum seal. He had a tight belt that divided his belly in two, although not evenly. I would later find out that his limp was because of his gout. In fact, his gout would become a daily feature story when I would work for him. He kept trying to join the young kids' conversation, in line at the DMV, and finally found his "in" when I'd asked if you needed to fill out the organ donor card on the back of the license. "I mean, like, if I died, and someone got my organs, would they get my parking tickets too?"

The man with the seal head laughed way too loudly at my hu-mor and started standing nearer to us, laughing, smiling, bobbing his slippery head, moving towards us as if he were already in our club—or maybe he was doing a trick at Sea World—I wasn't sure which. He'd overheard me brag that I'd been fired by Gilchrist's for shoplifting, dressed as a clown and that I was an Avon Lady for two houses until I got high, and I lost my will to work. He offered me a job on the spot.

"Just for now, maybe, because I'm going to be a movie star eventually," I said. But that day in line at the Boston DMV, Lou Lane had said, "You only need two things to work for me; first thing is—a *cah*," he said in the accent that needed some "R's."

"Nope. I don't have a car. My parents never gave me a car and I don't know how I'm supposed to get one now." Everyone around me in line shook their heads at my bad luck, admitting that you were supposed to get one when you graduated. It was the law.

Lou immediately rescinded, "Then I'll find you a *cah*."

"What's the other thing I need?" I asked, feigning interest.

"You need to be a *had* worker. Are you a *had* worker?"

"I don't know! I've only been a waitress."

"I *gawt* a feeling about you," he said. "I'm very psychic. *Yaw* going to *wowk* out just fine. You *gawt* something, kid." Lou was what they called an "insurance runner." He drove a gold Seville, wore a fur coat, matching diamond pinky rings, and liked everyone to call him "Uncle Lou." The window ladies at all of the Eastern Massachusetts DMVs judged him behind his big back, despite the gifts he showered on them.

"*Yaw* waking *fah* that insurance *runna*, Uncle Lou?" the window workers would ask with their suburban Bostonese.

He told me that my job would entail standing in line. "That pretty much there is the whole shebang," said Lou with his usual flair for the English language. "Can you do that?"

"Stand in line? You mean stand in line? You mean just stand in line? That's what you do?" I kept repeating it as if that would change the answer somehow. "No, I can't stand in line. I hate standing in lines."

"Good. That right there is the *numbah* one reason why I have such a good business. I *wawk* for the insurance agencies and the *cah dealaships*. We register people's *cahs fah* them. My company's motto is: 'Sit down, relax, we'll stand.'"

"Well, okay, I guess," I finally said. I'd heard that when it came to jobs you were supposed to play hard to get, like it was a relationship, but I didn't know for sure, since nobody had ever taught me how to get a job, or a car. But I knew what the square root of 49 was!

Lou found me a car, bought it for me, and took the payments out of my paycheck every month. He knew everyone in the business and *gawt* me a great deal on a '68 aqua valiant with a red racing stripe down the side, which I promptly named Phoebe, after my deceased aunt. An old woman had driven the car to church once a week. That was what the salesman had told Uncle Lou.

"Yeah, sweetie, and she went blind crocheting doilies for starving children in Rwanda and had to sell her car. Uncle Lou sounds like a *winnah*!" said my mom, mocking his accent. Months later, on the job, while at the Revere DMV, an older man stopped me to ask if I'd just bought that car a few months ago. "It was mother's, she only drove it to church." he said. Life sometimes works out.

Pretty soon, Lou's gout started to suck the very life out of him, curtailing his dancing days, certainly making his line-standing career a burden, so he began unloading more and more responsibility onto me. He was preening me to take over his insurance runner's business, and pretty quickly I felt trapped, yet indebted, like I was going to let Lou down if I didn't take over his line-standing empire. I immediately insisted we hire me an assistant since I was overwhelmed by the responsibility of standing in more lines to cover Lou, so he hired my roommate Hilarie. I started teaching her everything I knew about the business, which was precious little. "You stand in this line, and you register these cars. Then you stand in that line, and you register those limos. That's pretty much the whole shebang," I said, as I limped away.

After five months of working for a living, and after Hilarie was secure in the job, I decided to go back to graduate school so I could back up my movie star plans. "Well, who's going to pay for that, Deborah?" asked my father on the phone. "I've already re-mortgaged the house to pay for that summer camp you called a college."

"Lou Lane will pay for me!" I screamed back. "He loves me. He believes in me; he thinks I'm special!" I sobbed over the phone until my father offered to pay for part of my graduate school. I supplemented my parents' graduate contribution with a loan I'd gotten from The Student Loan Society of New Jersey. I started Penn State College University the next fall, moved into a graduate dorm that was mostly inhabited by rich Iranian exchange students. The Shah was still in control, and these were the privileged children of the upper crust in Iran. There were also a few Pakistanis, one Korean who had an obsessive-compulsive disorder, and a Turkish gal who was always hot. "I *em zo* hot," that was the sum total of her English. *Did they not have weather in Turkey?* I was pretty sure they had plenty of hot over there.

No matter what mid-eastern country they hailed from, they were the wealthy from those countries. None of them had borrowed a yen or dinar to come to school. They drove the finest American cars, smoked imported European cigarettes (which they had sent over from Paris). I was the poor white trash with the old aqua valiant and the plain wrap cigarettes that were made in some state that didn't care to have its name associated with them.

I got a job as a waitress on Saturdays for extra spending money, and I'd wait on these rich foreign students. One day, my boyfriend Peter's roommate, started bragging about Sara Tec, and how he was their best employee. He was best known for getting drunk at night and betting people ten bucks that he could eat a beer mug. He had apparently won this bet several times, and although I'd never seen the actual glass eating, he bragged that his favorite part was the handle. "It tastes like chicken."

I was waiting on a group of American students one Saturday at my waitress job when I overheard again—Sarah Tec. One of them said, "I work for Sarah Tec." Everyone kind of laughed, a few half-smiled, like they were secret members of KAOS, and Sara Tec was their headquarters.

Sara Tec was a technological place as far as I could tell. Yes, some sort of technology that I would never qualify for. I was getting my Master's degree in theatre, which was pretty much a guarantee I'd NEVER be employable, but I wouldn't have to worry about it for a few more years. I'd at least thought ahead that much. Sara Tec, it turned out, was a blood lab that paid people for their blood. I'd never heard of such a thing. God! I loved America. What a country—you can sell blood and hair and the gold out of your teeth and your rock collection at a garage sale. This was the best country in the world. There were opportunities here, man. People came from all over the globe to grab a piece of American pie. I entertained the idea, knowing it would be less tiring than working in this burger joint, but then I feared that my blood was probably mostly filled with cranberry juice and vodka, with a splash of donuts, so I shrugged the idea off.

"They pay $7.50 for a pint of blood. Cash. No questions asked," my new best friend Samme told me a few days later. That could cover two movies, a bucket of popcorn, and a few packs of Juicy Fruit gum. "It's also a great place to meet men," urged Samme.

That Saturday, I called in sick to my waitress job, thinking it wouldn't be a lie, for after I'd had a pint of blood taken from my stash, I'd probably feel weak, perhaps even faint. I thought about my mother's reaction when I would tell her that I was selling my blood to get by. She'd send me some dough for certain, for fear someone in her bridge club would find out.

In the waiting room at Sara Tec, I met a twenty-something guy from The Soviet Union who whispered, "You can do this *tvice a veek*," then he clicked his cheek like I'd better write this down so I don't forget. His color was not human, like sauerkraut, maybe he was already a quart low. "That's *vifteen American dollars, ca-lear.* God bless America," he said, nodding out. It turned out that Boris was there to get a pint back—he didn't feel so well.

"It don't work like that, Jack. Your platelets are gone," said a Texan wearing overalls and a tee-shirt that said "WHAT?" on the front. "This ain't no pawn shop here. This is America. They don't hold onto things, they sell em. We're not a country as much as a clearinghouse."

"But I am zooo tired," said Boris, his voice trailing off. I had no idea how the body worked. I guessed that your body would replenish its blood, so I asked that out loud.

"Your body is a turbine of blood. It's actually good to turn it over and take a pint out every now and again. It just gets stale sitting in there all these years," said a guy from Kentucky across the way from me.

"What do they do with the blood?" I finally asked, stumping the whole waiting room. My turn came, and they called me into a room and gave me a blood pressure test. The nurse seemed perplexed, taking the test again and again, squeezing my arm tighter with the strangling belt—until she finally sent me back to the waiting room to wait. I took the empty seat next to Boris, who now looked like he had slipped into a coma, his skin tone a shade lighter than his eye whites. I shook him lightly. "Boris, Boris?"

The nurse came out with another white-outfitted co-worker, and they both called me into a private room that had charts all over the wall. It was the kind of room where people in white take patients to tell them they are dying. A room that was in *a lot* of movies.

"We can't use your blood," said the meaner of the two. Her face was pock-marked, no doubt a victim of teenage acne. *Probably didn't go to her high school prom, and now she's taking it out on my blood.*

"Why? I'm American. You got people in your waiting room from countries I never heard of," I cried, my tears rising to my throat. Suddenly, I had to have that seven-fifty.

"You need to go to a doctor. You might have mononucleosis."

"The kissing disease? But I haven't kissed anybody in months!"

"You could've caught it from a toilet seat. There's always an opportunity," said Nurse pock-face.

"Or it could be Leukemia," added the nice one, like I was ordering food at a restaurant, and she was suggesting a better side-dish. "Your blood pressure is so low. We don't know how you walked here."

"You have no pulse. How do you feel?" The other asked.

"Well, I'm kinda tired, come to think of it. I have to work on Saturdays, you know! I'm a waitress at a burger joint. And all my school work. It's a hard life, and *not* nearly what I expected."

"We're not ruling out yellow fever," said the nice one. "With all the Brazilian students on campus, they could've brought it with them."

"Or you could just have low blood pressure," said the homely one who I was starting to like much more.

After three lost nights of sleep, and a blood test at the infirmary on campus, it turned out I merely had very, very low blood pressure. "Which is good," said the doctor. "It's very good. When you're older, you'll thank your lucky stars."

"Something to look forward to," I mumbled.

That night, I called home, but not before weaving this into a dramatic tale of fear, poverty, and pestilence, only emboldened by my stalwart resolve to keep going on and deliver burgers to the foreign students. I knew my mother would offer to slip me some graduate school spending money when she found out I had almost died trying to sell my blood. I knew she'd want me to make sure that this tale of unfit blood, yellow fever, and a Russian named Boris, never got back to her circle of friends. I knew she'd worry about what they would all think. But as it turned out, I didn't know squat.

"Well, that's wonderful," she said, sounding a bit Lawrence Welk-ish. "You kids are so lucky. When I was in college, we had to give our blood away. There was a war on, we all had to donate blood for the American Red Cross. You didn't have a choice. They'd come right into our classrooms and just take it. You kids got it made. Imagine, selling blood! You are so spoiled. Well, I'm proud of you! How very enterprising. You can probably sell a pint a week," she encouraged before she hung up.

I called her right back, and both she and my father answered the call at the same time, from two different extensions, each assuring the other that they "had it," which was always a signal that the other person should hang up ... but neither would give in this time. I finally said, "Hello?"

"Who's that?" asked Dad.

"It's Debbie, but I'm sick. I'm weak. I might have Leukemia."

"Well, who's gonna pay for that?"

"For *chrissakes*, Bob, we'll pay for her leukemia. He didn't mean that, Debbie—your Leukemia's on us."

"Jesus Christ! She's the most expensive child we have. I spend more money on your purses than you three brother's entire wardrobes. Why do you need so many purses?"

"Shut the hell up, Robert."

"You shut up, Shirley. I don't need your crap, not today. I don't." And with that, my Dad hung up the phone.

"For *chrissakes*, I don't need your crap any day, *goddamnit!*" she screamed into her extension and hung up, too.

"Hello? Hello? But what about my Leukemia?" I dropped the phone into its resting spot and got ready for my waitress job. I figured I could handle it for one more day—even though my blood pressure was beneath sea level, yes I could muster up the energy to wait on one more table, knowing that I was going to be a movie star, eventually. No, I wouldn't have to be a servant forever, not me, I was special. Even Paul Newman said so. He went to school with my parents.

Colonel Klink And
The Pipe In The Suitcase

The movie *Midnight Express* freaked me out for many, many years. Even now, decades later, on occasion, when I close my eyes at night, I can still see that hairy Turk raping that poor actor slammed up against the prison wall. If ever there was a good reminder to try and refrain from drug smuggling.

Several years before, my international drug smuggling career came to a screeching halt. In 1974, thirty unkempt classmates and I flew to Germany for a semester abroad. It was the end of my freshman year at Windham College in Vermont, when I signed up for the Beer Hall tour. (The college claimed it was a German literature program.) There were several meetings with the professors who kept warning us that American hippies were not exactly the guests of honor in Germany at this time, that our unruly hair and patched denims would cause us trouble. It was even suggested that we sew Canadian flags on our backpacks, because Canadian students were preferred. I was personally offended, as were others. Many of us carried on with our American flags sewn boldly onto the seats of our jeans, back-packs, or our head wear. Either way, we were ordered and then begged to leave all contraband behind to avoid incident, so we did.

But there were to be no incidents—we danced through customs like priests and children, when we arrived in Luxemburg, which really is more of a town than a country, (I think Poughkeepsie is bigger.) Weeks passed, and we crossed many international borders without one check, frisk, or raised European eyebrow. It was as if we didn't really matter, which irked us. Like paying for health insurance your whole life and never once getting sick—it's distressing. Eventually, you get sloppy, throw caution to the wind, you start smoking cigarettes, eating cheese whiz, and skipping around in traffic.

About a month into our German beer drinking and hash smoking curriculum, my friend, Debbie, and I went to Amsterdam to seek a better class of high. The hash in Amsterdam was legendary, it was smoked anywhere, which was an allure to all back-packing students to pass through there, and even stay. After our weekend binge, we hitched a ride back to Munich with two mangy-looking Vancouver hippies driving a ramshackle van. They were scruffy-looking enough to be Americans, so we called them Mutt and Jeff. By the time we boarded the retired love bus, another coed named Carol from California joined us, and the five of us left Amsterdam heading down the road, puffing spliffs, listening to The Grateful Dead and their song that you were supposed to listen to while going down the road. Within an hour, we were best friends, a merry band of soul travelers, free spirits trekking a mutual path—at least for this day. When we neared the German border station, we aired out the smoky van while Mutt or Jeff asked quickly, "Nobody's carrying, are they?" *Now you ask?* I thought.

"No!" I snapped, forgetting all about the dirty hash pipe that was carelessly splayed right on top of my pajamas shut inside my suitcase. Yes, I had gotten sloppy. I'd canceled my insurance.

Perhaps we looked like a heap of trouble, or maybe our number was just up, but our van hadn't even come to a full gestalt when the German border guards ordered us to get out of the van.

"Oussen!" they hollered.

Before we were even de-vanned, the Gestapo started unloading suitcases and backpacks, carting them off to a back room in the border station. My heart sank below my hip-hugger bell-bottoms. Someone barked at us in guttural English to take seats against a sterile grayish wall in the border station.

It all happened so fast. We had hardly even sat down when a guard ran out, waving my tin foiled pipe in a *Hogan's Heroes* kind of accent, "*Aha! Das ist eienen haschpfeife!*" Another man, apparently the boss, narrows his eyes the way Germans do in the movies.

"Who is da owner of dis hash pfeife?" he said in a strange mix of Germanglish.

I stood up and raised my hand, "Das ist meinen. Der haschpfeife ist meine." I was proud. I had no idea that I'd been paying attention in German class, but here I was! It's a shame my German professor wasn't there, he'd have been so proud.

"Aha!" said the man who suddenly looked like Colonel Klink, missing only the monocle.

Within five minutes, there was a team dismantling the van, removing armrests and unscrewing bolts that held the seats in. The Canadians shot me a dirty look when the man showed up with the German Shepherds who went to work with their noses. It all seemed so over-the-top until the German Fraulein arrived, then it turned into parody. The German woman pointed at me first with her crooked "come vit me" finger and led me into a small room, ordering me to take my clothes off.

"Offenzie mitt der clothes."

Knowing the dirty hash pipe was all they were going to find, I started mouthing off, "But we just met!"

She wasn't amused. Germans rarely are. I'd recently heard stories where the customs inspectors checked your cavities so I started to take this seriously. After she found nothing on my body, she made me bend over, ass up in the air, but searched no further than the glance. Neither of us wanted to take the relationship to the next level, *thank God*. She walked me back to the line and pointed to Carol. As I sat back down, Carol stood, turned around to the other Debbie next to me, with her back to the Frau, reached into her bra like a stripper, pulled out a nickel of pot and dropped it on Debbie's lap! Debbie's reflexes threw her hands over her crotch to conceal it. I was blown away that this cool cucumber sat in this line for hours, never letting on, even to us, that she was the one who was "carrying." Carol headed into the strip room behind the moustached woman. When the body inspector returned with Carol and came for everyone else, they all followed suit, passing the nickel bag off to one another while spinning around to drop it, and it was never to be found.

The Germans seemed frustrated that they couldn't find anything else on any of us, so I was taken into the interrogation room, and Colonel Klink barked, "Sitenzie!" So I sat-en-zie. Colonel Klink began to ask me ridiculous questions as he filled out a form, licking the pen between answers.

"Where did you get da haschpfeife?"

"From a guy at Oktoberfest."

"Aha! From a guy at Oktoberfest," he repeated writing deliberately, like he was solving a crossword puzzle.

"Vat vas his name?"

"John Doe," I replied without pause.

"Aha! John Doe! Is this the first time you have smoked die hashish?"

"Oh, no. My brother Reid turned me on back home."

"What is your brother's name?"

"Reid Kasper. R-E-I-D," I helped. "He lives in New Jersey."

"I do not know this New Jersey."

"That is your good luck."

He continued with his ridiculous questions, asking where New Jersey was and how old Reid was, licking his pen and recording everything I said. At the end of the buffoonish interview, Klink handed me the violation like it was an invitation to a better life and sent me back to my group—where nobody was speaking to me. I found the Germans to be warmer than my soul travelers at this point.

Right outside the waiting room, I saw that the van was sitting on the ground, tires lying off to the side, and a few guys were unscrewing the glove compartment, the seats, and the trunk. Then we all watched as they put the van back together and had a little summit in a room off to the side.

After about eight hours into the detention, the clock was heading toward midnight when Colonel Klink entered the main room and announced to Mutt or Jeff that we couldn't come into Germany because the front tires on the van didn't have enough tread on them!

We all headed back to Holland exhausted and spent the night at the apartment of a gracious Dutch couple we met at a bar. They enjoyed our story, helped us smoke the nickel of pot that had been in everybody's underwear, and we all mocked the meticulous Germans who missed the obvious. The dogs, the inspectors, the body searchers, Colonel Klink with the hash pipe in the office—they all missed it.

The next morning, we took up a collection to help the Canadians buy tires, with my chip-in being the biggest. I had to give them the next week's allowance just to keep from being skinned and run up a Dutch flagpole.

I've never been back to Germany since, and when I got home to the states, I warned my brother, Reid, "By the way, don't go to Germany!" He didn't seem to care enough to ask why, so I left it at that. And I never smuggled again—well, except for that one last time.

Roasting Dad: Take Your Father's Ashes Off Of My Mantelpiece

When my father died, there was no fanfare, no service, or circus. We had nothing planned, even though it was hardly a surprise. He'd been withering away for a long time right in front of us while we watched helplessly. It was an awkward time since nobody had a clue where to direct their sadness. Dad was a die-hard atheist till the bitter end. He didn't want any mention of GOD, or a memorial of any kind. His final wish was to be cremated and set on our mantelpiece in an urn, so he wouldn't miss out on any good stories.

So, we gathered our family grief and told stories about Dad, knowing he would've loved it. When friends heard that he'd passed, they came with food or drink, and they'd sit with us. We told more stories, and we laughed; some cried. It was like we were sitting Shiva without the Judaism, a wake without the Irish. We ended up roasting him like a panel of has-been comedians. We had the food, the booze, and the funny stories, which all went on a little too long like most roasts do. By nighttime, the party would evolve into a highly competitive game of Trivial Pursuit, Dad's favorite, which we played until someone cried or quit, just like he'd taught us.

My father was a big man, and his matching voice could blow you across a room if you weren't sober. His laughter boomed as well, and often. Nobody loved a good story like he did—our house was always filled with laughter and friends: my parents' friends, the four kids' friends, friends of friends. Our living room became a performance salon, many evenings. Someone was always taking the stage and entertaining. Reid had memorized the early Cosby records and could perform the "Noah" bit by age fifteen. We'd laugh hysterically. "Noah! WHAAAT?" We'd gather around the stereo to listen to Vaughn Meter impersonate President Kennedy, or Alan Sherman sing his way thru hilarious parodies. We'd all laugh as one, melting away any generational rifts. The laughter would catch on around the room like fire and sizzle all night long. If ever there was someone in the house that hadn't heard Dad's crazy college years' stories, he'd segue to them, "When I went to college at Middlebury ..." We'd all groan and roll our eyes. We'd heard all his wild tales a hundred times, and honestly, they were the kind of escapades where you really had to be there. Dad didn't care—on he'd go, never happier. "When I was at Middlebury College, our arch-rival was Dartmouth ..." We'd listen again to his most precious story about college, which he always lamented was "the best time of his life." Laughter was our family's mantra—topping each other was the goal.

My father's final wishes, his dream really, was to be cremated, set on our mantelpiece in an urn, putting him smack in the swing of things for all of eternity. There he'd rest under our fake Winslow Homer, above the fireplace, where we could include him in political discussions. Maybe Mom could continue the argument they'd been having for forty years, yelling at his ashes from time to time, finally getting in the last word. Then, when people came over, Dad insisted we should say, "Have you met my old man?" walk them over to the urn and nod toward it. He laughed like a maniac each time he played the scene out. Sometimes he would prance around the room, demonstrating vocal inflections we should use, as if only he and Red Skelton knew how to pull off a joke. Everyone thought he was kidding, so we'd chuckle along with his dark humor, even add a few riffs on the subject.

"Yeah, then we'll all eventually go in urns and sit up there in diminishing sizes like Russian nesting dolls," said Reid.

We assumed he was just telling one of his stories, but then Dad died, and we came face to face with the bitter fact that we had no better plan for his ashes. So, we sat frozen as to what to do after the four-day roast. We had him cremated, but nobody went to pick Dad up from the Funeral Home that day, or the next day, either.

After a little too much time had passed, we picked up his ashes from the crematorium. It had been seven years, and the funeral home had to threaten to dump the ashes before my brother drove the mile over there and saved our father's remains, practically pulling them out of a box marked "to go out." We were embarrassed as a family, and no one wanted to be the one to go, so we sent the youngest, Joe. We were still really clueless on what the hell to do with Dad. Mom wanted no ashes in her living room, (except the ones jumping off the ends of her cigarettes), but we had no plan B. Joe brought them straight to the house, and much to her horror and objections, he staged the urn on the mantelpiece as Dad had wanted. We kind of laughed, waiting for some company to come on over so we could try Dad's line out: "My dad loves a good story.

Do you know any?" Then we'd lead them over to the urn and invite them to start with our nod.

After ten minutes of the four kids going back and forth, my mother threw a fit. "Get your father off of there! Take him down. Put him somewhere else. It's macabre. I will not stand for this. Do you hear me, Robert?" She walked over to the urn and started yelling at it, "I simply do not want you on my mantelpiece. You can hang out in the closet with your shoes." My mother was half-kidding but meant it, at the same time.

"But Mom, it was Dad's final wishes!" Robbie preached.

Joe added, "Just think, you can finally win some fights with him."

Mom dragged on her cigarette, rolled her big eyes and walked away, meaning that was that. The Pope has spoken.

After Dad sat in a musty closet amidst his remaining size thirteen shoes, for some time, the family decided to take him to Vermont and spread his ashes there. We also decided to finally donate his shoes to someone tall, who could fill them.

Vermont has always been a special place for our entire extended family. My parents, aunts, grandparents all went to Middlebury College, and as a young family, we took many trips there for their reunions. Dad's favorite stories were all about "college this and college that." Each trip, he took us to a waterfall that he loved called "Texas Falls," gushing waterfalls that rage over rocks into several pools along their trek back to the ocean. The falls lay in a hidden meadow where he and his wild fraternity brothers, the DKEs, swam and partied as college students. We drove the six hours to Vermont to take my father back to a place that brought him joy and undoubtedly, plenty of laughter—Texas Falls.

It was a beautiful summer day in the Vermont woods when

we arrived at Dad's final resting place. The water was particularly disturbed that day, and while we were letting go of Dad's remains to rejoin the falls of his youth, we started remembering his stories, and we told a few one last time, verbatim, but in a slightly mocking tone. Mom smoked her cigarette and watched her children scatter her husband into the swell, then promptly wash away with a gush. We all laughed at his stories just like our father had taught us to do, for so many years.

On our way home the next day, somewhere in Connecticut, Mom offered up her final wishes. "While we're on the subject, I wouldn't want you to go through all this trouble for me," said Mom. "You don't have to worry or feel guilty."

"Great," I said, stirring some laughter.

"Just leave me anywhere. And I mean it!" Mom insisted.

"Well, we can't really just leave you anywhere, Mom. I mean, what? Do you wanna go to the mall or somethin'?" Joe asked, laughing at his own joke (something he'd learned to do very young).

"In front of what store? Macy's?" Reid asked.

"Just throw me in the fountain by the movies."

"Would you like to see the movie first or just go for the swim?" asked Reid. Then we laughed, and riffed and one-upped each other all the way home, to commemorate that we were a family—*this family.*

Don't Share Your Feeling With Anybody: Nobody Cares

Pretty quickly, after my father passed on to the poker game in the sky, I became my mother's traveling companion, which is slang for chauffeur. Mom enjoyed sitting upright in the shotgun seat, blowing smoke out of the crack at the top of the window, while the disappointing world went by. Dad's ashes were still at the crematorium when Mom was already pitching a trip. "Let's just go. Let's just fly like eagles into the future. Let's take our Chevy to the levy till the gas tank goes dry!"

"Mom stop listening to my FM radio. You don't know what you're talking about."

"It ain't the meat—it's the motion, babe," she sort of sang. My mother had taken to calling me "babe," which was kind of hip, yet annoying, simultaneously.

"Do you even know what 'it ain't the meat, it's the motion' means?" I scolded.

A trip with Mom and her constant companion of disappointment was not inviting. (I would have rather set my hair on fire.) She'd raised me singing the anthem: "A son is a son, till he takes him a wife; a daughter is yours for the rest of your life." Sung as a warning, not a compliment or even an homage to *me*. "Come on—let's go trucking' like The Dead. Whoaaa—Yeaaaaa!" Like it or not, if my poor mom was to get away—it had to be with me. The only other person who could possibly travel with her had just died.

It was the mid-eighties when my mother and I did our first road trip from Los Angeles to San Francisco but not in a straight line—more like a parallelogram. To my knowledge, Mom hadn't yet cried over her dead husband, so I was hoping to have some mother-daughter time, feel our feelings and then set the pain free. This was a tall order—Shirley Kasper was a tough old broad who just didn't like to let things show, the kind of woman who wore a girdle under her muumuu.

A few days into our vacation, chugging over the Sierra Madre mountains of Yosemite, I brought up my dad for the second time.

I mentioned that I was feeling a bit "sad." I'd planned it, rehearsed it in my mind, and presented it badly, like an actress in a community theatre play. No one in our family was very good at communicating. We chatted, we told stories, we laughed, but transmit a feeling? Not quite. Our dog, Sam, was the only one who could express his needs clearly. If you had a feeling in our house growing up, you were usually sent to your room until it passed. If you dared complain, Dad would butt in, "Go clean the basement—then you'll have something to complain about."

My mother responded the way she always did when I spoke of emotions—she lit another butt and blew her smoke toward me, which always dropped an emotional curtain between us. I coughed dramatically, waving my hands like there was a kitchen fire in the car.

"Sorry," she said, but she never really was. She rarely paid attention to where her exhaled toxins sprayed, and smoked like it was still the fifties when you could light up in hospitals, libraries, even at your gynecology appointment. Your gynecologist might examine you with a cigarette sticking out of his mouth, too, making it a *come-at-your-own-risk* kind of appointment. Mom just couldn't accept the fact that the country was becoming a no-smoking zone, holding onto her nasty habit the way a tick clings to its dog.

The twisty roads that wound around some of the tallest mountains in America were slippery, and my little Datsun could barely make the chug around the turns. We'd been required by the national park's regulators to have tire chains in the trunk, in the event that it snowed up on these passes, which it usually did this time of year. We were in the part of the country where families had eaten each other to survive one winter. "I couldn't imagine eating another human being, especially without ketchup," I mentioned to Mom to break the silence.

Mom pointed her unlit cigarette toward the rugged peaks and said, "Your ancestors crossed these mountains in covered wagons, some even on foot." Mom was referring to her people who were part of the great Mormon migration that traveled west, crossing the great wide plains and then the Rockies in pull carts, covered wagons, even on horseback to find their Garden of Eden—Utah.

"Our ancestors traveled over the Rockies, Mom, not this far west."

"Same difference," she corrected. "They were trailblazers—they climbed on foot; they had frostbite and lost toes," she pressed on. "These are tough people, your ancestors. The women would have a baby and not even stop walking. The babies weren't born, they just kind of fell out. You didn't see *them* eating each other. My great grandmother was born on a stump in a blizzard."

"No, she wasn't," I said with a laugh. "Wasn't your great-grandmother from Scotland?"

"Who knows? I wasn't even born yet. Nobody complained, nobody cried," she continued.

"You don't know that at all. For all you know, the women whined all the way across Kansas."

"They were pioneers, Deborah! Of course they didn't complain. Don't you read books? Haven't you ever seen *Wagon Train*? They experienced real hardship. Your generation does nothing but cry about everything. You kids think your emotions are interesting to others."

Just then, an elk dashed right in front of my car so abruptly that I had to jam on the brakes, and we were both thrown inside the car. Mom was thrust forward, holding onto her breasts while bumping up against the dashboard. But still, not a peep out of her. She patted the top of her hairdo to make sure it was still there and re-staged her girdle. "They would skin that elk and eat him raw," Mom said without missing the beat to drag on her cigarette. She shook her head back and forth as if overwhelmed with the lecture du jour, and now we should just digest the information in the quiet. My mother spoke the truth—her people were hardy, and she inherited the mother lode of the clan's cold blood as well. When my father died, she didn't shed a tear. I was not letting this trip go by without a conversation about losing him. The woman needed to let something out! If necessary, I was prepared to just squeeze her until she oozed out some sort of a liquid—eyes, nose, any hole would do.

After Dad had passed, we had kind of an ad hoc wake at the

house. My parents were atheists, so no burial or service was offered. Instead, we had an awkward several day-long gathering where people stopped by with food, drink, sometimes both, and we'd hang out, drink too much, and tell stories.

On about the second day of our impromptu wake, I sat down in our den, away from the crowd, to take a moment to enjoy a private tear, which wasn't something I did often, either. In the middle of my crying, my mother walked through the den, tracking down another bottle of bourbon. She stopped in her tracks, "What's wrong?"

"What's wrong!?" I said, incredulous. "My dad died. That's what's wrong!"

"Oh," she said, surprised, "are you still on that? That was days ago."

I was shocked. I knew the woman was marbleized, but this was over the top. When she left the room, I cried harder.

"Mom, don't you think it's dangerous to keep things inside?" I asked as we neared the snow-carpeted Yosemite Valley.

"What things?" she asked.

"You haven't cried over Dad, yet," I shot back. "What's wrong with you?"

"I am crying on the inside. I don't want to bother you with my problems," said Mom.

Who are you? Lady Macbeth? There is no inside crying. That's ridiculous! It doesn't cry inside—it turns to disease! You're going to have a heart attack if you don't let it all out. It's not human. Let a tear or two out. I promise you, you won't rust!

That's what I thought, on the inside—but said nothing. Instead, I took a deep breath and then gushed over the majesty of the Sierra in front of us, grateful that we were in a car and not a covered wagon.

After that trip, I was always trying to scare up a traveling companion for Mom. But no one else could stand her snoring, her smoking, her coughing, and her utter disappointment with everything and everywhere. If she ever wrote a travel book, it would be called: *I've been around the world, but it all looks like Jersey to me.* She'd gone to Europe, only to return, saying it was old. She thought the Alps were nice. "Nice? I never heard anyone call the Alps nice. Stupendous, magnificent, indescribable, beautiful ... breathtaking, but never nice, Mom."

"They were *very* nice," she conceded.

"What about Aunt Janet? You love her." (Everyone loved Janet.) "Janet would be perfect. You two have so much in common. Call her up and see if she wants to take a trip somewhere with you." When Mom made me fork over some examples as to what they really had in common, all I could come up with was that Aunt Janet liked king crab legs, too.

"She doesn't like them as much as I do!" Mom shot back. "And she doesn't like me to smoke in the hotel room," she said as she sucked in another of her butts.

"Ma, nobody likes you to smoke in the hotel rooms! They already smell like other people's bad habits!!"

Mom had stopped flying and stopped going to movies since smoking had become verboten in so many places. The non-smokers were starting to turn on the smokers, making me joke, "That the next Civil War was brewing. Smokers v. Non." Mom's social life was *smoking*, so her world was getting smaller. It was starting to look like she'd have to stay home to enjoy herself. My mother smoked three packs of unfiltered Kool cigarettes a day and coughed up four. She'd smoke, then she'd cough. Sometimes she'd cough as she was smoking. She could no longer make it through a whole night of sleeping without getting up to cough. And while she was up, she'd always have a cigarette. And she snored. Sleeping with Mom was an oxymoron. The covers would practically get blown off me with each snore she let rip. It was like trying to sleep with Popeye. Her nicotine addiction was so furious by age sixty that she had taken to huffing her cigarettes like you'd smoke a joint. Later on, in an attempt to clean up, she started smoking the filtered Kools. And she never let us forget her huge concession. "Get me a carton of filtered Kools. Don't forget the filters. I smoke filters now, *goddamnit.* I'm on a health kick. Don't say I'm not doing my part in keeping it clean over here."

While packing for our second trip, which I had dubbed "The Great American Lobster Tour" since we were heading up along the coast of Maine, my mother's neighbor knocked on the door. We'd been holding her mail for the few weeks while she toured Europe on a widow's bus and truck tour. Her hair was over teased and dyed a strange orange color which I felt certain looked better in her mirror than it did in our living room. Otherwise, why would you purposely wear Halloween on your head? Her face lift had expired sometime that year, and she knew everything. I asked her how her trip was, although I already knew. "Eh! The brochures are so much nicer than the countries. They have a helluva publicist over there. I'll tell you that!" and that summed up her trip to Greece. She and my mother were snobs together—they enjoyed turning up their noses whenever occasion demanded.

Our plan was to drive up through New England, into Maine, and on up into Montreal and Quebec City. Our first stop was Newport, Rhode Island, where we toured the rich people's mansions, which always brought out a mixture of awe, yet ripe jealousy for us. We both wanted a better life than we were having. We went back to our four-star hotel, drank away our sorrows, and ate a few lobsters for dinner. After some drinks, I asked my mother if my father had been a good husband.

"Yes," she said with no explanation.

"So, he never beat you or anything?"

"Of course not!" Then she ordered some after-dinner drinks, and the flow of the discourse headed in another direction. She was one tough nut to open, like a pistachio with no crack, you just weren't getting in there without tools.

The next morning, we headed up to Maine and arrived by lunch, where we had lobster, of course. When the waitress asked her what she would like, she said, "Well, lobster, of course." The waitress shook her head as she left, slightly put off by Mom's haughty attitude.

"You sound like a snob, Mom"

"Well, I can't help it. We're in Maine; what were we supposed to order? Rocky mountain trout? When in France...!"

We went out to dinner that evening, and we picked our lobsters from the tank and asked the waiter to slaughter them for us. "We'll take the two on the bottom of the stack—they lack ambition," said Mom. "Always pick the lazy ones. The ambitious ones have muscles, they're tough," she lectured.

On our fourth day of "The Great American Lobster Tour," I was getting sick of eating crustaceans, exclusively. I'd had six lobsters in three days, and honestly, they were starting to taste like trout. Mom showed no signs of slowing down. For brunch the next morning, she ordered an omelet stuffed with lobster, I ordered pancakes. As we planned our drive into Canada the next day, Mom pitched the idea that we just stay in Maine. "Who needs to see Quebec?" she said.

"You've had enough lobster, Mom. We're not cutting out Canada so you can keep eating them!"

Mom continued ordering lobster for our last few stateside meals. The last night, after dinner, "Mom, ever wonder who cracked open the first lobster? How did they know that something so wonderful would be inside?"

"Dumb question. Obviously, man copied the animals. Shall we have an after-dinner drink?"

"Dumb question. If man copied animals, how come we have toilets? Which animal gave us that idea?

"Smart ass."

We stayed later than all the other customers, having one more drink, and then one more. Mom fondled the check and was about to drop her credit card on top of it, when she opened herself up, just a crack. "Lobster makes me feel like someone else. Someone with a different life ... your father and I ate lobsters on our honeymoon, every day, and every night. Dad could eat two in one night...the taste of it takes me back to when ... I had everything to wish for. Now I can only think of wishing for lobster. He promised me we'd be wealthy enough to eat lobster every night. I just didn't imagine that I'd have to lose him to make that dream come true. Oh Robert ..." she sighed.

I patted Mom's arm lightly, to let her know that I understood, and I did. Then, something happened that I'd only seen once or twice before, and certainly not in this decade: my mother cried. It was just a tear or two at first, but then more started falling out of her eyes like a light rain, and then a short but heavy downpour fell—because it *had to*. She cried the tears of a thousand disappointments. And it embarrassed her, like maybe she was disappointing those stalwart ancestors who climbed the Rocky Mountains so long ago? The tough people who thought feelings were for sissies.

I awkwardly handed her my dirty linen napkin to dab her eyes, then I dabbed my own as well. "Don't cry, mom, you'll rust." That's all I could think to say. Now, so many years later, I wish I had said, "Good job, Shirley, it's all right to cry on the outside."

After a long and loaded silence in that restaurant that night mom finally said, non-chalant, "What time do you want to leave for Canada, tomorrow? I hear they have excellent French Onion soup in Quebec."

I Don't Like To Brag, But My Daughter's Dating A Bank Robber

I suppose if a Puerto Rican transvestite hooker ever gets stabbed and bleeds to death in front of your apartment door, you really shouldn't talk about it, even if it is Easter. But I just couldn't help it.

"You are one lucky gal," my mother said as if I'd just been nominated for a Peabody Award. "Everything happens to you, Debbie. Wait till I tell the girls."

"Well, I hope I don't get murdered too!" I screamed back into my end of the phone—never a shred of motherly concern from this lady.

"What if I'm next? People die every single minute in New York, you know—this isn't Altoona, here!"

"I can't hear you—my garbage disposal is on!" she shouted over the sound of grinding eggshells. "Call me later—after *Jeopardy*."

My mother always made out like she had no control over appliances that were on, like maybe she had no hands or even the skill to turn things off. So, we'd just have to wait for them to run their course. Sometimes an electric carving knife would interrupt a rare intimate moment between us, and my mother would act as if "What are ya gonna do?" rolling her eyes—a helpless victim trapped inside the harsh prison of modern technology. "I can't hear you, I'm using my battery-run eyebrow plucker," or "I'd like to chat, but the new electric weed whacker is whacking the lawn ... and oh Jesus! now it's headed next door—I have to go!"

Sometimes I felt like Mom was merely taking my calls so she'd have something to say to "the girls" at bridge club. By the next morning, I knew she'd already be on her second polish of the transvestite stabbing story, in time for Wednesday's bridge club, which was really just a suburban "Open Mic Night" with cards. Ellen, MaryAnn, and Nancy would all sit there in their pearls and polyester, sipping their dry Manhattans, swapping silly stories about their kids—none of whom would ever even dare dream to have a transvestite hooker bleed to death on their Manhattan doorstep on Easter or *any other holiday,* for that matter. Mom would wait for the perfect moment, sometime between the second and third highball. She'd throw the cards into her electric card shuffler, while Nancy would speak above the dull hum of a buzz, blab about her daughters who were both married and breeding. My mother would nod politely, unable to hear her, and wait quietly until someone would ask, "So what's new with Debbie? Is she still dating that bank robber?"

"No, but a Puerto Rican transvestite hooker bled to death, knocking on her door. Two spades."

I'd actually only had one date with the bank robber almost two years before, but they just could not let it go! I'd even unwittingly dated a child molester since, but my mother couldn't twist that one into a light-enough story for the girls.

"Where in heaven's name did she meet a bank robber?" they had asked.

"At the bank!" my mother would've quipped. They'd all laugh. Then they'd all work it: "She was making a deposit; he was making a withdrawal. Well, at her age, she can't be too picky—at least she knows where he is nights." And on and on. Oh, they were funny, those four, during their afternoon rodeos, posing as bridge games. I would always be the girl that dated a bank robber. Until now. A dead transvestite trumps a bank robber.

The cops had labeled the transvestite's death as an occupational hazard, lecturing me on the phone from his precinct, saying, "He died 'cause of his lifestyle.'"

"Her," I said

"What?" the cop asked.

"Her lifestyle," I said. "Her lifestyle. He's a her."

"But she had a penis. That was as much a man as me, except for the bra—double-wide," he snickered.

"But he wanted to be a woman. She called herself Chi-Chi and referred to herself as "she." I think since she took the time to stuff herself into a Betsy Johnson jumper, the least we can do is call her a 'she.'"

"We ain't going to be calling her at all, Mrs. Kasper since he's stabbed dead."

"Ms. Kasper," I corrected. "It's what she wanted," I persisted.

"I bet what he really wanted was to not be dead," he replied.

I told Officer McBigot on the other side of the cordless that I was scared for my life. A personal promise of mine was that if anybody in my immediate nucleus was ever a victim of a violent crime, I was leaving. It seemed a good time to move out of NYC. I told the cop

I was thinking about moving out to LA right about then.

"LA? Why? So you can get drive-by shot by a gang member? Better to stay here and get mugged. And FYI, don't worry, the chances of another *moider* in the same building are a bit unlikely," he said with a hint of a chuckle. "You're actually really lucky. You're in a good spot. The chances of two people living in the same building, statistically, both getting *moidered*, are about a million to one. So, unless you're a prostitute too? Hey, why were you out so late?" he asked suspiciously. "Where were you last night?"

"I'm a comedian. I work nights."

"Yeah, don't we all? Life's a bitch, and then you die," he said, stealing from a tee-shirt. "The chances of getting raped in the subway are high at this point. So, take the buses and walk. But don't move to that sunny septic tank with palm trees. My sister's kid moved out there, joined a cult, and changed her name to Raisin."

I had actually missed the whole stabbing ordeal. I was away at my gig in safe Princeton, New Jersey, forty-five miles from Manhattan. I almost drove home at 1:00 AM after my set—but stayed at the hotel at the last minute to revel in the oversized bed and the extra channels the room's TV had to offer. At approximately 2:00 AM, Chi-Chi had reportedly belly-crawled down the two flights of steep steps of our pre-war walk up—knife still in her and bled out on the chipped white tile right in front of my door. She was clearly trying to knock for help. When I got home on Sunday morning, there was blood on my door and some red residue on the tile in front of the door, along with a yellow body taping. Happy Easter.

Robert, the homeless man who lived on the stairs in our lobby, saw nothing. We called him "our bum," but he drank Perrier and slept by scented candlelight, every night sprawled across our lobby steps. He'd open the door for me when I'd stumbled home sloshed, sometimes lecturing me about how I shouldn't drink so much or stay out so late in the mean city—that I should love myself more. Made me wonder *who the bum really was.* He never liked any of my dates and had no problem asking them what their intentions were when they stumbled home with me. Most of them intended to wake up with a hangover and get on out of there.

Robert weighed about 300 pounds, with a stomach the size of a bean bag chair, leaving us all wondering how he could have afforded to feed that lumpy beast. He had a wrapped bum leg, swollen to the size of a side of beef. It looked like someone wrapped the leg up with a crutch still in it. Robert claimed he had a lawsuit brewing, and pretty soon we'd be seeing the last of him, but he'd still swing by and pick us up in his limo if we want; then we could, "go to a circus or something," he'd tempt. He'd been living in our lobby for over a year and generally knew what time everyone came home, who ran out for what when, but he saw and heard nothing about Chi-Chi. He was a sound sleeper, and quite often I'd have to shake him hard to wake him up when I got home, since his bloated body made it impossible to pass through the tiny lobby steps over his sprawl. We all assumed the *moiderer* stepped right over Robert, which upset him.

"That just make me wanna throw up," said Robert. "It's time for me to find a safer place to sleep. This is a dump."

I sensed the cop was winding down with me on the phone, so I turned into Nancy Drew. "Do we have any leads?"

"We think he died because his John didn't care for his schlapinki. Can't really blame the guy. Most Johns don't like dicks on their whores, if you'll excuse my language. That makes one too many as far as I can tell," he said in an accent suddenly thicker. "I wouldn't *want a hooka wid a dick, would you? Would jew?"*

"No!" I said quickly. It was a no-win question he'd thrown my way—a bit unfair, really.

"Did you know 'he' wasn't a 'she?'" he asked.

"Yes, sir, I did." I always called cops "sir" lest they ever decided to turn an investigation toward me or haul me in. I hadn't done anything to be hauled in for, but how could we know for sure? I'd seen all the corrupt cop movies in the '70s. I saw *Serpico*—twice—and never looked at NYC's finest the same again.

"How'd you know?" he asked, suspiciously.

"Well, sir, she had a beard. And she was really, really big. And, uhm, there was hair on her knuckles. And she had a deep voice," I said, trailing off, wondering how quickly I could pack up and leave.

"Sounds like you two spent a lot of time together." Suddenly I felt like I was on the phone with the block yenta, not the desk detective from the 128th precinct.

"She wasn't very pretty or anything," I continued. "I mean she wasn't even a good looking transvestite. She looked a bit like a redwood in a dress."

"A redwood in a dress!" McBigot said with a laugh. He covered the phone and started throwing my simile around the room at the precinct. I asked if they thought they'd find the guy that did this heinous thing.

"Nah," he said as if I'd asked if he wanted a schmear on his bagel. "We don't really care about a Hispanic transvestite prostitute. Good riddance, we say, good riddance. These people eventually *extoiminate* each other and then themselves if we let them go. If only we could get the rats and the roaches to *toin* on each other too, then we'd have a nice place here for decent folks to live."

"Then why did you call me? Why are you gathering evidence?" I asked, already knowing the answer. He *was* a yenta, and even he had never—in his life—seen a dead transvestite hooker. This was bigger than both of us.

"File," he said as if I should have known. Ah, yes, the "file," the proverbial file. I remembered all about files from watching *Hunter* reruns.

I joined the neighbors gathering in the lobby stairwell, relaying to them that the cops didn't give a rat's ass about our moidered transvestite.

"They left him lying there all night. You're so lucky you weren't home," said Betty, a dancer who lived upstairs. I hadn't spoken to her since I organized the rent strike the fall before. She was a ballerina-in-training at Lincoln Center with a ballerina body—long and thin like pulled rope, her hair brushed back in a tight ballerina knot, and sunken, hungry cheeks. I liked to offer her treats, just to watch her hunger weep. I doubt she'd had a cookie since Jimmy Carter was president, and she was so self-absorbed, I doubt she even knew that a Jimmy Carter *was* president. We had several ballerinas in the building, but I never saw any of them except on their way to their rehearsals, which was all the time. They'd stride bowlegged down Columbus Avenue, like graceful praying mantises, passing all who got in the way of their dreams. They might have been a hazard on the street, but they made great neighbors.

"Maybe I could've saved her life," I said sadly. "She came to me, I'm the only one in the building who was nice to her."

"I was nice to her," argued Robert. "I liked him-her-him, that person. I liked that person a lot. Never turned a mean look on me, always asked how I was. Most people don't ask me that."

"Well, we know how you are, Robert, to be fair," I said. "You're living on our steps, we can *see* how you are. And just for the record, I ask you 'how you are' all the time." Then I sighed, "Geeze. I coulda saved his life."

"Her life," corrected Betty Ballerina.

"How do you think I feel?" asked Robert. "I didn't even know she was a prostitute. I thought she was reading palms. I mean she was a little BIG to be a prostitute."

A bit like the pot calling the kettle black, I thought.

By late Easter night, I'd worked the story in my head into a morality tale where she had slid down the stairs and bled to death in front of my door, trying to get me to help her, lifting the last of her strength to knock on my cold door, perhaps crying out, "Hey—! Call that number! Nine-something. I know I haven't had time to have you over, but could you help me anyway?"

"If I had been home (which I almost was), I would've gotten her help. She would've lived!" I said, with eyes moist. "I liked her," I lied. The truth was, I didn't like Chi-Chi at all. It just wasn't the right time to mention that. Her white fru-fru dog yelped constantly, and her doorbell rang like a Mr. Softee truck in July. She was the pied piper of perverted gimps, creepy night-crawlers, and horny old geezers. I preferred the clean little ballerinas who made up most of the building. You never even heard a can opener or a potato chip crunch from their apartments, and when they did date, the men would always be collegiate and pressed. And there was the one time when the transvestite's sink overflowed and leaked through my ceiling lighting fixture.

When I stormed upstairs to tell her, she stood there all a-flutter, in a fluffy robe, holding it shut in the front, like I wanted to peek.

"Good heavens! Oh my I'm sorry," she brayed, her voice trying to cling on to a woman's register, while her Adam's apple betrayed her. When we went into the bathroom to see that the tub was indeed overflowing and spilling gallons of water onto the floor, she froze. She motioned with her eyes that I was the one who would have to take control and turn the water off! Like *I* was the man in this bathroom scenario! So I did, while she vamped there in feathers and boas, a bloated Blanche DuBois depending on the kindness of this stranger.

But she wasn't sorry enough, and I knew she was turning tricks in the building, so I ratted her out. I called the landlord and told him that one day my buzzer buzzed, and I let a short, hairy old man into the building who banged on my door by mistake, screaming, "Is the redhead here?"

"Oh, is that what color that's supposed to be?" I said, cracking the door just enough to see his face.

"Yes—the redhead is indeed here. She's upstairs, in 3N. I'm the dishwater blonde in 2N, so keep climbing, Hairy." He had eyed me up and down with little interest and passed on upstairs to the redhead. I knew he'd be sorry once he got there. Even if he liked transvestites, he wouldn't like this one—she was a linebacker. So, I bolted my door quickly in case he decided that I wasn't so bad after all. That's when I knew that Chi-Chi was turning tricks, right upstairs. When I told the landlord, he told me I had to get some hard evidence.

"The constant stream of balding old men going up and down the steps isn't evidence enough?" I screamed into the phone.

"She could be selling Tupperware," he suggested feebly, "You never know—this is America." He was Polish and was not above slipping into his first language when the questions got uncomfortable. I gave this information about the encounter with the bald man to the cop, wondering if that perhaps could have been the man who *moidered* her. McBigot didn't seem to care much, didn't even offer to send an artist over so I could have him sketched. No, I didn't like her, but still, maybe I could've saved her.

"Would you have opened the door at three in the morning for a bleeding transvestite?" asked Tina, a teacher who lived in the building and had just joined our stairwell meeting.

"I hope I would have." I sighed. "Yes. Definitely, of course."

"It was awful," offered another hungry-eyed ballerina. "The cops had him roped off like a sideshow. They left him lying there all night, still bloody, mascara dripping down his cheeks, stab wound in plain view, skirt hiked up around his chest, and his boner still erect, like a tent pole!"

"We were held hostage by a dead woman's boner," said Betty. They wouldn't let us pass on up to our apartments. I came home—I was on a first date—the place was a crawling zoo!

"You'll never hear from *him* again," I pointed out, offering her a thin mint to soften the blow. The stairwell meeting broke up, and we all gave one another hugs, knowing we might not all be together again for months, perhaps until the next rent strike or maybe the next tragic event.

I cherished that evening, although sad by definition, I loved the way we, as neighbors, all came together to commiserate. There's something sublime about the way a tragedy can bond the most unlikely people to one another, even if only for a slice of time. Nobody but our stairwell klatch will ever know what it felt like to be a part of that grievous Easter, it was ours, alone—it belonged to us. And from that point forward, whenever we would bump into each other, it would be with a knowing nod, a nod that bumped up our acquaintance to the next level.

As I lay in my bed that night, packing my apartment in my head, I worried for a moment about Chi-Chi's mother. How in the world would she ever know that her poor "daughter" was dead? I also wondered if they'd even spoken, recently. I wondered if Mrs. Chi-Chi was ever able to brag to her bridge club about her daughter. or if she approved of her lifestyle.

By Wednesday's bridge club my own mother would've spun the story with her own flair: "If Debbie had decided to drive home after her gig, she would've come face to face with the murderer. She could've been murdered, too. Maybe he would have stabbed out her eyes so she couldn't identify him! One spade."

"She's sure lucky, that Debbie. Two hearts," said Nancy.

"I've got nothing. I'll pass," added MaryAnn.

"Maybe a nice single man will move into that apartment above her," said Ellen. "Or is Debbie still dating that bank robber?"

Don't Let The Dogs Eat You

My dear friend Arlene recently asked me to be the maid of honor in her late-in-life wedding. No sooner had I accepted than I started bragging to everyone that I was going to be an "old maid of honor," and those of us in our sixties thought it was funny. But then that bad taste of the bygone label, "old maid," hit us, which wasn't very funny. It's one of those pejorative phrases for women you don't hear much anymore, like "spinster," or "butter churner." Words which conjure up images of wrinkled old biddies wearing corrective shoes and bifocals, living alone with a single goldfish swimming in a glass bowl. Those of us who survived the sixties and its bastard son, the seventies, remember sadly that it's what they'd think about you if you were unmarried beyond the age society deemed "appropriate," or past the childbearing age. And as if the label weren't bad enough, they made a *card game* out of it, "Old Maid." If you picked the hideous and wrinkled old woman out of somebody's hand of cards, you lost, right then and there—ostracized from the game, just like old maids were spurned by society.

During the eighties, I was technically an "old maid" because I never did have children. My eggs (if I even ever had any) were probably over easy in the seventies, and completely fried by the nineties. Now, I guess I'm an older, old maid, with hard boiled eggs, maybe even deviled, by now. We had more than our fair share of unmarried people in our family: two old maids and one bachelor, all of whom were my personal role models. One of my old maid aunts even had a hunch back and wore corrective shoes. A movie costume designer couldn't have made the point any better.

Because of these trailblazers, it occurred to me early on that you didn't have to get married and have children to validate and carry on with your life. You can work, live alone, grow a hump, grow cats, and nobody's head would explode if you did. You'd still get invited to family weddings. People might whisper, but you'll have a seat and a plate of Chicken Kiev, that you could weep right into.

I have always been ruffled by the fact that there's no derogatory counterpart label for men who never got married. Old butler? Crusty unmarried fart? Angry old man? No, men who don't ever get married are merely called bachelors, sometimes even swinging bachelors—it was not only acceptable but envied, *even exotic.*

My mother's younger brother, Uncle Ron, was a confirmed bachelor. He lived in Phoenix and visited the Kasper family of six in New Jersey every couple of years for a few weeks. My Dad accused him of coming to visit us whenever he started thinking about getting married and having kids. Two days into his summer vacation with the chaotic Kasper household quashed that inkling. We'd all have a good laugh at our own expense, but Ron never did marry. Ron ended up adopting over ten dogs and becoming a hermit. My mother was always stressed about his sad, lonely life, deathly afraid he would die, nobody would ever know, and his ten dogs would eat him.

"He's down to eight," I interjected the first time she played this horror movie for me. (Clearly it would be better to get eaten by eight dogs?) Throughout a few decades, Mom brought that nagging fear up to me over and over again. Give her a few bourbons, and she'd tell you twice in one night.

It got to the point that if my mother ever started a sentence with ... "I'm a little concerned ..."

I'd cut in and say in my monotonous, repeating voice, shaking my head back and forth for effect, "Uncle Ron's dogs are going to starve to death and eat him."

"No," she'd say, "I'm concerned that my new green carpet is going to clash with your father's chair. What's wrong with you, Debbie?"

Another time ... "I'm worried about ..."

"Uncle Ron's dogs eating him before he even dies, that they just start taking bites ...?"

"No! That's a terrible thing to say. Thank you for putting that image in my head. You have a very sick imagination. I don't even remember what I was going to say."

She had a routine where she'd call her brother every single Sunday without fail, always relieved to hear his Arizona "HEL-lo." They emphasized on the HELL in this part of the country, perhaps inspired by their weather. Sometimes my mother would make me get on the other extension in the den to say "hell-o" to him, too.

I'd say, "Hi, Uncle Ron! How are you?" feigning enthusiasm.

He'd say, "Hiya, Debbie. I'm good, good." And how are you doing there, Debbie?"

"Good. Thanks for asking." That was about all we could think to say to one another. "Well, I have to go pick Joe up at the library. Bye!" And I'd hang up the phone before anybody could say, "Joe? Library? Hey, hold on a minute there, Missy!" There was no way in hell I was ever picking any of my brothers up at any library—police station, reform school, school detention—yes. Library—no.

"How are the dogs?" my mother would always start the phone call with.

"Fine, fine."

"Good. What do you feed them?" she'd ask, not so much out of concern or fear, but truly, there just wasn't much to say to a retired man who used his mutts as witnesses to his will. "And, how are you?" she'd ask, already knowing that he'd say, 'fine.'"

"Fine, fine," he'd say, like a beginner's English class. "How, uh, are your gardens doing this year?"

"Very nice. My roses are blooming. And how are your cacti?"

"Oh, very good. You know, they don't go anywhere. They'll be here long after I am," her brother said, starting to wind the conversation down a bit. "Well ..."

My mother's favorite Aunt Beth was what one would call an old maid, in fact, that's exactly what my dad called her behind her back, but to her face she was "Hello, Beth." Beth was old even when she was young. She looked sixty at forty, and by the time she hit sixty-five, her skin was well on its way to the floor. She'd retired and enjoyed her meager pension yet still dressed like she was coming to take dictation, not relax at her niece's house. Beth was so thin when she put on her pearls, her weight would change. Her hair was dishwater blond and curled tight on her head like she'd just removed the aluminum clips, leaving the pin curls sitting there like tiny coiled cobras. My mom's aunt wore button-down polyester shirts with sewn-in scarves and wouldn't leave her room until she was completely dressed, and with lipstick on.

My great aunt would stay long enough that she had her own toothbrush hole in the bathroom—generally about a month—and everyone had to shift beds around, like an orphanage does when somebody gets adopted, so Beth could have her private room.

Each time she came, by about week three, my mother's silver hairs started splitting away from the rest of her hairdo, reaching out to try and strangle Beth. When it was time for her to go, Mom would lie, "It seems like you just got here."

Aunt Beth was a Mormon ... of sorts. My mother's whole extended family on her side were Mormons, but her parents ex-communicated from the church because they'd rather enjoy a cocktail. (I'm sure there were some other issues, which nobody chose to clue me in on). Beth would have her fingers wrapped around a rocks glass of scotch before she unpacked, "Scotch on the rocks," she'd say as if there were a chance we didn't remember. Who could forget the time she drank until she fell sideways out of her chair, taking the chair down with her? Her teeny body hit the ground and actually bounced. The fall didn't even wake her, but that was the last time we sat Beth in an armless chair. Who could forget all the stories she'd tell about driving up the coast of California with a girlfriend and stopping at all these roadside speakeasies and getting "snookered," and each story ended similarly—"We never did eat!" I started figuring out that Beth's 89 pounds were primarily Johnny Walker.

One time I asked Beth, "Aren't Mormons supposed to not drink?"

"That's just in Utah, sweetheart. This is New Jersey." She told the story about her doctor advising her that she could have one drink before sleep. "It was based on that advice that I began taking naps." Everyone would laugh at Beth's dry humor. "Originally, he told me to quit drinking, so I got a second opinion. I asked Jose, the cashier at the liquor store. He also told me to cross liver off my organ donor card. I told him that my organs were going to live long beyond me, they've already been preserved in there." My family was so alcoholic, even our Mormons drank.

If you asked her if she wanted coffee after dinner where she'd finish five scotches, she'd yell, outraged, "I never put out a fire." You could set your birth control to that response. My brother Reid came to visit from college, I told him I could predict what Aunt Beth was going to say if I asked her if she wanted coffee.

"I doubt it," Reid said.

"How much do you doubt it?"

"Five bucks."

I screamed out, "Beth, want some coffee?"

"No, thank you." And then ... nothing. Reid and I stood in silence, waiting to see who won the bet ... but nothing.

I was shocked and slightly befuddled as I handed Reid a five-dollar bill—just as it hit his itchy palm, she yelled into the kitchen, "I almost forgot to tell you, I never put out a fire!"

I snatched the five back like it was on a magician's string.

When I got older, into my twenties, I once asked her why she never got married and had she been in love, ever? My great aunt told me she was in love with the same man for years, who she had some sort of relationship with, but she purposely obscured the facts, leaving out juicy chunks of story. Beth knew how to parse words. I tried every trick I knew to pry the secret loose, but she was protective of this memory. I couldn't tell how often they saw each other, or whether he slept over—it sounded to me like he was married. She teared up when she spoke of Steve. She loved him for fifty years, but she never told him. When I asked her "why?" she said, "It wasn't any of his damn business! You don't need anybody's permission to love." That made me sad, it was as if she knew he didn't love her back. Suddenly, my career role model melted into a tragic woman who died alone with a broken heart, getting snookered night after night to try and wash the touch of Steve away.

My aunt started getting hard of hearing, and she could no longer understand my questions, "Aunt Beth, did you ever want children?" Either she pretended like she didn't hear me, sipping on her scotch, or it was something she didn't think was any of my beeswax, just like Steve. She'd taken to sitting still like she was meditating, with her eyes open, and her highball glass wrapped with fingers. When Mom told her, "YOU NEED A HEARING AID, BETH!"

Beth said, "I'm not hard of hearing, I'm *tired* of hearing."

After my mother died, I called my uncle, her brother, for the first time ever. She'd begged me to stay in touch with Ron since he had no one. I never had anything to say to him—I'd always found it difficult to find a common bond with a hermit who played checkers with dogs. After the "hi, how are yous?" our conversations always quickly dried up to an uncomfortable desert.

On this summer evening, I'd called him for my mom, and I have to assume it made his month—it sure made mine. Ron and I must have talked for an hour, and it flew by like a paper airplane. We laughed, we confessed, we cried and we held each other with our voices over the phone. During this talk, I ended up thanking him for making my unmarried and childless life valid, for paving my way. He laughed. "I'm glad I could finally give you something," he said with his slight cowboy accent. I ended up asking him why he'd never married, assuming it was because he was just a loner. My uncle then unraveled the saddest story for me. He had been in love! He fell madly in love in his twenties. I could barely fathom my uncle as anybody's heartthrob, but in his late twenties, he met the girl of his dreams, and she broke his heart. He'd bought a ring to propose, and she turned him down and not very nicely, he said gently, using a cadence slower than usual to emphasize the gravity of the story. I teared up over my poor uncle's lousy luck.

It made sense that he was protecting himself. He drank a case of beer every day, toting it around in the front as his belly. That should have been a clue that he didn't want anyone getting near, using his girth as his "moat." He told me that night that he never wanted his heart touched again. Thirty-five years later, her name was still too hard to say aloud. "My dogs never hurt my feelings., most people let you down." Then he went on to tell me that he found life disappointing.

I tossed and turned that night, flipping my pillow, trying to shake the image free in my head of my Uncle Ron, so harmless, so alone for his whole life, rescuing dog after dog trying to fill the void.

My role models were not trailblazers—they were two lonely people who both spent a lifetime yearning for someone they would never really know. They each turned to their own way of coping. Beth died alone in a hospital, with a second cousin at her hospital bed. When Ron passed, he had five dogs, and it took days for a neighbor to know that he'd died—it was the piled-up newspapers which clued her in. I didn't ask for any details about his death. But I will never forgive my mother for putting that image in my head.

Jonathan Livingston Seagull Was Not Just A Dumb Bird

Soon after my new roommate, Amy the depressive, moved into my Upper West Side apartment, she gave me my first self-help book. One mid-morning, she opened her bedroom door—just a crack—stuck her hand out and slipped the book to me, like a joint. Just her way of saying "hey." Her door then snapped shut like a bank vault on a timer, and I heard her click the latch. Some days, that was just the best she could do.

"Make yourself at home!" I yelled after her—I was taking baby steps to be a better me. Amy had just moved in, and I wasn't sure how it was going. She would lock herself in her bedroom, which was about the size of a toaster oven, for hours on end. When she came out, she'd say something nice-ish and go back in for a rewind, like some new age cuckoo clock. I felt badly when she told me she was a depressive, which I assumed was like being manic-depressive, without the "up" days.

I guess my mother had technically given me my first self-help book. *Jonathan Livingston Seagull* was a best-seller—all the rage in the seventies. I remember that I liked it, I think. But then again, I just thought it was about a dumb bird. I didn't get the parable about being free and finding your own true self. I don't think my mother did either—one thing she didn't need to impart to her four misfits posing as children, it was, "Dare to be different, my little birds!" She believed that self-help was sad and religion was for people who didn't have friends, and enjoyed a nice bazaar. I was brought up by atheists: hard-core atheists, although my mother did admit to me late in life, that she *did* believe in God ... she just didn't like him. Mom needed to be in society's loop, so she gave all four of her kids this book for Christmas the year it came out.

By the late eighties, most people were trying to do better than they did in the seventies and love themselves (and all of mankind as well). I was starting to stand out like a mole on a baby's face—a cynical atheist spewing negative thoughts thinly disguised as sarcasm. I no longer fit in. Even people I liked were starting to imbibe in the self-helperies. Movements, workshops, and bumper stickers were erupting out of the vomitous love. The "Positive Thinking" aisles at the bookstores were expanding faster than the universe which inspired them. Twelve-step programs came to light and were hooking innocent drunks right off the streets—come, come! We've got coffee and clichés, and there was a lot of hugging going around. If someone hugged me, I'd wilt like a bag of fish—no arms or hands, just a lifeless sack. It was a scary time for me. Cynicism was like cocaine—people were still doing it but only in their lofts with close friends.

Even my hostile brother Rob thought I was getting really negative. He'd sobered up that month and suddenly had hope, *damn him!* Everyone was turning on me. I had just stepped out of his blue Volkswagen blaring "Truckin'" way too loud. I slipped onto the bus back to New York City without so much as a "bye." We rarely used the pleasantries in my family. No thank-yous, no hellos, hardly ever any goodbyes—there were never beginnings or endings in our existences—just middles.

We were raised as heathens and were usually too busy interrupting each other and taking the Lord's name in vain to entertain pleasantries. We never even uttered a "God bless you" when someone sneezed. There'd be this long, blank stare while we waited for the awkward silence to pass. Sometimes my mother would say something supportive like, "Well, it's a good thing you let that out or your head would've exploded." Sunday mornings, while all the nice families went off to Church, or Mass, or whatever, we had our own rituals. My parents would look out the window and laugh at all the poor people who needed the crutch of religion while they glug, glug, glugged on their drinks.

I was living in Manhattan and had gone to Jersey to check in with the Mother ship: my ancestry of cynical don't bother raining on my parade—it's already been canceled—kind of philosophy which was from my father's side of the family. My mother and her brew had passed me: alcoholism, sarcasm, and hopelessness. It had all culminated into a kind of self-loathing that needed medication to mask. My self-esteem had gotten so low that one night, a man had called me the wrong name in bed, and I gave him another guess. Clearly, I didn't love Debbie.

I'm open-minded and will read the first couple of sentences of any book before I decide I don't like it. I'd even read *The Bible* once, (drunk), just so I knew what I was arguing against. I opened the self-help book with the rainbow on the front cover, which Amy had given me and I began my new life on a Trailways bus bound for New York. The first sentence of the rainbow book was bold. It said, "Life is simple. You get back what you put out."

"Hmmm." I was intrigued. I hadn't ever thought of that. I read on a bit, and the first page of the rainbow book clearly claimed that you can create anything you want just by "affirming" it, by doing affirmations. You can create joy, good health, love, and meaning. You see it, you say it, you get it. This kind of blew my covers off, like that last, loud snore—the one that finally wakes you up from a deep sleep. The author claimed that she had cured herself of terminal cancer by affirming good health. The book went on to let me know that an affirmation is really just a positive statement, like "I'm beautiful." You say it and say it and say it, and before too long, you actually believe that you are beautiful. Then allegedly—eventually you become beautiful, or after a while, if you don't become beautiful, you at least go out and buy new makeup and maybe a new hairdo so you're at least prettier or, at worst, less ugly.

My two-decade-long vodka therapy had stopped working sometime earlier that year, and I too, wanted to find a better me. I'd tried taking some action on my own to attempt a self-cure. I tried mixing my Popov with tonic instead of cranberry juice. I then switched to wine—a huge concession (to me, anyway). I tried cutting the wine with soda, I even drank Miller Lite on the rocks (which didn't slow me down much, it just gave me the wherewithal to drink more.) I tried smoking more pot while cutting back on the liquor and the blow, which I was trying to do only on weekends and special occasions like Tuesdays. Although my hangovers were less frequent, something was still missing. That day on that bus, I had a positive thought: *Affirmations seemed harmless enough. They're really pretty basic and not religious or anything creepy like that,* I justified. Then it occurred to me that cavemen probably even did affirmations. Perhaps a Neanderthal would grunt at his woman, "I get dinner now," then off he'd go to club some Mastodons. I doubt he ever left the mud hut saying, "I'll probably never be able to get me one of those hairy behemoths, and we'll starve to death this winter, Snookie." Those that did probably died off, taking their skinny wife and hungry kids with them—survival of the fittest working hand in hand with positive thinking. I was having a little breakthrough right there on a bus, but there was no way I could've known that then. I did feel something. I briefly entertained the idea that I was coming down with the Swine flu. *It was around, and that would be just my luck,* I snorted. Then I thought that *that* was a negative thought. So, the better of me got me, and it occurred to me that, *hey, yeah, I could do with a piece of "me pie."*

I didn't necessarily want to be beautiful, never a priority for me (which turned out to be convenient), but I wanted something, so I tried a few affirmations. I stood in my living room and kind of affirmed and kind of ordered …"I have a boyfriend." I waited a moment, and when nobody came, a truly miraculous thing happened—I didn't give up—I tried again. I didn't have a clue what I was doing—all enthusiasm, and no talent like Tabatha in the episode of *Bewitched* when she discovered she could twitch her nose, I started flinging affirmations around my NYC apartment like they were spells: "My dentist lost my root canal bill—That cute guy I met last week at the bar is calling me. I have a BMW. My phone is ringing. Now! It's Ringiiinnnnnng Nowwwww. Nowwww! My phone is RIIIIIINNNNNG—"

Another miracle happened ... right at that moment, my phone rang. It was my best friend du jour, Janette. "Oh-my-god. I put a spell on you. I told you to call me, and you called me," I said to Janette. "The rainbow book says I can have anything I want,"

"Oh, I read that. I do affirmations all the time." said Janette in her ever cheery attitude. She'd called to report her weight loss that day. "One half a pound, again." We were dieting together, but I was failing.

"Great!" I faked. Janette had been hired by the SlimFast people to lose weight and become one of their before and after TV commercials where you have to admit in front of the world that you were a big fat pig—in an ad! Nevertheless, it was looking like she was going to be thin, and I wasn't. "What if an ex-boyfriend sees it?" I'd asked. I was always concerned with ex-boyfriends and what they would think. I don't know why—mine were all dead, gay, or in rehab. "I'm hanging up now," I affirmed, and I hung up. I was chomping at the bit to practice my newly acquired witchery some more. "I'm thinner than Janette," I affirmed. "Janette's fat, and I'm thin," I quickly added. Clearly, my spirituality had some growing up to do, since at this point, an affirmation was less about getting what I wanted and more about making sure others lost something in the mix. But I had made a big stride, since not that long ago my sole source of spirituality was rock and roll lyrics, "what goes up must come down," "you can't always get what you want," or "knock three times on the ceiling if you want me."

I sat there, contemplating my soul, when a cockroach walked across my coffee table. This one wasn't even scurrying—it was more of an arrogant, "You don't even bother killing us anymore, so why *rush?*" walk. I aimed my new powers at this little creep. "You're dead!"

And I just kept saying it until I splattered him with the bottom of my coffee cup. There were a few other cockroach types around, slowly walking toward wherever they were going, so I repeated, "You will all die now. I deserve better than this." Everyone knows it's useless to crush cockroaches—more just appear and then you need professional help. There was said to be a billion cockroaches in New York City, and that they would outlive a nuclear war, they were so indestructible. It's never seemed fair to me, when butterflies are so fragile that they can't even withstand a heavy rainstorm.

Somewhere around the third death affirmation, I put on my coat trance-like and slipped into the cold and nasty Manhattan night to buy some roach motels. "I have my limits," I said, when I returned and scattered the traps around my place, like a dealer at a blackjack game. I was beginning to get how this affirmation stuff worked.

"Your subconscious hears you and backs you up," said Amy. "Your subconscious is very, very powerful." She had actually read the whole rainbow book. I didn't have that kind of time—I was negative, and that was extremely time-consuming.

"Ah. I see." I nodded. And I did. Amy then snapped her door shut like she was on *Laugh-In*, and it was Joanne Worley's line. I was beginning to feel some power at my fingertips, and I thought maybe it was time to set my goals a wee bit higher than roach motels. I couldn't help but noticing that the book had suggested we affirm world peace ...

"I have a BMW," I blurted. BMWs had always lured me. It meant "I have arrived." I was pretty clueless where one arrived to, or how I was going to get there, but I did know that wherever it was, I would be driving a BMW around. "I have a BMW. I have a BMW!" I screamed. "I need a BMW!" I chanted it faster and faster, louder and faster. In fact, it got so loud and so fast it actually began to sound like the Buddhist chorus, "Nom Yo Ho Renge Kyo." I knew this chant well. An annoying Buddhist who had just moved in on the third floor used to sing it daily at 6:00 AM, at which point the sound would burst through my rear bedroom window by 6:01 AM The chant was loud and haunting like horror movie music. "NOM YO HO RENGE KYO."

I didn't usually get home until way after 4:00 AM having been out either working, or partying. On about the fifth morning of this, I threw my window open and screamed in the scariest voice I had, "SHUT THE FUCK UP—LOSER!"

The Buddhist stopped on a dime—"NOM-YO—!" Right there in mid-chant and she never crooned a "Kyo" or a "Ho" again. I was proud, as I had created that.

"You probably killed her," my mother said. "You can't go around raining on people's parades, Debbie. You'll never get a husband." I found that statement sadly ironic, as it was from her side of the family that, we not only learned *how* to rain but also how to figure out what time the parade was scheduled, so it would ruin the most floats.

"I don't want a husband," I threatened, lighting a cigarette.

"That was cute when you were twenty, but now you're forty, and your career? Well, where is it?"

"I'm thirty-five, Mom."

"Oh."

January was drawing to its dank close, and I continued with my chant, "I want a BMW." I played with the form, like a bored jazz man in the sixties, GIMME a BMW. GIMME, GIMME, GIMME. B-M-B-M-W ... NOM YOHO RO... Help me!

One shitty winter night, the temperatures had dropped below

zero, and the winds were railing around like beasts. I bundled up and went out to the world's largest parking lot: Manhattan. It was time to move my car, a ritual you had to perform if you were insane enough to own a car there. They street-clean every other day, so to avoid getting a ticket (or even towed), you had to move it from one side of the street to the other. Then the very next day, you had to go back out and do it all over again, like Sisyphus and his rock—back and forth, north to south, east to west, rain or shine. Every other day, I was sentenced to an existential theme park, "Sisyphus-land."

"You're lucky you have a car to move," Amy said as I bitched my way out the door. By this time, she was only coming out of her room every third day to say upbeat things and then fleeing. All her positivity was starting to get on my nerves. It was December in New York, nothing to be happy about.

I got to 78th street, between Columbus Avenue and Amsterdam Avenue mid-block, exactly where I had squeezed the car in the night before—but it was simply not there. I looked around for several minutes, tricking myself into believing that it had somehow moved itself, not wanting to see the truth—but my Nissan Sentra was gone! I couldn't help but notice that there was no BMW in its place. For a brief moment, I did enjoy a thought: *Maybe the universe had to remove the Nissan to make room for the BMW?* The whole thing was a bit coincidental to not have been rigged. *There definitely might possibly be a BMW coming.* The thought pushed on as I wondered if this was the right time to order the color. "RED!" I affirmed out loud, just in case it was. "Convertible," I quickly added.

Then the old Debbie returned like I had Turrets syndrome, "The fuckers stole my fucking car," I affirmed. "My fucking car's been stolen." I shrieked to a few other people at the car mover's theme park. "My fucking car's been stolen." Nobody seemed surprised. "So cynical," I said under my breath.

"Just part of the ride," grumbled an old man who got into his Impala from some decade I don't think I was even alive in. He rolled down his window to continue belting out his bitter song. "That's what you get for buying a new car. You played right into the stealer's hand. My car's older than my prostate surgery. They both still work. I come out every other day, and it's always here. And if it isn't, who gives a policeman's ball? I hope someone does steal this piece of shit. I'm tired of moving it every other *God forsaken* day. The only thing I want off it—is my plastic Jesus from the dashboard, so I take that in every night with me. I set it on my sink, next to my Preparation H. They'll take anything." He left without a "bye."

"People are just a tad too negative in this town for me," I said to myself on my way home. By the time I'd reached my apartment building, I'd already put three fucks into the sentence. "Be careful what you ask for," Amy said when I told her that, "My fucking car had fucking been fucking stolen."

"It's all gonna work out. You'll see, I really wish you could see that."

"I thought they'd let me keep the Sentra till the BMW came," I whined. I tried to keep her engaged, I knew she was about to flee. I had come to be able to detect it, maybe a twitch in her left cheek-bone—or a mad look in her eyes—so I blurted, "Wait—I mean if my BMW comes, and it's waiting at a lot, say in Connecticut, how am I going to go pick it up, with no car?"

"I gotta go," she lied and quickly disappeared into her hole. It was only 6:00 PM., but that was all of this day she could take, so I was on my own. I finally figured out that I was just supposed to wait for the BMW to arrive. I guessed that the BMW could figure it out on its own.

"Bet you fifteen bucks your car's been towed again," my mother lectured on the phone that night. "You park anywhere you damn feel like it. You're very careless, you know? And there's always red stains on your shirts. Switch to white wine." I thanked her for sharing and hung up. Something was shifting in me!

One morning a few days later, Amy emerged in her bathrobe. "Sometimes you're supposed to just be happy with what you have," she recited in an ominous tone. By now, she'd read the whole rainbow book and its sequel—the one with a sun on the cover. She was the closest thing to a guru I had, so I assumed she knew what was going on.

"Ah," I improvised. I wasn't sure if she was implying that I should've been happy with the Nissan or if I were supposed to find happiness now, with no car at all, although it didn't matter, as neither optione appealed to me.

Part II
You Can Always Get What You Want, Mick!

It began to really come down outside. Snow in the city is beautiful and pure for about five minutes, when it first meets the slanty skyline, but the minute it slides onto the dirty old buildings, it turns a brownish, sooty blech color while it slithers down to the streets to cover them in that same blech. Winter in New York is like an Ingmar Bergman movie: long, dismal, and hard to get through without alcohol. By mid-January, the New Yorkers get mean, and the sun sometime sets early just because it's had enough of that day. I don't like Januaries, mostly because I know it's followed by another month I don't like even more. I started pining for Florida or better: May. A lot of New Yorkers head for Florida in these dismal months. So many, in fact, that I nicknamed February "Miamuary." It made Amy laugh.

Amy and I were both stand-up comedians—so nothing ordinary made us laugh. Nuances, deliveries, inside jokes, and made-up words would get us going. "Miamuary," Amy repeated, doubled over. "That's the funniest thing I ever heard." That couldn't have been possible, she seemed to be over-reacting, but I took the compliment.

"I wish I could go on a cruise," I told Amy a few days later.

"You will," she said on her way to her bedroom.

"Will what? Will what!" I screamed after her, but it was useless, she'd already shut her door. What did she know anyway? She was nuts. "I'm going to the Caribbean!" I affirmed. A broad sweeping statement directed to nobody in particular. I called Janette and told her I was going on a cruise as a comic.

"That's fabulous," she said. Janette was the least competitive person I'd ever met. The kind of friend you needed in your chorus, always happy for your good fortune, always supportive. Of course, what did she care? She was skinny. *Everybody had everything except me*, I thought for the slightest minute. Then I turned my angst into an affirmation, so I too, could have some things.

"I'm going to the Caribbean. I'm getting booked on a cruise ship. Everyone got that?" I said aloud as I flung my hopes around the apartment. "My phone is ringing now! NOWWWW!"

A few days later, as the sun sadly set over the rigid shadows of Manhattan, my phone rang. I had no way of knowing that this phone call would change the rest of my life.

It was the *Publisher's Clearing House* of wake-up calls. On the other end of my phone was a cruise ship booking agent from Florida who called herself Candy Casino. A few nervous jokes stuttered out of me, as everything is an audition in comedy land—"It's a good thing you didn't go into nuclear physics with a name like that. I guess you found your calling. Booking cruise ships or stripping were pretty much your career options."

She by-passed the trouble of laughing at my ad-libs and pressed on, "I need a girl comic for a cruise to the Bahamas next week. I hear you're funny. I hear you can handle a cruise ship. I hear you can do an hour clean. I hear you're kinda pretty. They like that on the ships."

"What do you mean, 'kind of pretty?'" She didn't take the trouble to answer that, leaving an awkward pause—one that Harold Pinter could've driven a cruise ship through. So I asked, "Hey, The Bahamas aren't in the Caribbean, are they?"

"Hell if I know," said Candy. "I book 'em, I don't map 'em." Candy spoke like Tonto. After we'd been working together for a few weeks, she'd call to rebook me on a ship and just say, "Pack 'em up. You're going to St. Thomas," like I was a contestant on her game show.

"Do you realize how powerful you are, Debbie? Everything that you want, you get," said Amy with awe. Before I could negate that compliment, since it still just seemed rude to let people say nice things to me, she and her demons fled back to her toaster oven for forty-eight straight hours, long enough to have been stripped, cured, and smoked. I tried to scream after her, "I still don't have my BMW!"

But even I, the president of the Northeastern chapter of the "Nothing Good Ever Happens to Me Club," had to believe that something was weird. For the first time in my life, something was fucking changing. I sat, wondering for a speck what Candy meant by "kind of pretty." I hoped that, that wasn't something people were spreading around. I didn't need that kind of press. Then I traced my mysterious fortune back a bit.

Hmm, I guess I had mentioned to a few people at a few clubs that I wanted to go to the Caribbean. I remembered that I had been blabbering about it for a while, maybe even complained a bit to some comedians about my career. So then, they must've told two friends, and then they must've told two friends, and so on until that shampoo commercial pyramid marketing technique worked—a comic named Richie, who was a big shot on the ships, told Candy in Florida. I was beginning to see how these affirmations work! You have a goal, you express it in a positive light, it gnaws at you so much so that you take some action, tell people, and voila! You're a witch! *So, an affirmation is really just a complaint with a deadline,* I concluded. It seemed that the "nothing good club" was going to have to elect a new leader. I was going to the Bahamas!

Janette chimed in with her usual support. "You're amazing. But you already told me last week." I explained to her that last week, it was merely an affirmation—this week, it's my life. I suggested she start doing affirmations so when I became rich and famous, we could still be friends. I now knew that my entire life was on the drawing board. I had proof.

A cruise ship is really just a floating shopping junket of bitching, sunburnt travelers. I met people from Des Moines who hadn't been outside of Iowa since a two-dayer to the Indiana State Hog Eating Fair in 1977, and still had the nerve to find fault with Barbados. "There was too many flowers. It stunk," said a southern farmer's wife at dinner one night, even though nobody asked her opinion. I too, found fault with Barbados, but being from New York City and not Slippery Eel, Alabama, I felt I had big city superiority. I had decided that the beaches were too narrow and rocky. I'd gone to Barbados in the third week of my cruise career. The first two weeks in the Bahamas worked out, and I was re-booked, and now I was in the Caribbean, just as I had affirmed.

It was Miamuary, and I was now on a ship that docked in seven ports in seven days. The Jesus Tour: St. Thomas, St. Johns, St. Kitts, St. Lucia, St. Maartins, St. Barts—islands so beautiful they had actually been sainted. It was a miracle. Thank God I had no car back in New York to worry about. Who would've moved it from side to side of the street? Mick Jagger's cry came to mind, "You can't always get what you want, but if you try sometime, you'll get what you need." *Oh no, Mick...you can get what you want, too, at least Debbie Kasper can.*

After the Saints, the ship went onto Barbados, Grenada, and ended up in Puerto Rico. Then we'd park in the same ports the next week, with a different group of floating complainers, for whom I had to do one show every five days. It was the best job, *ever!*

I think what shocked me the most about the eye-poppingly beautiful Caribbean was that it could also be so hideous. Everywhere you looked, the Windex colored sea lapped manila beaches. Each island seemed more aqua and more manila than that next. But once you pull back off the beaches and off the American and European owned resorts, you're in a third world country, make no mistake about it. Scrounging natives roam the edges of the coiffed properties, begging for your trade. There were a lot of dark, gangly women who wanted to braid my hair. Their own hair would be a Mardi Gras of beads and bright bows, and they wanted to weave their native ideas onto my head. They'd ask once, sweetly, then back it up with a whiny beg, and before you've even said "no" for the second time—they'd hurl insults.

"You're hair's too stringy anyway. Leave her alone; she don't have no money. She must work on the ship." They knew the ropes. Their fathers, brothers, and husbands were selling coconuts that were carved to look like Eleanor Roosevelt, right on the beaches. Others pushed live palm trees woven into living hats or monkey hair vests, and coconuts made into everything: coconut coffee cups, coconut pen holders, lopsided diaphragms.

Most of the kids weren't selling anything but pity. "Can I have one of your American dollars? I'm hungry!" Filthy goats roamed the islands freely, like big ugly dogs. They just ran around like it was part of some master plan, but not in any particular pattern or direction. They didn't work together like buffalo or wild horses or even cockroaches. They worked and traveled alone, like comedians.

St. Barts is the exceptional island on the saint tour. The land is owned by rich French people and is completely goat-free, which relieved me when I got there. I asked the sales lady at an overpriced boutique on St. Barts where the poor people on the island stayed—she pointed into the harbor and said, "On the cruise ships." I repeated that to my audience the next night on the ship—they didn't laugh.

I saw one cow in six weeks and twelve hundred thousand goats. I was not going to order meat at any Caribbean restaurant. I asked the waiter in a cafe on St. Maartins (a half French, half Dutch island), whether they ate goats or not. "Naaaah," she brayed. I'm not sure if she was teasing me, but I wasn't about to order a burger and have to pick the bristles out of my teeth to find out. Our waitress was blackened from her ancestry or perhaps the sun, or maybe even a little of both, and I had already managed to insult her. I knew better than to piss off a waitress—they can lick your food. She smiled through her teeth which looked like chipped china. "Oh, I see it. You're from

New York, are you then?" Her accent had a brogue to it,—kind of French, kind of Jamaican, kind of goat-like. I was tired of people asking me that question. I guess I wore New York like a tee shirt.

I tried to reign in my attitude and be as uplifting as the rainbow book had tried to teach me. "Well, I am from New York, but I've changed, and I love everyone now." She winked at me and asked for my order. I then said, even more Mary Richards than before, "How's the lobster?"

"Sad. He's in a freezer, don't you know? He's cold, almost dead, and he's about to be drawn and quartered because some American has ten bucks." She didn't know she was screwing with a professional. I wanted to slam dunk her through the heckler hoop when I remembered the healing, loving message of the book. So, instead, I molded my disdain into a phony smile and politely ordered a lobster. Then quietly flipped her the bird under the table.

I was lunching with my new best friend that day, the ship's magician "Mark the Magic Man." Mark was entertaining some children at another table by pulling his napkin out of one of his nostrils, saying, "Help, my brains are falling out of my head!" Even the kids only found it funny the first time. I riffed to myself for a while on the goat theme, working up a bit for that night's show ... "So I ordered some ribs, and they came with a beard." I jotted it down in my notebook, knowing I could make it funny later. I had found trust since the book had appeared in my life. I could do anything I affirmed. I could even pull a napkin out of my nose. I just didn't see what that would get me.

"When my lobster came, I swear the claw looked like a goat's hoof. It wasn't pink, it had hair hanging off the shell!" or so I said on stage the next night. "You ever try to crack a hoof?" The audience brayed. They, too, saw the goats. This was how you played a cruise ship, inside jokes about the cruise, the buffet, the Norwegians, and the goats. My goat bit was going to be a classic before we even hit Grenada.

Grenada is stunning, the super model of the Caribbean, but it's so poor—the goats were begging. Now that I'd been around the Caribbean a bit, goats had come to symbolize the third world. They'd stick their smelly heads right in your rented car's window and bat their eyes at you. Goats aren't very bright, or at least the one that got his head stuck my Jeep's window wasn't. Richie and I had been booked on the same ship, and we rented a jeep to check out the island. At a stop sign, a goat butted his head in on my side. I panicked and began to roll my window up slowly, as that was my solution to world hunger at that moment, but the goat didn't retreat. I then rolled the window all the way down to free him, but he still refused to take his head away. "Maybe this is some tactic they learned at goat begging school," I said to Richie, as he drove away, with the goat's rammed head still hanging from our window frame. It hoofed along for a few minutes until we sped up. They were some persistent mammals.

I had never even heard of Grenada until America invaded it a few years before. Thank God for wars or we'd never know where anything is. It was big news, we hadn't invaded anybody since Viet Nam (at least nobody we civilians knew about). We were saving Granada from the evil clutches of Cuba's communism, which was only a few hundred miles away, as the eagle flies. History will say that our Marines had landed, and democracy prevailed.

The truth is that these people were hungry. Grenada is still the un-raped rain forested island of the Caribbean. A rainforest, as it turns out, is just the new name for a jungle—probably coined by some marketing genius who couldn't get as many people behind "saving the jungles" as he could "saving the rainforests." The big score in Grenada, aka The Spice Island, is that you can buy saffron by the ounce for two dollars. I bought some, and I still have it, every yellow speckle. I didn't really want the saffron, nor was I sure what it even did. But all the other cruise women were giddy over the two dollars of it, and I just got caught up in the insane sport of it all. Let's just say that a lot of saffron left Grenada that day on its way to a better life in America, and I helped.

After the saffron liberation frenzy, I hooked up with some new best friends—Methodists from South Carolina. We hired a man named Alto on the second day in Grenada, to be our tour guide, and drive us around the dirt and gravel streets of this spectacular island.

The Methodists and I had all made a thirty (American) dollar pot for the day—which is enough to own an Alto and his mini-bus for six hours in Grenada. We chose him out of a motley line up of Grenada's finest goat herders, basket weavers, airport transport drivers, plantain pickers, and coconut painters. We chose Alto for very scientific reasons: his van was less dented than the other tour guides, and he used verbs in his sentences. But Alto had the smallest head I'd ever seen. He looked like a grown man wearing a cootie head. He drove like a drunken teenager coming home from prom. "He's barely able to see over the steering wheel with his baby-head," said one of the Carolinians.

"He speaks English, you know, Sugar. You can't just talk about him right in front of him like he was Italian," said her husband. She responded by rearranging her saffron stash in her purse.

Alto was in over his tiny head with us. We were curious and smart. He tried to answer our questions, which came fast and hard. At first, it seemed his English was bad, then I discovered his information was bad. He made things up.

"So, are there many phones here?" I asked.

"Yes, I mean no. I'd say around five hundred," stuttered Alto.

"Five hundred phones?"

"No. I mean three."

"How about TVs—do yaw'll watch 'People's Court?'" asked a particularly vapid man from the capital of South Carolina.

"Is that the Caribbean or the Atlantic down there?" I asked.

"Yes," said Alto.

"What was the sentiment when America invaded and saved you from Communism?" a Methodist preacher asked.

"We had already been invaded by Columbus," he said.

"Do you people eat goat here?" I had to ask.

"Only the stupid ones," replied Alto.

"The stupid people or the stupid goats?" I quipped, not able to help myself. I was always working. After a while, the Grenadian inquisition tapered to its natural end, as Alto didn't know much more than an Eleanor Roosevelt coconut head.

I rented a car in Puerto Rico by myself since I was getting sick of all my new best friends. It seemed like all anybody did was complain, and complaining seemed "so yesterday." Besides, for the first time in my life, I was starting to like me. "I like me," I had been affirming every night in the ship's bathroom mirror. "I really like me." The car came with a map. Not of Puerto Rico but of, I think, Bolivia. I don't know who laid out this map, but I doubted that it had been updated since the Caribe Indians had first canoed to this Emerald Isle. The map led me to routes that ended in swamps and dirt roads that wended their ways to parks that were closed off. Some roads inked on the map would just stop in mid-line—due to lack of anybody's ambitions to finish them, I assumed. Puerto Ricans are maniacal motorists. I suspected that they had been to the Alto School of Driving. They'd think nothing of driving seventy-seven miles an hour, slamming on their brakes in the middle of what they call a highway—to jump out of their cars and pee on the side of the road. It was like some ancient Olympic event that died off, The De-uri-thon. Their cars were all smashed up. I was scared, but I was in the Caribbean. Amy would've said that I had created that.

Late one March afternoon, the sun bathed me with its love. I was spread on a deck lounge chair like mango chutney on a pork chop—warm and sticky. In the quiet of my afternoon, a thought whispered to me: *Maybe I should get out of New York, the people there are so negative.* I slurped some more of my frozen margarita and said almost aloud, *I'm a new me. I like turquoise way better than grey, and the sun is my new best friend. I fit in here. Maybe I should move onto a cruise ship and be a cruise ship comic for the rest of my life.* The brilliance of that thought suggested that I sit up to accept the full impact of the idea. *That's it! I'll live here, right on the Norwegian Cruise Ship. I'll marry the Purser! Which one is he?*

By the end of my sixth week as a cruise ship comic, I'd changed my mind. Although I was a way better me, and I was so very awfully grateful to have had the Caribbean experience, and I really didn't like to complain, yet, I had to admit that I was getting a little bored of it all. I was sick to my stomach of carved-out pineapples filled with pink drinks. I was tired of drunken Norwegians in their wrinkled whites making lewd comments to me in their Nordic lilt. I was claustrophobic in my cabin, which was so small that I had to close my closet to floss. I'd grown weary of magicians pulling stupid things out of weird places. I was perpetually stuffed from the midnight buffets. I was tired of all my new best friends leaving me every single week. And would that sun never stop shining? How about a little rain here, people? Even my new favorite color turquoise was starting to look phony to me, or dare I say a little too *Caribbean?* Not complaints, mind you, just facts.

I'd bought an "I Swam with the Dolphins" mug on St. Barts. I'd seen the volcanic Pitons smoke on the Island of St. Lucia. I'd snorkeled in pirate's coves. I'd gambled in St. Maartins, bartered in St. Thomas, bicycled in St. Johns, mingled with Moroccans, bingoed with Brazilians, and meditated with Methodists. I'd drunk rum with Buddhists at the factory where the fine people of Ron Rico make it— but more importantly, my comedic riff on goats was honed and funny. It was time to move on. *But the sun is so healing. New York is so gray.* I must have thought that out loud because a row of tanned German sunbathers (an oxymoron) all perked up and said, "Vas?"

I tried to suck my pulpy Pina Colada up a chewed and clogged straw.

"That's it." I snapped. "This is too much. I need to live where the straws work. I deserve better than this!"

A German woman said, "Vas?"

"Maybe this is a good time to move to California," I whispered so that the nosey Germans couldn't hear me. I shook my head like an Etch-A-Sketch, in fear the idea might actually lead me to getting up and doing something about it. After spending six weeks in the lazy Caribbean, the thought of doing something was repugnant. The Caribbean was not known for inspiring ambition. "I'd have to pack, and then I'd have to go," I said to the sun-blessed air. But the image of Los Angeles reappeared in my Etch-A-Sketch-head. "Yeah, I think it's time," I affirmed. "I'm going to California. I'll need a car.

I'll get a red BMW." I pulled a postcard out of my purse and dashed a note off to Amy.

> **Dear Guru:**
> **I've decided to move to California and become a famous movie star. Thanks to you, I think I can make that happen. The apartment's all yours. Enjoy it!**
> **Love, the new Me.**
> **P.S.: Miamuary!**

I thought for a moment how Amy wouldn't have to close herself off in her bedroom anymore, she and her depression could roam the joint freely like a goat on Grenada. I wondered what she did in that bedroom of hers. Probably affirmations! *She probably affirmed that I would go away, and she would get the apartment!* The witch! That's what the old me thought—for a second. But the new me didn't care. *This is my true self. I am me, and I am content,* I smiled. I was tired, so I affirmed that I would take a nap, and so I did. I fell off asleep under my new higher power, the sun, dreaming about my BMW and world peace, and in that order.

If I Die, Make Sure My Silver Gets Polished

When my mother hit her mid-sixties, she lost her central eyesight due to macular degeneration, which is a proliferation of blood vessels behind the retina. She could see blurs, shadows, and my character flaws, but not much else. She noticed it one morning when suddenly her central vision was zigzagged.

I bounced down the split-level steps to our living room where Mom was seated holding her hand, with perma-cigarette lodged in yellow-stained fingers, firmly over one eye. I watched as she switched the whole process to the other eye: blink, rinse, and repeat. This was her "at home optometry kit."

"Is there something wrong with your eyes, Mom?" I asked, overly aware that even if there were something wrong with her eyes, she'd NEVER go to an eye doctor.

"It's nothing, Joe," she said.

"It's Debbie, Ma. You need to go see an eye doctor."

"That's ridiculous."

"Joe's six feet two with a moustache. I'm the girl."

No, she'd never go see an eye doctor. She'd sit on her couch ad infinitum, running her own tests: squinting, switching TV channels to see if ABC was less fuzzy, making pirate faces, blinking slowly, blinking more rapidly—like a distorted Morse SOS code to no one. The tests would go for days, but no doctor would be alerted. Not a chance.

"Eye doctors don't know a damn thing. They're not even real, you know. They're eyeglass salesmen who took a few night courses. They're nothing more than eyeglass pimps."

"That's Optometrists."

"Exactly. Try having a heart attack while reading an eye chart— you think he'll know what to do? He'll send you home with some Visine. They're not doctors—that's all I'm saying."

"You don't believe in doctors anyway."

"Exactly," Mom replied, stabbing the word "exactly" with her teeth to let me know this leg of the conversation was over.

My mother loved to read and never got used to her lack of specific vision. Then one day, through no urging from anyone, she made a sort of peace with her malady. "I've been thinking about it. I've decided that I'd rather lose my eyesight than my hearing. Can you imagine never being able to hear your grandchildren's laughter? Never being able to hear what people are saying about you? No, thank you; I'd rather lose my eyesight."

"Well, then you're a winner, Mom," I said, lamely.

"Never hear The Beatles again?" Mom pressed on.

"You hate The Beatles."

"Yes, I do, and I enjoy that privilege."

My mother just did not believe in doctors. "It's a scam. They don't know what the hell they're talking about. Betty Hahn had a tumor the size of a lime on her intestines, and the doctors didn't even know. Told her to cut out ice cream."

"Well, she did weigh in at 250. A weight loss wouldn't have been a horrible idea," I offered feebly.

My mother had gathered all the hard evidence she needed to keep her distance from doctors. This grape didn't roll far off that vine, for I, too, perform at-home tests, examinations, quizzes, and various mathematical equations before I'll consider a doctor. My very first gynecological visit had scared me away from that type of doctor for life plus ten years. A wall-eyed braless female at Planned Parenthood inserted the speculum and, after complimenting the shape of my cervix, grabbed a hand mirror and placed it between my legs. She made me sit up and look into the mirror so I could see inside myself. You really only need to see one cervix in your whole life.

My sister-in-law Ginny tells a worse story about her male gyno who inserted the speculum (vaginal car jack) into her vaginal vessel (his words, not hers) and began to sing "Getting to know You—Getting to know all about you," ruining *The King and I* for both Ginny and me for the rest of our lives.

I usually forego mammograms, preferring to perform my own breast exams—continually searching for lumps, along with every American woman over the age of forty. I don't usually check in the privacy of my own home. I don't want to be alone if I get bad news. I don't think my mother ever checked her breasts, home or otherwise—seemed to me that she recklessly shoved them in their brassiere and moved on to ignore another part of her body.

Mom had been told thirty years ago that she needed a complete hysterectomy, so she got a second opinion—she asked me, and I said, "Well, that sounds awful!" It did sound horrible, particularly the way she described it.

"They want to take out everything from here to here—to here!" She demonstrated, placing one hand under her breasts, while the other hand started chopping just above her pelvic line. I couldn't even imagine what would've been left. Everything my teenage limitations could think of seemed to kind of lie within those cut zones.

"What do they put back in there—stuffing?"

"I won't be able to drive you anywhere for weeks, and you'll have to make all the beds every morning, cook dinner, do the dishes, probably drop out of ice-skating lessons."

"No," I said. "No hysterectomy—out of the question."

That was it. The decision had been made by a fifteen-year-old. She never got an X-ray or a blood test, never had her pap smeared. Her idea of a breast exam was a quick brush of her 40 double Ds and a nod. All clear. The last GP my mom saw told her to cut back on her drinking, and quit smoking. She immediately switched from unfiltered Kools to filtered Kools, pushed cocktail hour back an hour from 3:00pm to 4:00pm and never went back to that doctor again. To mom, a doctor was where you stop off on your way to the end of your life. Doctors were merely the front men for the undertakers. To her, preventive medicine was a bottle of Maalox, a pot of coffee, and a snide remark. She had lots of evidence:

"Doris was fine, she only had a little sore throat (for ten years), and she was very active, still singing in the Church choir (yeah— down to two notes). When she finally went to the doctor, he gave her cancer. Three months later, she was dead. Didn't even make it till Christmas, and she'd already bought all her presents! That's why I shop on Dec. 22nd. Mrs. Pearlman down the street—one day healthy as a horse; next day, the doctor told her she had one year to live. One year to the day. Mrs. Pearlman died. Who needs that kind of pressure? I'll die when I am damn well ready to die. No, thank you. I don't need a doctor. I need a silver polisher."

My mother came from a long line of stoic Anglos. They worked hard, they drank harder, then they died, asking for no pity. She entertained weekly, throwing dinner parties for other disappointed suburbanites who drank too much to wash away yesterday, and try not to think about tomorrow.

Like most mothers in the sixties and seventies, Mom had inherited family monogrammed silver, and it was all kept in locked-up chests for no one to see or use, with only a few choice pieces on top for the tease, like a stripper in a club threatening to take off her top. If you walked by the buffet where it was kept, she'd prod you with a finger, saying, "Keep moving that's fine stuff there, that is. It's not for looking or using, it's just for the being." And she'd never use her good stuff for just us. We drank out of converted jelly jars, we ate off of plastic Flintstone plates, and for the holidays, she'd taken to opening up the breakfront in her dining room, dusting off her silver and her bone-colored gold-plated Wentworth china. She'd stack it up on her dining table, watch it for about a half-an-hour and smoke. That night, at dinner, she'd casually say, "You all know I have fine Wentworth family china, beautiful antique engraved family silver, don't you?" We'd nod "yes."

"Good, because this year, for Thanksgiving, we're eating on plastic—I'm *damn* tired of doing dishes. That stuff has to be hand-washed, you know." I always applauded her when she cut out dish-washing—I was the only daughter in a family of six, so the bulk of the kitchen duty fell on me.

My mother's big extravagance was the black maid who came in once or sometimes twice a week to help her with the house and polish up her silver that sat proudly on the buffet. Our family silver was to be adored but never used, to be walked by but never fondled, to be worshipped but never kissed.

Lola drove a very long Cadillac. My mother drove an Oldsmobile, an old one. Each Thursday, Lola parked her land boat right in front of the house, stretching from one neighbor's curb to ours, the smashed-in side facing our house so the neighbors wouldn't see. My mother was always concerned with what others thought. I guess she wanted the neighbors to think that our maid was wealthy. I didn't quite get the point.

Lola had one long boob that streamed across the top of her chest, like a flesh shelf, high and proud. She was always smiling (sure, she drove a Cadillac) and was the most devoutly religious person I'd ever met. She was always praising The Baby Jesus. People in the suburbs didn't generally mention religion in public. My mother was an atheist and didn't usually hang out with people who invoked Jesus, Joseph, Mary, or her little lamb. My mother didn't care for religion or religious incantations, but for some odd reason, Lola had a special dispensation. They had a bond that baffled my brothers and me. I have no doubt that at some point, the two of them came to terms with religion, but I also have no doubt each left with their spiritual convictions intact.

To Mom, Lola could do no wrong—it was as if she were blood. She was from Camden, New Jersey, which is the nation's latrine. To call it a toilet would be flattery. In fact, it was world-renowned as a dump. You could travel to the Great Wall in China, and mention that you were from Camden, and the guard would probably say, "That place is a piss hole in the ground that stinks like ass meat!" But it was the dormitory for all the housekeepers for my suburban town, Cherry Hill, New Jersey.

Lola was the worst housekeeper in the world. My brothers and I couldn't decide whether she was lazy or just awful at cleaning, but we agreed that she was taking advantage of our mother's failing central eyesight. We laughed, telling our stories, "She turns on the vacuum and puts her feet up and sighs, 'Oh yeah, the place is dirty this week, Ms. Kasper. Whooo! I'm workin' my fingers to the bone here today, Ms. Kasper.' Then she pops a bon-bon in her mouth and turns the vacuum off after ten minutes."

"And the silver looks like shit, since mom's eyesight faded," Reid added. Does she even know?"

But when we tried to tell Mom what we thought was going on, she came to Lola's rescue like she was a wounded bird. "Lola's as honest as the day is long. Every week, I leave a dime and two pennies on the floor, just to see what she'll do. I put it right there on the floor next to my dresser like they fell off. And every week, she picks that twelve cents up and stacks it on my night table. She wouldn't steal a penny." My mother defended her as if she were one of her own.

"Ma," I attacked, "Who would steal a penny?"

"Twelve cents!"

"What are you going to do with twelve cents?"

"Well, you could buy a stamp," she offered brightly.

"Mom, it's 1990. Stamps are twenty cents. The Great Depression's over. Try leaving a thousand cents around and see if she takes that."

"Why would I want to leave a thousand pennies about? I'd have no place to walk, then, would I? Do you know how many pennies that is? I don't have time to count out a thousand pennies. That would be like having a job. And, smart ass, one time I did test her, and I hid a five-dollar bill under my bed, just to see if she'd take it. It's still there. Go ahead, look. It's still there. She has not taken it to this day."

"Ma, she has not cleaned under your bed since you lost your eyesight! I'm sorry to be the one to tell you this, but she's not cleaning your house. It's not clean." Then I added the always hurtful: "People are talking."

I got on my hands and knees just to prove my point and looked under her bed at the layer of last year's lint, lost pennies, and wayward pillow feathers. "Oh, look who's here? Judge Crater!" Then I spotted the fiver. "There he is." I pulled the five out, shook off the layer of dust. "It's disgusting under here. DISGUSTING! I have to go take a shower."

"Well, why don't you clean it, then?" chimed in Mom.

"Excuse me, but I was under the impression that you had a maid?"

"Why should Lola clean under my bed? She's a grandmother, for *chrissakes*. I don't want her on her hands and knees cleaning under my bed—she might get hurt. You're right there. You clean it."

"Okay, but I'm taking the five."

When my mother died, Lola came to the service and back to our house afterward. She was the first to arrive, remembering to face the Cadillac's smashed side in, so no one would know. My mother would've liked that. Nobody had contacted her, but she clearly read my mother's obituary, and she and The Baby Jesus showed up, teary-eyed, and bereft as if she'd lost her own mother. She hugged me hard, pushing her breast shelf against my grieving body, "Oh, Ms. Kasper, I loved your mama. She was kind. She was my favorite house to clean."

Sure she was, she made you watch Jeopardy with her. She told you to put your feet up. She made me pick up your slack.

"Your mother was so afraid of doctors. I drove her to the doctor, you know? She'd lost her sight to the macula generation. She couldn't drive."

"Yes, Lola, I know. Thank you so much. She loved you, too. Her dying words were about you."

"Yes," she continued, missing my sarcasm and contempt. There she stood, the woman who took advantage of my mother for years.

"I drove her to the doctor. She got her test. They said she had the cancer. They saw it on the X-ray. The cancer. In the lung. Right in the lung—it was all over that lung. She thanked the doctor. Didn't shed a tear. She walked out the room, filled out her papers and said, 'thank you.' I wouldn't thank no doctor who gave me no cancer. He looked at her like it was your mother's fault. I wanted to slap that man right across his face. She was quite a lady, your mother was. Quite a lady. I drove her home, she didn't say anything. We got home, and I fixed her a bourbon on the rocks, and she lit a cigarette."

"Of course she did," I smiled.

Lola continued. "I asked if she was okay. She said, 'I should never have gone to the doctor. Should never have gone. Now I gots the lung cancer. He gave me the lung cancer.' She smoke that darn cigarette and smiled. I polished up her silver and went home." Lola stopped at that moment, and she looked over at my mother's buffet. She saw the silver—tarnished, abandoned, looking more like a junk pile of sad pewter than family heirlooms. I glanced over at it as well. Lola's mouth dropped open, like a drawbridge. Her sawed-down teeth trembled in horror. "Oh, your mother would be upset. She wouldn't want anyone to see that."

I wondered *who would ever polish it now. Who would care? How would I ever divide this up between my brothers and myself. None of us wanted it, but no one would want anyone else to have it, either.*

Lola slipped out of guest mode and into an apron she grabbed from the hook under the sink. She pulled out the polish and grabbed a gob of paper towels, yanked the tarnished silver off the buffet, and began to polish right there as people were starting to arrive. I never saw her move so fast. It was like she was at a silver polishing competition at a County Fair. This was not the Lola I knew.

She left early that night, not wanting to overstay her welcome. I followed her to the front door, gave her a longing hug, and *I meant it.* I tried to slip her $25.00—I knew my mother would have wanted me to do that. Lola pulled it out of her pocket and slapped it back in my palm like a drug deal gone wrong. "No, thank you, Ms. Kasper. I loved your mamma. We was friends." Her eyes became gooey and warm; she shook her head back and forth in small strokes like someone who just ate a really good piece of cake. "Your mother ..." Lola didn't know how to finish her thought. "I will never forget her."

I watched Lola shuffle down the front lawn and get in her Cadillac. She turned and waved sadly to me. I stood there, wondering what a Jesus-loving uneducated teetotaler from Camden and a white bridge-playing atheist society wannabe could possibly have had in common. I will never understand, but I could see it, just the same. A blind person could see the years of affection Lola had been carrying around for my mother.

Hey! Don't You Know Me?

When I was younger, I never forgot a face. My mother always bragged that I bumped into people I knew everywhere I went. "Debbie knows people everywhere—all over the world, everywhere we go, Debbie knows someone." She'd widen her big eyes as if she were marveling about the new cold-water Tide.

"Yes, Debbie has always been quite popular," one of her life long best friends, Ellen, replied.

My mother corrected her, "I didn't say anybody knew her, she just knows them. I don't call that popular. I call it crazy. Wherever we go, a restaurant, a movie theatre, the beach, she stares at everyone. Then she runs up after them. It's embarrassing." It didn't take much to embarrass my mother—long grass, a dented car in your driveway, a chubby daughter.

If I have ever laid my eyes on your face, it will forever be etched in my memory like a metal plate for a lithograph. What's worse, if I saw you and thought we'd met before, I'd hound you to the gates of hell to figure it out, tracking the clues in our paths like an Indian. I think the reason that I always sought out familiar people is that I have always yearned for a sense of belonging, and recognizing a face gave me a feeling like we were all in this stupid mess together. Ultimately it made The Beatles' song come true for me—"I am he, and you are he, and you are me, and we are all together, goo-goo-gajoob." I might stare at you at the theatre, squeezing my hazel eyes together to figure it out, or perhaps I'd throw furtive glances your way in a Parisian Cafe, asking the waiter what you'd ordered, hoping that would spur a memory. "Cafe Au Lait, huh? Well, that's very interesting. If he pays with a credit card, please tell me his name," the waiter flitters off. My French sounds more like Spanish—it's really "Sprench," so the garcon misunderstands, thinks I want to pay the man's check, and brings it to me.

Once in the mid '70s, before my sophomore year at Windham College in Vermont, I was at my parents' home in New Jersey, packing, getting ready to leave for Germany on a semester abroad. We were only allowed 40 lbs. of crap, and I was hovering at 70 and couldn't part with even one pair of earrings. Frustrated, I hit a party with some high school friends who were also still home for the summer, where I bumped into Bill Mason, who I didn't much like. Bill always had to one-up me, and I'd get competitive, so I'm pretty sure he didn't much like me either. (But I feel certain I didn't like him *more*.) Our conversations were always short, and on this night, he asked me what I was up to, so I said, "I'm flying to Munich on Monday for four months."

"I'm flying to Sweden on Monday for five," he said.

We both walked away, each shuddering over how much we

disliked the other.

I was heading to Munich via Icelandic Air, which took hundreds of thousands of students to Europe in the seventies. It was a cheap airborne party. On our way to Munich, our plane stopped in Reykjavik to refuel. We de-planed at the crack of Icelandic dawn, and when I stumbled, hung-over through the airport flanked by my college crew, I saw Bill Mason ahead, surrounded by a few of his friends too (although he didn't have as many as I had). We spotted each other several feet away and both snapped our heads back slightly as if to say, "What the hell?" When the two moving clumps of students neared one another, I spoke first, "Hi, Bill," I said in an intentional, almost mocking monotone.

He nodded slightly like he wasn't thrilled to see me again so soon, either, "Oh, hi, Debbie." he mocked back.

And we both kept walking, never to see each other, again.

My friend, Sharon did a pretty big double-take, yanking at my arm to stop me, "Who the hell was that?"

"Bill Mason."

"How do you know that guy?" she practically grabbed me by the lapels and slapped me across my face a few times to help me change my mind.

"He's from my hometown. He's from Cherry Hill."

"Bullshit. If you knew him, why didn't you talk to him?"

"Because I don't like him. I don't like him in Jersey, and I *really* don't like him in Reykjavik."

"That's ridic-ya-vik," said Sharon, creating a word we ended up tossing around all over Europe when something bizarre or outrageous happened.

During the seventies, American students were backpacking all over Europe. It was practically our birthright, so it wasn't unusual to bump into people you knew in, say, The Hoffbrau Haus in Munich or on a train platform in Luxembourg. At least it wasn't unusual for me because my beady green eyes were always searching, searching.

Sometimes people would make loose plans to meet a friend in some far-off country. "Hey, meet me at the Spanish Steps on Tuesday in July; I'll be there." You'd be required to go to Rome's famous hang-out every single Tuesday while in Rome until you found your friend. Maybe you'd leave a note with the Dutch guitar player there, who always sang "Knocking on Heaven's Door" to his small fan club, in the event that next Tuesday he sees a blonde American wearing a denim jacket that says "Dead Head." The note would tell him that you went on to Barcelona, "So let's meet in front of the Gaudi museum any Saturday in August." How we ever found each other in those days, beats me. You had to leave an intricate network of clues, carrier pigeons, or smoke signals, and only the very ambitious and clever would find one another. The seventies was a series of scavenger hunts, pay-phones, and hiding in dark alleys, like living in a bad spy movie waiting for Peter Sellars to pop out from behind a phone booth, wearing sunglasses, and send you to your next designated mark.

I went to see *HAIR* at the West End while I was visiting London during the hiatus from my German abroad program. (There were a slew of students there from my school on an English Literature Program.) At the end of *HAIR,* the cast urges the audience in the orchestra section to jump on stage and help them sing a rousing reprise of "Let the Sunshine in." That night, my traveling mate, Debbie, and I saw the show, hanging over the balcony from cheap seats, clapping along, celebrating our generation's very first musical.

I then began to stare into the crowd of amateurs flapping around on stage in search of a familiar face—of course.

Dusting off my binoculars, I was peering from face to foot, trying to find someone, I couldn't give it a rest for a minute. I looked back over the bad dancers again, desperate. There must be someone here I know. Within minutes, BINGO. There—doing a frenzied Calypso like dance with the floor—as if he were trying to get thrown out of the joint—was Neil Wagner from Windham College in Putney, Vermont, 05346! I gasped loud enough that my whole row turned on me. I grabbed Debbie's sleeve and pointed in horror to the birdlike idiot doing the cool jerk on stage, mouthing, "He's from Windham. He lived in my dorm!"

"That's ridyavik! she screamed. He wasn't on any abroad program, so it was weird that he'd be there. I grabbed Debbie by the hand, yanking her out of the theatre for fear of having him see me, too.

Neil lived in my dorm freshman year and had a stalk-like crush on me, which did nothing for my popularity. He was a weird loner with long but filthy black hair, who preferred the company of his dog, Dartagnan, to anybody, except me. Or perhaps everyone preferred the company of anybody but Neil, leaving him with only Dartagnan to hang out with. He would drop acid and camp out on the floor in the dorm lobby, fog up his wire-rim glasses from flop sweat and talk to his dog, who looked bored. Don't get me wrong, he wasn't making doggie conversations like "wanna go for a walk?" No, he would have those intensely existential, psychedelic conversations that you first contemplate in college, where you discuss the meaning of life, or you intellectualize the center of a bubble or question how dogs in Mexico learn to speak Spanish. Conversations that required some sort of mood elevator to inspire them.

In Frost dorm, my home freshman year, everyone left their doors slightly ajar, particularly if you were open to a visit. One night, I was lying on my bed, reading, the door cracked, just a bit (which meant I might be up for a visit, depends on who you are), when I heard Neil whispering outside my door in the hall, "Dartagnon ... push the door open. Push it with your nose, yes, the door Dart, open Debbie's door, go ahead." It all happened so fast—Dartagnan pushed through the door and ran into my room, jumped on my bed, followed by Neil who was vamping, "Oh Dart, bad boy! Debbie's probably studying." And then Neil took a flying, leaping, belly flop on top of me, too! Then he pretended he had slipped. A few of my male dorm mates had to come and pull him out of my room. He still followed me around that whole year, skulking behind columns in the quadrangle always coincidentally being on my end of the dorm, always the one to pick me up in his green Volvo when I was hitching to town. The whole thing made me sick. Here he was, thousands of miles from Vermont in London, dancing like a drunken scarecrow. It was time for me to get out the hell out of Dodge. Neil was clearly stalking me internationally, now.

The next morning, there was a crazed series of knocks on the door of the flat where we were staying. A few of my dorm mates from college were in London, so we were staying with them. It was six o'clock in the morning—the knock woke up four hung-over nineteen-year-olds. It was Neil Wagner, screaming "I hear Debbie Kasper's here!"

My friend Patty, who knew his obsession with me, cracked the door, saying, "She left, you missed her. She said she was going on to Bulgaria and she'll see you there.'"

Debbie and I jumped a train and headed to Amsterdam on our

way back to Munich. We hitched a ride in Amsterdam with a pair of Canadian hippies who had a badly painted and poorly running hippie van with missing back seats. Instead, they had a bunch of dirty throw pillows, coloring books, and notebooks for people to comment in. The joints were always flowing, and you'd be encouraged to say something profound (read: stoney) in the book. If all you could say was "Debbie was here," you were discouraged from writing anything at all, so I didn't leave my mark. We ended up getting detained at the Dutch/German border because I was careless with a dirty hash pipe, so we spent more time than expected in the back of this leftover Summer of Love van. When the Canadians dropped us off in Munich a few days later to rejoin our group, they said, "Good riddance, Debbies. Bye ... Adios ... Auf Wiedersehen! Hide your hash pipes!" they yelled as we jumped out of the van, which had barely even come to a stop for them to dump us out.

After the semester in Munich, several of my friends stuck around and hitch-hiked, enjoying their birthright. My friend Susie said she was heading somewhere warm, maybe Greece. I'd personally had enough of Europe. In other words, my parents cut me off and suggested I come home and work for six weeks before heading back to college in Vermont.

One day, in the mail at my parent's house on Cherry Tree Lane in Cherry Hill, New Jersey, 08034, an envelope addressed to me, Debbie Kasper, arrived from Barcelona. I opened it quickly. There sat my New Jersey driver's license. I hadn't even noticed it was missing. Susie had thumbed into Spain and gotten picked up by two hippies in a love van from Canada. Susie was rolling around on the dirty cushions, and she dropped the pen she would use to write in their comment book. Reaching down between the cushions, she pulled out my driver's license. It apparently fell out while we were getting detained at the German border—the border guards had collected all of our licenses, and passports, and birthmarks. Now my driver's license sat in an envelope at my parent's house. I felt very close to the Canadians and my new friend, Susie and I couldn't wait to tell Debbie—that is until I read Susan's note.

I found this in the back of Jim's van from Vancouver. When I told them I knew you, they said, 'If we never meet anybody named Debbie again, it'll be too soon, ha-ha!

People continued to pop up for me—again mostly because I looked or stared until my eyes burned. My visual recall was always firing on all pistons, almost superhuman in my powers. I could actually look through people and recognize someone I knew standing behind them.

In the early eighties, my uncanny skill continued. I was waitressing in Manhattan at the time, and one day, walking down Broadway, I saw a lady who I recognized but wasn't sure how, so I stopped her. "Wait, I know you. Do I look familiar?"

"No," she said. Then I went through my litany of quizzes, "Are you from New Jersey? Did you go to college in Vermont? Been to Boston? Do you ... did you ... have you ...?"

"No, not me, no," she insisted. She flashed me a look that said, "Leave me alone, whack-o."

I kept her in my glare for several moments until I finally put it together; I screamed, "You ate at The Copper Hatch last year. I waited on you. You had a hamburger, rare."

The woman nodded, slightly wierded out, and then she dashed into oncoming traffic right in front of a bus and across the busy street to get away from me.

"You gave me a shitty tip!" I yelled after her. I sighed in victory. I knew I knew her.

After college, I was living in Boston, and I went to a party. The party was dimly lit with candles, but across the living room, I could still see a familiar face. There sat a blonde girl about my age, who I swore I knew. I yelled from across the room, "I think I know you!"

"Oh?"

My next question was always: "Am I familiar to you too?" She nodded vaguely. I said, "Don't worry, I'll figure it out. I always do. Are you from New Jersey?"

"No, Delaware."

"OK. Where did you go to college?"

"Florida," she said proudly.

"Vermont," I shot back, trumping her tone and state. It was so much cooler to go to school in the Green Mountain state than the national swamp. "My name is Debbie Kasper, is that familiar?"

"No. Donna Wells."

"Nope," I said. We both smiled uncertainly, and I turned away.

My date led me toward the kitchen to get a glass of wine while admonishing me that I was annoying her. "Let it be," he said.

"I can't. I know her," I whined. I had half a glass of wine with whomever he was, knowing that this would be our last date, when I darted back through the crowd to take another go at Donna. "Summer camp at Matollionequay, in the Jersey Pines?" I knew it was a stretch—I'd already mentioned Jersey, with no rise out of her.

"No," she laughed.

"Shit. I'll figure it out. I definitely know you," I said. I was starting to sweat since I was only 21 years old, and was running out of places I'd been. "Where do you live in Boston?" I asked brightly. It was a futile question since the familiarity was old. I knew this girl from the way back, not from some local liquor store.

A few hours passed, the party was winding down, and I'd run out of time, but Donna's familiarity was nagging at me like a tongue cut. I kept staring and stalking, running life movies in my head. I finally took the seat on the couch next to her by the lava lamp. By this time, she was pretty sure we'd met, too. Either I'd convinced her with my intensity, or she'd had a vague recollection on her own. But every time I neared her, she'd welcome me with a wave and hungry eyes. Finally, out of desperation, I said, "What's your sign?"

"LEO."

"Me too!" I said. "That's interesting. How old are you?"

"I just turned 21," she admitted.

"Me too!" I shrieked, squinting my eyes. "When's your birthday?"

"August 4th,"

"Me too!" I screamed out. "Now that's weird."

"Really weird," she agreed.

By this point, there was a pack of partiers around us, cheering us on. They all began to chime in with things like, "yeah, really weird."

"Maybe you were twins separated at birth," someone offered, lamely.

I don't know what prompted it, but suddenly, a memory of a vacation I took when I was eight years old came into focus. We spent my eighth birthday in Washington, D.C., and stayed at a hotel with a huge pool right outside in Virginia. It was a hot August day, and while playing in the pool, I met a blonde girl with my same birthday, which at that age was a magical event, almost incomprehensible to an eight-year-old. We played for hours in the water, and it was one of the best birthdays I've ever had. She was my everything that day—and it all came back to me, now. I looked at Donna and asked if she went to Virginia on her eighth birthday.

She was silent for a long few moments, then said, "Yes, we stayed at a big resort, and ..."

"... you swam in a pool with a girl named Debbie," I said proudly, "we played for hours. It was a great day!"

"Oh God! We had our birthdays together!" she said, trembling like she'd just seen the Lady of Fatima.

"You had a maroon bathing suit with a little navy skirt," I said with my knowing look.

"You had a two-piece with blue ruffles!" We both screamed with joy, the people left over at the party, applauded.

I'm not quite as sharp as I used to be. I'm still obsessed with finding people I know, but my skills have diminished. I've turned into the crazy lady my mother the prophet described.

I once gave a street beggar in New York City five bucks, her story was so sad. It was something about her daughter at the hospital and on her last breath, and she had to get there. It was a drama that Eugene O'Neill might've laid out. I said, "You're either telling me the truth, or you're an amazing actress. Either way, here ya go," and I handed her about five times as much as I'd ever given a stranger in my life. "Seriously!" I yelled after her, "that was brilliant."

A few years later, from my bedroom in Los Angeles, I saw my moocher in a TV commercial. I recognized her immediately, the voice, quivering when she found out she had cancer, and nobody would take her insurance. The tears, so familiar. Not sure whether she became an actress because I suggested it, or if she was trying to raise money for new head shots, that late night in Manhattan, and I helped pay for them. Either way, it sure looked like I helped make her dream come true. I watch her career now with pride. She shows up in movies, TV, commercials. I don't know her name—but she's my girl. I'm glad she's off the streets if she was ever on them.

I believe our paths cross with people from our past all the time if we take a moment to notice, and yes, maybe even stalk, if necessary. To this day, nothing makes me feel warmer than running into someone I know—completely out of context—from some place, some time, when I was younger. It frames my life in a sort of a circular rhyme and makes me the star of an existential riddle.

Sadly, it doesn't seem to happen so much anymore. It could be that I'm not really looking, or my eyesight isn't what it used to be, or maybe I don't leave my house enough, and the delivery boys who bring me food—well, I know them from the last time they brought it. That one is easy.

Turn Down The Grateful Assholes!

My phone rang Wednesday night at around 6:00 PM. on August 9th, 1995. It was my mother, "Well, now are *you* all right?" Her tone was as if she'd called every last person in her Rolodex on some tele-scavenger hunt and was just about done, then she suddenly remembered *me*.

"Yes, why wouldn't I be?" I shot back, a bit confused. It wasn't like her to make a general call asking after me. I'd moved from NYC to LA several months earlier, and we spoke often, but something was definitely off with this check-in call.

"Jerry Garcia died!" she said as if I'd just awakened from a coma. My mother found odd ways and strange times to bone up on her mothering skills.

"Oh, right," I said, chuckling slightly at her strange concern.

"Good, so they do have newspapers out there!" she gasped out.

"And restaurants where they require shoes."

"Well, you don't seem upset. It's the end of an era, you know." I smiled, knowing she got that from one of my brothers. I had three brothers, and we were all Dead Heads and had been for over twenty-nine years. I could hear her glass of ice and bourbon scrape the phone as she took her gulp. I knew she was sitting on her pale yellow couch, cigarette squeezed between two fingers, holding a drink, balancing the phone on her shoulder—all juggled together by sheer talent. The kind of skill only a mother of four could have developed. "Well then, all my kids are okay," she said with a sigh. I could hear her getting up to walk to the kitchen to mix another highball.

"You've spoken to everyone?" I asked, amused.

"Yes, of course," she shot back defensively like I'd asked if she'd showered that week. "Why wouldn't I, Deborah?" she asked a bit sarcastic, a bit hurt. My mother was a smoker, so the end of her sentences always fell short of their earnest beginnings. It often sounded like she didn't really care, but truthfully, she just never had enough air to finish thoughts anymore. "I called Reid first," she wheezed. "We talked for a long time. He was listening to some live Fillmore Album, with Lindsay and Robbie" (my brother Reid's kids, because our Dead Headiness was spilling into the next generation). "Then I checked in with Rob, who was upset—you know how sensitive he is. He and Jimmy had the *Steal A Face* record on."

Steal Your Face, I corrected.

"What difference? Dumb name. Then the second I took my girdle off and got into my evening wear, the front door burst open, and in came your brother, Joe. He stayed for three hours and told me about every single damn Dead concert he ever went to, for *chrissakes!*" hitting herself up with another gulp of bourbon. "I thought he'd never leave. Did you know they did an hour-long version of 'Going Down the Road' in Philadelphia at the Spectrum—'77?" she whispered.

"No, and I was there," I laughed.

"Now I can die."

I thought about my parents who listened with disdain for years to the muffled but ongoing riffs of The Dead seeping from our three back bedrooms. We each had the exact same compact stereo my mother bought with her green stamps, and none of them were going to waste. There came a point when Mom could no longer call us down for dinner—she had to climb the short set of stairs of our split-level home to bang on everyone's doors individually. Sometimes she'd call us on the upstairs number, but we couldn't hear the phone ring with Jerry Garcia rocking out on plastic record players from all three rooms. "Turn that music DOWN! And come and get it!" she'd scream, banging on our doors, like a rejected lover.

My father thought all rock and roll was crap, and anyone who wasn't Acker Bilk or Tennessee Ernie Ford was a hack. He used to goad us by saying, "What's that you're listening to—crap or shit? Who's that—'The Grateful Assholes?'" We had to laugh. "The Grateful Assholes" became our nickname for our favorite group. To this day, it cracks us up. But whenever our friends would meet us at our house to party before a show, my parents would open the bar, pour the drinks, and turn their noses away when we lit up doobies in our back bedrooms. They'd help us make the signs to hold up at the show so our Dead Head friends could find us at the overrun concert. Like parents at a football game rooting for their son the quarterback to score, they'd yell out the front door as we left, "Have fun! Hope you find everybody."

Reid became a Dead Head in high school, and Rob, Joe, and

I fell in line pretty quickly because we all liked what Reid liked. He was our light, our rock tour guide, and honestly, our life mentor. We wanted to hear what he heard, and we wanted to hear it like he did. In fact, we all wanted to be Reid. He was extremely popular and very cool, always with a constant stream of long-hairs, in and out of his bedroom, and he was rarely without an entourage of hangers-on, holding onto his every word, including his siblings. Chicks dug him, men wanted to be him, and dogs licked him.

The happy and freeing music of The Dead was always rocking from Reid's teenage bedroom, which was secluded at the back of the house. We'd hear him singing along with "Bertha," and "Sugaree," it would seep into our ears and work their way down to our hearts, and before we knew it, we were all Dead Heads, too. I was probably the least dead headiest of all of us. I'd often fail pop quizzes posed by Reid—or Rob, could never name all the members of the band—would blow the names of certain songs so they'd roll their eyes at each other and chide me as if I weren't a real Dead Head, but I was the best I could be. I had an undying crush on Bob Weir, so I figured that alone should qualify me. I had most of their albums, knew all of their lyrics, and most of my late teens, twenties, and thirties' memories were backed up by Dead songs. "Truckin'" was my favorite song in the world for a few decades. Even now, if it comes on, I swing into full party mode, dance around freely, and belt it out like it was 1971.

My brothers and I had probably been to about 200 concerts between us, and many of them together, or some combo of us together. I'd probably only chipped in ten of the 200, but it was enough to keep me in the group. I don't think I ever went to a Dead concert where at least one of my brothers was there. Some of us would even drive across several state lines to meet up at shows. That's what Dead Heads did. You went to as many shows as you possibly could, you wore tie-dye tee shirts and flashed peace signs to other Dead Heads. It was a whole culture club, and we took our membership in it seriously.

"Well, thanks for checking in on me ... last," I said, bringing the call to an end. I had a pint of Cherry Garcia frozen yogurt that wasn't going to eat itself. That would be my memorial. I would eat the whole pint, I decided right then.

Mom and I both knew that she didn't give a rat's ass about Jerry Garcia, nor could she have picked him out of a police line-up if he had personally snatched her purse off her shoulder and put on her lipstick in front of her. Yet, she knew how much he and the band meant to all of us, so she checked in like a family member had died, and in a way, one had. It occurred to me what a terrific mother she really was. I couldn't imagine listening to Joe drone on about The Spectrum and all the shows he saw there, including all the set lists, but I guess that's what bourbon is for. It does make other people more interesting.

I hadn't been to a concert in years, had sort of gotten over them, but now I was reconsidering, like outgrowing a doll until your mother chucks it, and now you want it back, and you cry until she digs it out of the trash.

I hung up the phone with my mother and put the *Workingman's Dead* cassette in my player and sang along with "Casey Jones." It was the first album of theirs I ever loved. Reid had given it to me for Christmas to welcome me to his club of cool. Each lyric awoke many thoughts and stirred my lodged memories. I smiled sadly, and tears trickled down my cheeks as I sang along to "Riding that train ... high on cocaine ..."

At once I was sad—even guilty that I hadn't felt worse about the whole thing. I hadn't kept up with my Dead Head membership except to eat Cherry Garcia frozen yogurt almost every day. Suddenly, I missed The Dead, and I missed my dad. So many memories were awake and dancing, and I cried.

Reid once made Dad sit down and listen to a few songs. My father threw his hands up, screaming, "That hurts my ears. I can't understand a thing they're saying. Glen Miller, now *that* was a musician!" Then he'd make us all listen to "Big Bad John" on his record player, waiting for us to say, "Oh yeah, this is music, Dad! You are right."

I'd always fantasized that my dad secretly loved The Dead but could never admit it to his four kids. Maybe he had his own copy of *American Beauty*, and there was a secret stereo in the basement, where he played all their albums like a real Kasper did, but when "Just a Box of Rain" came on, he was moved to sing, "Just a box of rain, no ribbons for their hair ..." and it would set him free.

The Night I Was
Billy Joel's Uptown Girl

I was never a big fan of Billy Joel's music, but that doesn't mean I couldn't have married him when I had the shot.

In the early eighties, I was a waitress at a nouveau-hot restaurant on the Upper West Side of Manhattan. Celebrities, politicians, rock stars came around and often. Ruelles had high ceilings, a chandelier, a gorgeous centrally placed round mahogany bar, and nothing but young, good-looking waitresses. The outdoor cafe ran the length of the eatery and was always a-buzz with people-watchers.

This was the summer of money, and I was in the right place at the right time. I waited on movie stars, rock stars, politicians, and pop artists until my eyes rolled up into my head when I saw them prance in. My memories of them all circled around how much they'd tipped; Dustin Hoffman—40%, Robert DeNiro—200%, Peter Max—20% and a doodle on his place mat (which my busboy spilled coffee on and scrunched up while I screamed "No!") ruining my chance to retire that week. The Rolling Stones came in sans Jagger and racked up a $150 tab in drinks and left me $2.00 (3/4 of one percent). But I don't hold a grudge. I'll never buy any of their albums, but I don't hold a grudge. I always preferred The Beatles, anyway.

Early one Saturday night, a limo pulled up out front. Out stumbled two guys who looked like trouble. I was drawn. I've always enjoyed a nice batch of trouble. I watched from my station on the balcony as the limo riders were led up the stairs to my empty section. The short one was disruptive, singing to the Billy Joel tape that was playing throughout the restaurant. He began waving from the steps like an emperor, claiming, "Hi, I'm Billy Joel! I'm Billy Joel!"

I wasn't sure it was really Billy Joel since he kept saying, "I'm Billy Joel!" It seemed to me that if you were Billy Joel, you wouldn't have to say that you were Billy Joel. To be fair, he might have been a little high, a good bet since it was the eighties.

As the hostess sat him at my prime "to be seen table," perched in the eagle's nest of the restaurant, he started drumming frenetically on his table to the Billy Joel hit that was still blaring from the quadriphonic speakers. "That's my song, 'You may be right, I may be crazy.' Rat-a-tat-tat!"

I was a Dead Head myself, and I wasn't sure if it was really him, nor did I much care. I mostly cared about my tips. This could go either way, I thought. Rock stars were iffy. Since I really wasn't sure what Billy Joel looked like, I asked the bartender, "Is that Billy Joel?" He gave me a "maybe" shrug, continuing on with his Saturday night mixing. I started asking around, "Is that Billy Joel?" No one was sure, but it seemed possible since he was a short guy who got out of a long limo.

The unruly customer using Billy Joel's name was waiting for

me when I slid up to his table. He jumped into a full-on cocaine kind of rant, empty of periods or pauses. "You're my waitress great you're gorgeous I'm Billy Joel what's your name glad I got you I love blondes I'm Billy Joel this is my lawyer it's my birthday I'm gonna have a hamburger he's having the duck you want rice with the duck yeah he'll have the rice make my burger medium with cheese you know who I am right we want two double white Russians!"

"Up or on the rocks?" I replied, shaking my head from information overload. I put his drink order in at the service bar, asking the bartender again, "Can you please look at this guy again and tell me if it's Billy Joel?"

"I guess," he shrugged.

Another customer took the table to Billy's left. Before they were even settled at their table, he said, "Hey, how ya doin? I'm Billy Joel." The man would just not give it up! He continued with his two-fingered drumming. By now, someone else's song was playing, and he was ruining it. *Oh, this better be a big tip, mister* was running on a loop in the deck in *my* head. I was glad I'd never bought any of his albums. Jerry Garcia has probably never once had to say, "I'm Jerry Garcia." Within ten minutes of him being there, my entire section was overrun with the Billy Joelness of it all. Everyone knew Billy Joel was in the joint, particularly Billy Joel. He kept flagging me over and flirting possessively.

"Hey I'm having a party tonight at Magique it's my birthday you can be my date I want you to come you're gorgeous I don't have a date!"

That's because you're obnoxious, I thought. "Thank you for the offer, Billy, but I'm working," I said, nodding around the joint, smiling in that "are you stupid?" kind of way to make my point.

"Working? Here? You don't have to work. I'm Billy Joel."

"Well, I'm Debbie Kasper, and Debbie Kasper has to work."

"You come, and you ask for me," he continued, as if I hadn't even spoken. At that exact moment, Marvin, my boss who was six feet tall at least, approached me and pulled me aside to yell at me for being late for the sixth time that week. Bill saw Marvin pointing at me in that "You're in trouble way" and jumped up from his perch, ran in between us, faced Marvin's belt buckle, and said, "You can't talk to Debbie that way. That's Debbie."

Marvin said, "Yeah? Well, I'm her boss, and I can talk to her any way I want. I own this place. Who the hell are you?"

I turned Billy Joel's body around and pushed him toward his table, saying, "Billy, go sit down! Now." I turned to Marvin to apologize and make sure he didn't think it was my boyfriend or anything. "I'm sorry, Marvin, that's Billy..."

"I know who he is. He's a pain in the ass."

Billy Joel was gone within 45 minutes. As he left, he slipped me fifty bucks and a piece of paper with his name on it—Billy Joel. "You'll be on my guest list. Make sure I know when you get there. And bring a hot chick for my lawyer." Then he danced out the door, still telling anyone who cared that he was you-know-who.

At midnight when my shift was done, I counted my tips. It had been a banner night. Well over $100! I grabbed a fellow waitress and we decided to go to the party. I wasn't excited about seeing him again, but maybe Roger Daltrey would be there. Now that was some sexy!

We decided to call Magique before taking a cab to the East Side since it all just still seemed surreal. I still wasn't convinced that it really was him. When I called, the woman on the other end of the phone barked at me, "There's no Billy Joel party here tonight!"

I hung up, turned to my friend and said, "Nope. Told you!" At least I was right, which was always the best booby prize.

I went to bed but not before re-counting my stack of bills on my futon, which was one of life's great joys in those days. I was happy I didn't part with the ten bucks to get to the other side of town only to be humiliated. I had to be back at work at 11:00 AM for brunch the next day, anyway.

When I walked into Ruelles the next morning, the bartender stopped me from behind his bar. "How was the Billy Joel birthday bash?"

"There was no birthday bash. That wasn't Billy Joel, I knew it."

"Oh really?" he baited. He opened the paper to the center gossip section where there was a double-paged picture titled, "BILLY JOEL'S BIRTHDAY BASH AT MAGIQUE."

There was my Billy Joel dancing like an idiot in love with a tall blonde gal, whom I could only see from behind. She looked like she might have been a model. Next to Billy was someone who looked exactly like Roger Daltrey, dancing alone.

When I told Mom the story over the phone that week, she took a deep breath, made a "tsk" sound and shook her head so hard her chin hit the phone. "You know what your problem is, Debbie? You just don't know when to say, 'yes.' Sometimes life is just 'yes.' It's just as easy to fall in love with a rock star as it is a busboy, you, know."

"One busboy, mom. ONE. I don't make a habit of it."

"You turn every chance into a story—while you are missing your life! You have the best stories around, but NO LIFE! I don't know when you got so cynical."

Soon after that, I read that Billy Joel and Christie Brinkley were married. I felt terrible that he had to settle.

At least that's my take on the story.

Acknowledgements

Thank you to my hilarious parents for always encouraging me in my art, and letting me skewer them. To my brothers: Reid, Robbie and Joe, for their relentless senses of humor, which has helped me get through life. And my sister, Susan who inspired me.

Bless you David Sedaris, for teaching me how to write and daring me to do so.

I have eternal love and gratitude for Janette Barber, Brad M. Bucklin, Paul Lyons, Cathy Ladman, Didi Rea, Lindsay Jones, Bob Keenan, Monica Piper, Arlene Schindler and in the "goes without saying" department: *Elissa Tognozzi and Pat Sierchio, who have always been on my team even during the rainy seasons.*

And there's all of you, whose names, stories, ideas, and lives I have depicted: Amy Foster, Saskia Ishii, Carolin Hatfield, Janet Taylor, Kathy Taylor, Chris Taylor and Jeff Taylor, Paul Flanagan, Janette Baber, Susie Frishberg, Debbie Lazar, Mom's bridge club, Lola, Pam Inelli, Mary DePolis, The Great Wall of China, Hilarie Jenkins, Liz Gram, The Mafia, Mrs. Mitrocsak, Mrs. Lutz, and Mrs. Selmi, Sharon Lockhart, Bill Mason (who I still don't like), Germany, and Billy Joel (please don't sue me).

And so many others, whose names I've changed—if you recognize yourself in a story ... you are probably right.]
Thank you all for letting me use you.

Thank you for reading this far,
others are off getting a snack...but not you!

Please go to Amazon.com and
Goodreads.com and leave me a review
Reviews are like
manna to writers
Please visit me at DebbieKasper.com
DebbieKasper2@Twitter.com
DebbieKasper @ Facebook
DebbieKasper/Writer@ Facebook.com
DebbieKasper@Instagram.com

or... just rent a plane and write "Hi" in the sky

Thank you, I appreciate you, with-
out you, I am NOTHING
Debbie Kasper, 2020

Made in the USA
Middletown, DE
23 July 2020